THE COMPLETE
BIKE
OWNER'S
MANUAL

THE COMPLETE
BIKE
OWNER'S
MANUAL

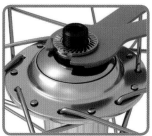

DK London
Senior Editor Chauney Dunford
Senior Art Editor Gillian Andrews
Designers Stephen Bere, Ray Bryant,
Katie Cavanagh, Phil Gamble
Editors Hannah Bowen, Katie John, Tash Kahn,
Sam Kennedy, Hugo Wilkinson
Managing Editor Gareth Jones
Senior Managing Art Editor Lee Griffiths
Publishing Director Jonathan Metcalf
Art Director Karen Self
Creative Director Phil Ormerod
Publisher Liz Wheeler
Jacket Editor Claire Gell
Jacket Designer Mark Cavanagh
Jacket Design Development Manager Sophia MTT
Preproduction Producer Jacqueline Street
Producer Mandy Inness
Picture Research Jenny Lane
US Editor Kayla Dugger
US Managing Editor Lori Hand

Illustrator Brendan McCaffrey

Consultants Luke Edward-Evans, Richard Gilbert,
Brendan McCaffrey, Phil Quill

Authors Claire Beaumont, Ben Spurrier

First American Edition, 2017
Published in the United States by DK Publishing
345 Hudson Street, New York, New York 10014

A catalog record for this book is available from
the Library of Congress.
ISBN 978-1-4654-5915-2

DK books are available at special discounts when purchased
in bulk for sales promotions, premiums, fund-raising, or
educational use. For details, contact: DK Publishing Special
Markets, 345 Hudson Street, New York, New York 10014
SpecialSales@dk.com

Printed and bound in China

All images © Dorling Kindersley Limited
For further information see: www.dkimages.com

A WORLD OF IDEAS:
SEE ALL THERE IS TO KNOW

www.dk.com

Contents

05 BRAKES 96

06 DRIVETRAIN 126

07 SUSPENSION 188

08 OWNER'S GUIDE 204

▶ THE COMPLETE BIKE OWNER'S MANUAL
Introduction

Bikes can take you far and wide, and to get the best out of every ride, you need to keep your bike in the best possible condition. Bikes do not run on your muscles alone; the interplay of pedals, chain, wheels, steering, and gear and brake systems gives power and control to your bike. In this book, we show you how to install, adjust, and maintain each part of your bike.

Whether you are a skilled mechanic or a beginner, learning how to fix and maintain your bike at home will save you time, energy, and money. It's also great to know that you can be miles from home and fix a problem in the unlikely event of mechanical failure.

This book uses high-quality CGI illustrations to detail every component of your bike. With no hands in the way to obscure detail and vivid imagery, the step-by-step instructions offer unprecedented clarity and get you close to every part of your bike.

Starting with the essentials

To lay the groundwork, this guide first explains the design and components of many different types of bikes. Advice on suitable clothing, rider accessories, and setting your riding position will give you the information you need to get the best use out of your bike in everyday riding.

The "Getting Started" chapter shows you how to set up a workshop and use bicycle maintenance tools. Setting up your own workshop is easy, and there are just a handful of essential and low-cost tools that you will need. As you decide to replace or repair certain parts of your bike, your collection of tools will slowly build. The chapter also shows you how to carry out routine jobs, such as cleaning your bike and lubricating moving parts, and provides information on dealing with emergency repairs.

Maintenance and repairs

Whether you ride your bike on the road, on a track, or over mountains, it will benefit from a good maintenance routine. Each chapter shows you how to care for a specific system on your bike. Chapters include advice on choosing the best components for your type of bike; an in-depth look at the key parts, with unique terms and names explained;

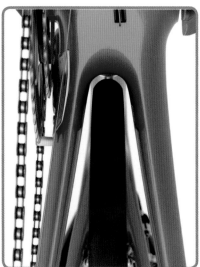

and information on how to set, adjust, and perform maintenance on particular parts. Annotated images and workshop tips cover a variety of models. There is advice on how to spot signs of trouble before costs spiral; detailed exploded diagrams and cutaways show you how each part of your bicycle works together, and how to make on-the-go adjustments without the risk of getting stranded on a ride.

Replacing and upgrading parts

Regular maintenance helps to stave off wear and tear. However, poor weather, grit, road salt, and general use will degrade most components over time, and these parts will need to be replaced.

Removing worn parts and replacing with new ones is tackled chapter by chapter with the step-by-step guides. While the general principles of braking, gear changes, wheel construction, and suspension have not changed, major brands often have their own proprietary systems–for example, for the size of bearings, the size of the chain or cables, or the way some parts fit onto the bike. Each chapter

covers the variations between the three major brands (Shimano, SRAM, and Campagnolo) and what to look out for when purchasing replacement parts.

If you want to improve your cycling performance, upgrading specific parts of your bicycle will help to make it lighter, make the ride smoother, and enable you to change gears faster and more precisely. Changing the handlebar, stem, and saddle are fairly straightforward tasks. More complex jobs such as replacing the drivetrain (the engine) of the bike or installing new suspension forks are expensive upgrades but will have a beneficial effect on performance. The step-by-step sequences show every stage of these procedures so you can tackle them with ease.

All of this information, together with a maintenance planner plus diagnostic and troubleshooting tips at the end of the book, will help you to enjoy efficient, safe riding for the full lifespan of your bicycle.

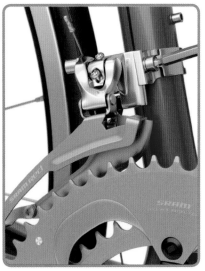

KNOW YOUR BICYCLE

Road bikes

Road bikes are sleek and lightweight, and intended for use on smooth asphalt. Their narrow wheels and thin tires mean they are able to roll quickly over smooth surfaces, enabling them to cover long distances at a fast pace. Drop handlebars allow the rider to sit in a more aerodynamic, forward-leaning position, thus transferring more power to the pedals. Racing bikes, hybrids, single-speed bikes, and e-bikes (electric bikes) all use components known as the drivetrain to power the bike, while gears make cycling easier. Frames are light and rigid, with steel and aluminum popular with the consumer market, and carbon fiber and titanium used more widely at competition level.

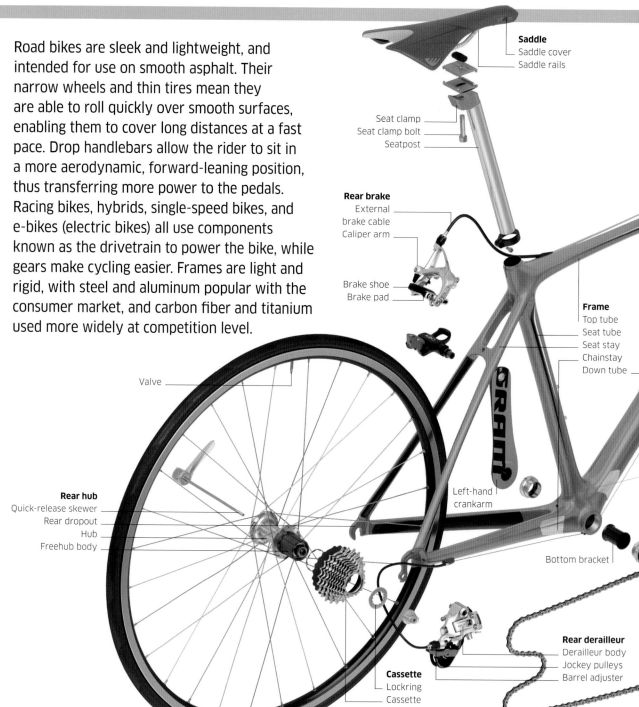

Saddle
Saddle cover
Saddle rails

Seat clamp
Seat clamp bolt
Seatpost

Rear brake
External brake cable
Caliper arm

Brake shoe
Brake pad

Frame
Top tube
Seat tube
Seat stay
Chainstay
Down tube

Valve

Left-hand crankarm

Rear hub
Quick-release skewer
Rear dropout
Hub
Freehub body

Bottom bracket

Rear derailleur
Derailleur body
Jockey pulleys
Barrel adjuster

Cassette
Lockring
Cassette

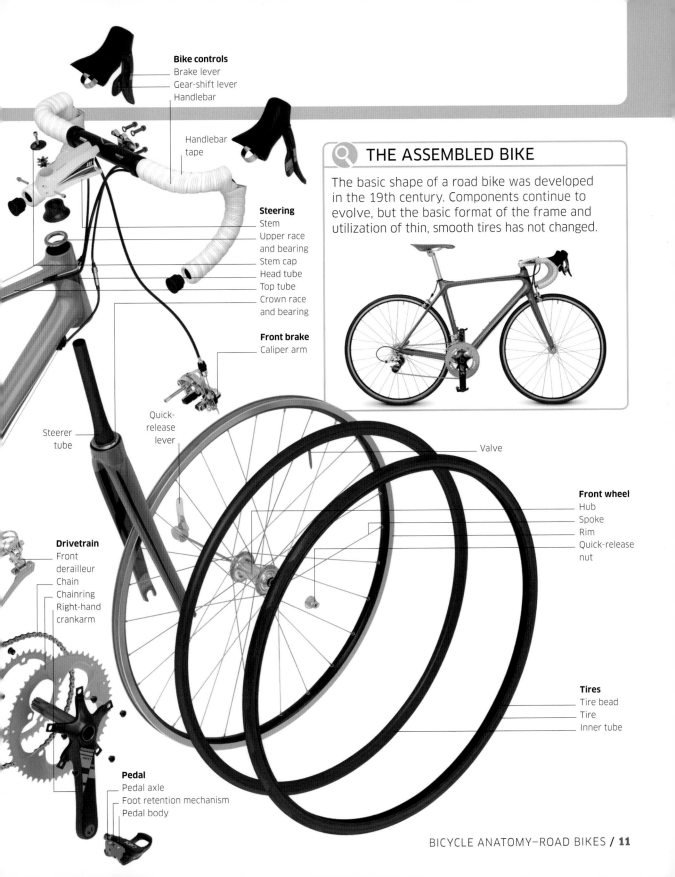

Bike controls
Brake lever
Gear-shift lever
Handlebar

Handlebar
tape

Steering
Stem
Upper race
and bearing
Stem cap
Head tube
Top tube
Crown race
and bearing

Front brake
Caliper arm

Steerer
tube

Quick-
release
lever

Drivetrain
Front
derailleur
Chain
Chainring
Right-hand
crankarm

Pedal
Pedal axle
Foot retention mechanism
Pedal body

THE ASSEMBLED BIKE

The basic shape of a road bike was developed
in the 19th century. Components continue to
evolve, but the basic format of the frame and
utilization of thin, smooth tires has not changed.

Valve

Front wheel
Hub
Spoke
Rim
Quick-release
nut

Tires
Tire bead
Tire
Inner tube

Off-road bikes come in all shapes and sizes. Most feature front suspension, and some have rear suspension as well. Front and rear disc brakes give the best stopping power, while tubeless tires allow riders to run lower pressures without the risk of pinch punctures. Cross-country racers usually have carbon-fiber frames, with larger wheels and 4 in (10cm) of front—sometimes dual—suspension. Enduro/trail bikes feature smaller wheels, wider tires, and 6 in (15cm) of dual suspension, while downhill bikes come with longer travel suspension and relaxed frame angles, making them stable at speed.

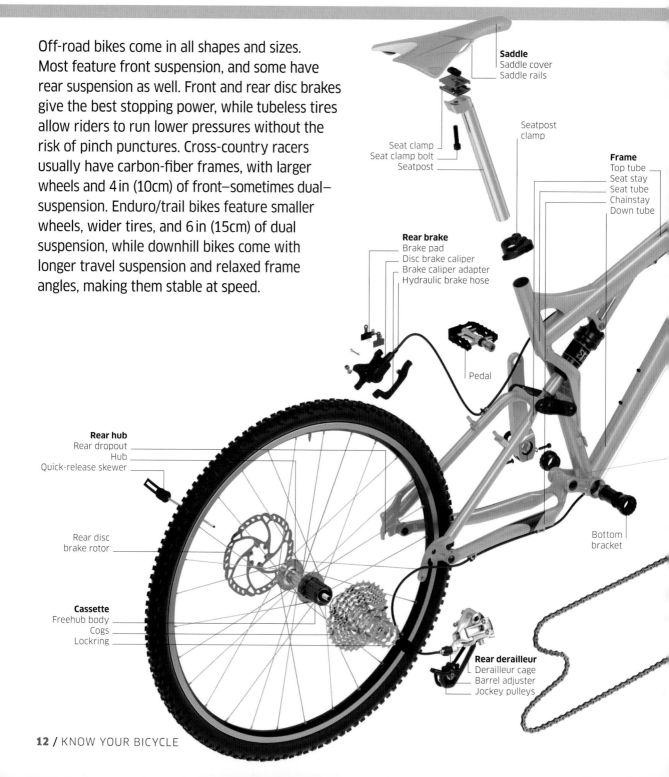

Saddle
Saddle cover
Saddle rails

Seatpost clamp

Frame
Top tube
Seat stay
Seat tube
Chainstay
Down tube

Seat clamp
Seat clamp bolt
Seatpost

Rear brake
Brake pad
Disc brake caliper
Brake caliper adapter
Hydraulic brake hose

Pedal

Rear hub
Rear dropout
Hub
Quick-release skewer

Rear disc
brake rotor

Bottom
bracket

Cassette
Freehub body
Cogs
Lockring

Rear derailleur
Derailleur cage
Barrel adjuster
Jockey pulleys

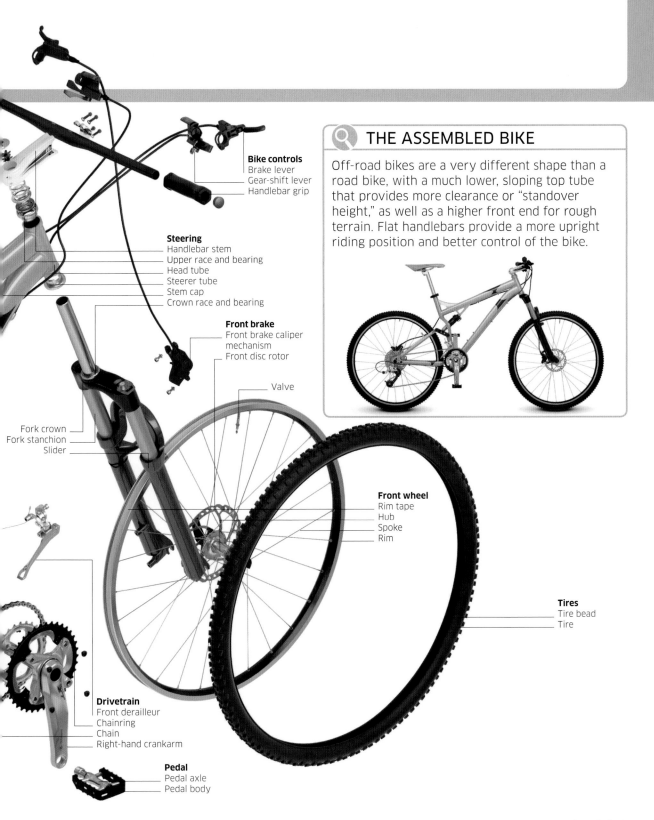

Bike controls
Brake lever
Gear-shift lever
Handlebar grip

Steering
Handlebar stem
Upper race and bearing
Head tube
Steerer tube
Stem cap
Crown race and bearing

Front brake
Front brake caliper mechanism
Front disc rotor

Valve

Fork crown
Fork stanchion
Slider

Front wheel
Rim tape
Hub
Spoke
Rim

Tires
Tire bead
Tire

Drivetrain
Front derailleur
Chainring
Chain
Right-hand crankarm

Pedal
Pedal axle
Pedal body

THE ASSEMBLED BIKE

Off-road bikes are a very different shape than a road bike, with a much lower, sloping top tube that provides more clearance or "standover height," as well as a higher front end for rough terrain. Flat handlebars provide a more upright riding position and better control of the bike.

Utility bikes

Being designed for reliable everyday use, rather than for sporting pursuits, utility bikes offer an ideal combination of comfort, reliability, and durability. They are heavier than sports bikes, but nevertheless easy to ride. Utility bikes often utilize simple, robust components and older technology, but are maintained in a similar way to newer designs.

⊙ COMMON COMPONENTS LOCATOR

With padded seats, flat handlebars, durable drivetrains, and sometimes luggage panniers, utility bikes are built for comfort and convenience. Some models feature front suspension to smooth over bumps.

24-speed gear system

Comfortable saddle

Flat handlebar

Rim brakes

Steel frame

Plastic chainguard

Gears Single speed, or may have derailleur or hub gears
Brakes Typically rim brakes; some may have hub brakes
Frame Steel or aluminum; children's bikes can be plastic

Handlebar Flat for a comfortable, upright riding style
Saddle Padded in soft material
Wheels Steel spoked, typically 12–26 in (30–65 cm) across

SHOPPER BIKES

Brakes Rim (pp.98–117)
Gears Derailleur (pp.140–149); Hub (pp.150–155)
Suspension None

HYBRID BIKES

Brakes Rim (pp.98–117); Hub (pp.122–125); Disc (pp.118–121)
Gears Derailleur (pp.140–149); Hub (pp.150–155)
Suspension None

FOLDING BIKES

Brakes Rim (pp.98–117); Hub (pp.122–125)
Gears Derailleur (pp.140–149); Hub (pp.150–155)
Suspension None

FIXED/SINGLE-SPEED BIKES

Brakes Rim (pp.98–117)
Gears Single speed
Suspension None

E-BIKES

Brakes Rim (pp.98–117); Hub (pp.122–125)
Gears Derailleur (pp.140–149); Hub (pp.150–155)
Suspension None

CARGO BIKES

Brakes Rim (pp.98–117); Hub (pp.122–125)
Gears Derailleur (pp.140–149); Hub (pp.150–155)
Suspension None

Whether intended for touring, racing, or even an intense commute, road bikes are designed with speed in mind, prioritizing performance over comfort. The most advanced bikes feature cutting-edge technology with computer-designed, wind-cheating carbon frames and razor-sharp, instant electronic gear-shifting.

COMMON COMPONENTS LOCATOR

Road bikes sacrifice both durability and comfort in the pursuit of speed. Slim tires and lightweight wheels are aerodynamic but provide little insulation from bumps in the road, while narrow sadddles offer minimal padding.

Drop handlebar

Aerodynamic saddle

11-speed gearing

Carbon frame

Rim brakes

Spoked wheels

Gears 2 x 10- or 11-speed derailleur gears
Brakes Typically rim brakes; may have cable or hydraulic disc
Frame Carbon, aluminum, titanium, or lightweight steel

Handlebar Drop bars
Saddle Light and narrow, often with minimal padding
Wheels 700c with aluminum or carbon rims

TOURING BIKES

Brakes Rim (pp.98–117); Disc (pp.118–121)
Gears Derailleur (pp.140–149); Hub (pp.150–155)
Suspension None

GRAVEL BIKES

Brakes Rim (pp.98–117); Disc (pp.118–121)
Gears Derailleur (pp.140–149); Hub (pp.150–155)
Suspension None

TRACK BIKES

Brakes None
Gears Single speed
Suspension None

TRIATHLON/TIME TRIAL BIKES

Brakes Rim (pp.98–117)
Gears Derailleur (pp.140–149)
Suspension None

CYCLOCROSS BIKES

Brakes Rim (pp.98–117); Disc (pp.118–121)
Gears Derailleur (pp.140–149); Hub (pp.150–155)
Suspension None

ENDURANCE BIKES

Brakes Rim (pp.98–117); Disc (pp.118–121)
Gears Derailleur (pp.140–149); Hub (pp.150–155)
Suspension None

Off-road bikes

Off-road or mountain bikes come in a range of designs, from entry-level models best suited to gravel trails to bikes designed for steep and rocky mountain descents.

Being equipped with wide, knobby tires that may be tubed or tubeless, mountain bike tires offer excellent grip and traction while the bike's suspension system limits shocks.

COMMON COMPONENTS LOCATOR

Good suspension and wide, tough tires are essential when trail riding on a mountain bike. Many models also feature disc brakes, which may even be hydraulically powered for precise braking control.

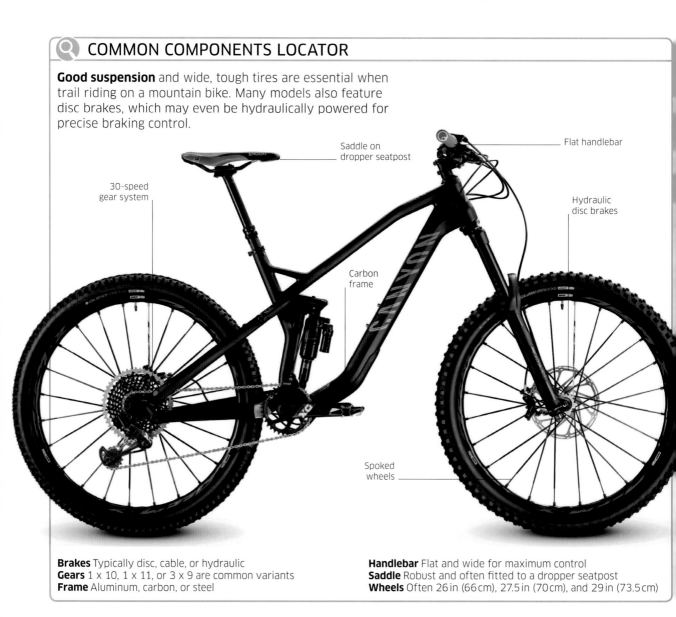

Saddle on dropper seatpost

Flat handlebar

30-speed gear system

Hydraulic disc brakes

Carbon frame

Spoked wheels

Brakes Typically disc, cable, or hydraulic
Gears 1 x 10, 1 x 11, or 3 x 9 are common variants
Frame Aluminum, carbon, or steel

Handlebar Flat and wide for maximum control
Saddle Robust and often fitted to a dropper seatpost
Wheels Often 26 in (66 cm), 27.5 in (70 cm), and 29 in (73.5 cm)

HARDTAIL BIKES

Brakes Rim (pp.98–117); Disc (pp.118–121)
Gears Derailleur (pp.140–149)
Suspension Front (pp.192–199)

CROSS-COUNTRY BIKES

Brakes Rim (pp.98–117); Disc (pp.118–121)
Gears Derailleur (pp.140–149)
Suspension Full (pp.192–203)

DOWNHILL BIKES

Brakes Disc (pp.118–121)
Gears Derailleur (pp.140–149)
Suspension Full (pp.192–203)

FAT BIKES

Brakes Disc (pp.118–121)
Gears Derailleur (pp.140–149)
Suspension None

DIRT/TRIALS BIKES

Brakes Rim (pp.98–117); Disc (pp.118–121)
Gears Single speed
Suspension Front (pp.192–199); none

E-MOUNTAIN BIKES

Brakes Disc (pp.118–121)
Gears Derailleur (pp.140–149)
Suspension Front or full (pp.192–203)

Road bikes

Road bike riding is all about riding your bike efficiently, so you can get as far and as fast as you choose. A good riding position that suits your desired combination of comfort, power output, and aerodynamics can help with this. First, you should choose a bike with the correct-sized frame (see box, opposite), and then adjust the contact points—saddle, handlebar, and pedals—to fit your requirements and find a neutral position for safe, efficient riding.

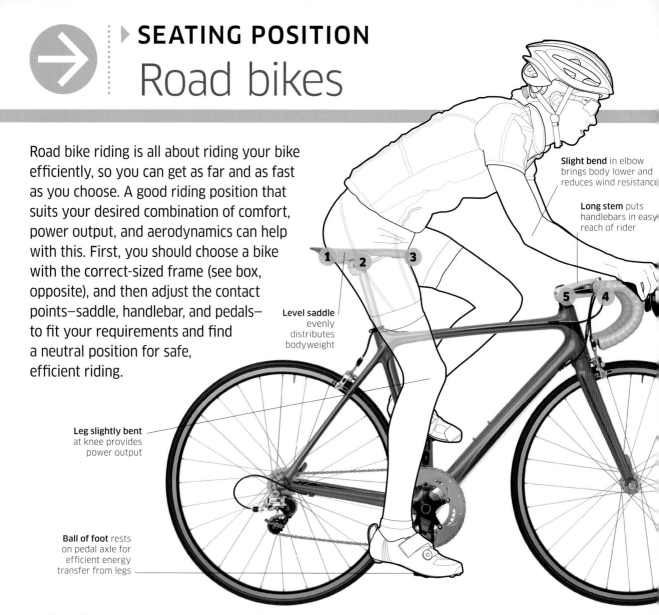

Slight bend in elbow brings body lower and reduces wind resistance

Long stem puts handlebars in easy reach of rider

Level saddle evenly distributes bodyweight

Leg slightly bent at knee provides power output

Ball of foot rests on pedal axle for efficient energy transfer from legs

BEFORE YOU START

- Collect a tape measure, spirit level, ruler, and hex keys.
- Set your cleat position (see pp.186-87).
- Set your bike on a level surface, ideally with the rear wheel mounted on an indoor trainer so you can sit on the saddle and pedal while stationary.
- Pump up the tires to the correct pressure.
- Put on your normal riding gear and cycling shoes.
- Record your existing set-up by measuring from the center of the bottom bracket (BB) to the top of the saddle; horizontally from the saddle nose to the BB center; and from the saddle nose to the center of the handlebar.

① SADDLE HEIGHT

Find an efficient pedaling position by ensuring you have a slight bend in your knee when your leg is extended. To check this, adjust the seatpost until your leg is straight and the heel of your cycling shoe barely touches the pedal when you are sitting in the saddle when the lower crank is at the 6 o'clock position.

Straight leg with slight bend in the knee

Heel of shoe just grazing pedal

5 STEM LENGTH

Your stem length needs to be long enough that you can grip the hoods comfortably without feeling stretched. A good technique to ensure you have the right length is to hold the drops and look down at the wheel hub. The handlebar should obscure the hub. If the hub is visible in front, you need a longer stem; if you can see it behind the handlebar, swap the stem for a shorter one.

Clear line to hub

4 HANDLEBAR HEIGHT

Adjust the height of your handlebar for your needs by moving it in relation to the mid-point of your saddle. For recreational riding, set the bar level with, or 0.4–0.8in (1–2cm) below, the saddle. For a more aerodynamic road bike riding position, set the bar 3.14–3.93in (8–10cm) below the saddle. To alter height of the handlebars, you can remove the stem and reposition the spacers, flip the stem, or install a high- or low-rise stem.

Spacers

3 SADDLE FORE/AFT

Move the saddle along its rails to adjust your center of gravity and ensure that you are well balanced when riding. Position the saddle so that your forward knee is over the pedal axle when you sit with the cranks horizontal. To check, sit on the saddle in your normal riding position and hold a ruler against your kneecap; the end of the ruler should pass over the pedal axle.

Knee in line with pedal axle

End of ruler passes pedal axle

2 SADDLE ANGLE

Ensure your weight is evenly distributed through the sit bones of your pelvis by setting your saddle at a neutral angle, with the front two-thirds of the saddle horizontal. You can alter this angle by up to 2 degrees for comfort, but any more than this may cause painful pressure on your groin and perineum and excess transfer of body weight onto your arms and hands.

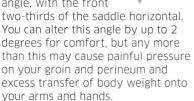

ROAD BIKE SIZING

- **Road bikes are sized according** to the length of the seat tube, and are described in cm—from 48–60cm—or as S/M/L/XL.

- **Check you have sufficient** "standover clearance" when standing with your legs either side of the top tube. 1–2in (2–5cm) between your groin and the frame is ideal.

- **Consider a bike's "stack" and "reach"**—the distances vertically and horizontally from the center of the bottom bracket to the top of the top tube—when buying a bike, since you cannot alter these later.

▶ SEATING POSITION
Off-road bikes

Mountain biking is a more fluid form of cycling than road riding. Riders shift between different positions for climbing, descending, jumping, or absorbing bumps, and to respond rapidly to twisting trails, rough terrain, and changes in gradient. Finding the right position involves setting the contact points—saddle, handlebar, and pedal cleats—to suit your riding style.

Relaxed wrists provide grip and control

1 ◦ **2** ◦ **3**   **4** **5** **6**

Slightly angled saddle improves climbing position

Bodyweight evenly distributed for effective suspension and traction

BEFORE YOU START

- Gather tools—tape measure, straightedge, level, hex keys
- Set your cleat position (see pp.186–87)
- Adjust suspension to normal riding settings (see pp.194–95; 202–03); set dropper seatpost to normal (see pp.70–71)

1 SADDLE HEIGHT

Adjust the seatpost to set the saddle at a comfortable position. For trail riding, a good benchmark is to set the saddle at hip height. For efficient pedaling when climbing, use the road-bike saddle-height method (see step 1, p.21). Downhill, technical riding is easier with the saddle 1–2 in (2.5–5 cm) below the hip.

2 SADDLE ANGLE

Changing the angle of the saddle helps you adapt your bike and riding position for the ride you are on. For trail riding, angle the saddle slightly nose-down for a better seating position on climbs. For downhill riding, angle the saddle slightly nose-up so you can grip it between your thighs on fast descents and corners.

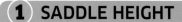

Set saddle angle a few degrees from horizontal

3 SADDLE FORE/AFT

Slide the saddle along the rails until its center aligns with the midpoint between the rear axle and bottom bracket (BB). This puts your body in a position that gives balanced handling, even tire traction, and efficient suspension performance.

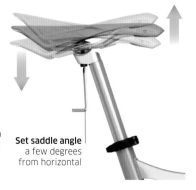

Set saddle to avoid cramped or stretched position

> **Workshop tip:** High tire pressures (40psi) suit aggressive, fast riding on dry trails, while low pressures (25-35psi) are better for muddy riding. Tubeless tires allow very low pressures (20-25psi) without risking pinch flats.

7 GEAR/BRAKE LEVER ANGLE

Angle your gear and brake levers at a slant of 45 degrees from horizontal for a neutral, relaxed wrist position with good access to the controls. For a personal fit, adopt your normal riding position—seated or standing on the pedals—and angle the levers so your wrist is relaxed and straight.

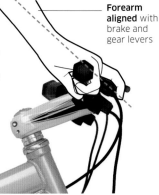

Forearm aligned with brake and gear levers

6 GEAR/BRAKE LEVER POSITION

For optimum braking power and steering control, place the brake and gear-shift levers where you can easily reach them. Holding the grip in your usual riding position, slide the brake lever along the bar until you can pull it with just your index and/or middle finger. Next, with your hand still in its normal grip position, set the gear-shift lever where you can easily reach it. (You might need to slot it in between the grip and brake lever to achieve this.)

Brake with one finger for best power and grip

5 STEM POSITION

Choose a stem that suits your style of riding, but make sure you are not cramped or overreaching, as this can cause lower back pain. Shorter stems (2-2.75 in/50-70mm) are best for rapid steering; longer ones (3-4 in/80-100mm) are best for climbing. Stem angle also affects handling—a high-rise stem gives a stable position, but steering will be less precise. Use a low-rise stem or place the spacers above the stem for a more agile position.

2-2.75in (50-70mm)
3-4in (80-100mm)

Spacers on top of stem for lower position

4 RISER-BAR ANGLE

Most mountain bikes are equipped with riser bars—the ends rise up and sweep back from the middle of the handlebar. Release the clamp and twist the bar so that when viewed from the side the rise is angled parallel with the front fork. Angling the bar farther back will place pressure on the wrists and back; farther forward puts excess weight over the front wheel and impairs handling.

Low-rise stem for precise steering

MOUNTAIN BIKE SIZING

- **Mountain bikes** are sized by seat-tube length, usually in inches—from 13 to 24 in—or as XS/S/M/L/XL.
- **If choosing a new bike,** check for sufficient "standover clearance." You should be 2-3 in (5-8cm) above the top tube when standing astride it.
- **"Stack" and "reach"**—measured vertically and horizontally from BB center to top of top tube—are the key dimensions for figuring out whether a bike is long and high enough for you.

Essential gear

There are some pieces of equipment that you will use on almost every ride. Some are necessary for personal safety, and others make cycling more convenient or comfortable. All are essential tools for a cyclist, so it is worth taking the time to find the best pieces of gear for your needs.

INNER TUBES

Inner tubes vary according to the diameter of a bike's wheel and the width of its tire. Their valves vary, so make sure you have the right pump.

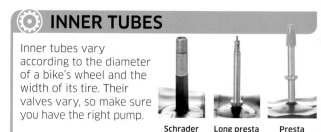

Schrader valve tube   Long presta valve tube   Presta valve tube

SADDLEBAGS

Clip a small, discreet saddlebag to the rails of your saddle so as not to restrict movement when riding. It will generally have space for a spare tube, a puncture repair kit, tire levers, and a small multi-tool. Larger versions also allow you to carry spare clothing.

Tool bag

Traditional

Waterproof

PUMPS

Pumps with broad, long barrels are easy to use when inflating wide tires but may take longer to reach the high pressures required on a road bike.

Screw top

Valve head

Rubber grip

Mini-pump   CO₂ inflator   CO₂ canister   Frame pump

ON-ROAD TOOL KIT

Consisting of a multi-tool, tire levers, and a puncture repair kit, a basic tool kit is useful for all basic repairs. Make sure that the multi-tool you take with you on a ride is equipped with tools to suit the fittings on your bike.

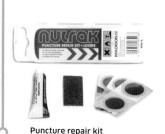
Puncture repair kit

Spoke wrench

Nylon tire levers

Tire lever

Chain breaker

Hex keys

Pick tool

Multi-tool

WATER BOTTLES AND STORAGE

Hydration is essential when riding, not just in the summer months. Road bikes often have bottle cages, while off-road cyclists frequently use hydration packs.

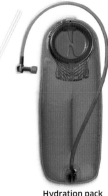

Mouthpiece

Bottle cage

Bottle

Triathlon bottle

Hydration pack

Backpack and hydration pack

LOCKS AND STORAGE

Many types of locks are available, with multiple security devices required in some cases to padlock the various parts of your bike.

U-lock

Chain lock

Cable lock

FENDERS

Fenders keep your clothes and bike clean in the rain. Off-road fenders need regular cleaning to prevent them from clogging up.

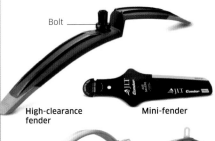

Bolt

High-clearance fender

Mini-fender

LIGHTS

Modern LED bike lamps can rival car headlights. Flashing lights alert traffic to your presence, while high-powered beams are great for off-road riding.

Battery pack

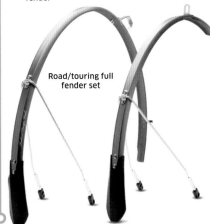

Road/touring full fender set

LED with rubber clip

Clip-on light

Emergency front and rear LEDs

Night-riding lights

Bike and accessory manufacturers are quick to develop and adapt cutting-edge technology. In particular, GPS has transformed bike navigation, largely eliminating the need for you to carry maps. Heart rate monitors and power meters make tracking your performance much easier.

⚙ COMPUTERS

Even the simplest bike computer will calculate your speed and the distance you have traveled. Wireless devices are more expensive but look neater.

Wired digital bike computer

Large-screen computer

⚙ GPS

Super-accurate, smaller GPS devices are increasingly common. Higher-end versions can be uploaded with detailed maps and offer turn-by-turn navigation.

Compact model

GPS watch

GPS phone

Mini GPS

Full-color GPS

⚙ HEART RATE MONITORS

Heart rate monitors are an affordable way to ensure that your training is both targeted and effective. Modern versions can be linked to your smartphone and any training apps you may have.

Built-in heart rate monitor

Heart rate watch

Strap monitor

Velcro monitor

Monitor helmet

⚙ POWER METERS

A sophisticated training tool, power meters track the amount of effort you are putting into your cycling to give you an instant measurement of how much you are exerting yourself. In addition to recording your training progress, you can use them to keep yourself cycling at the correct intensity for the duration of your bike ride.

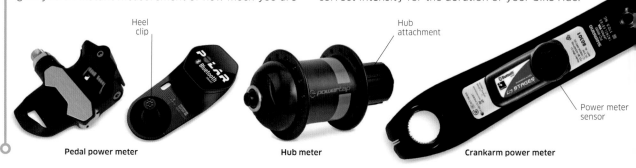

Heel clip

Hub attachment

Power meter sensor

Pedal power meter

Hub meter

Crankarm power meter

Smash-proof lens

CAMERAS

Mounted on a helmet or directly on a bike, a lightweight camera is a helpful piece of equipment that can be used to relive downhill exploits or record evidence of any accidents.

Helmet-mounted camera

Cycle camera

Camera light

POWER GENERATORS/DYNAMOS

Modern generators are a convenient way of running lights and are more environmentally friendly than battery-powered LEDs. Some versions can even simultaneously charge your smartphone.

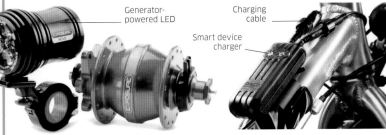

Generator-powered LED

Charging cable

Smart device charger

Generator and light

Smartphone charger

MISCELLANEOUS

New devices use GPS technology to make it possible for you to navigate or keep track of your training progress with a single glance, while the latest powerful mini-speakers can now fit in a bottle cage.

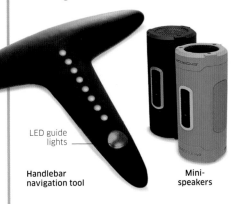

LED guide lights

Handlebar navigation tool

Mini-speakers

Optical touchpad

Smart eyewear with heads-up performance display

SAFETY AND SECURITY

Radar sensors warn you about nearby traffic, while light-up helmets ensure that you will remain visible in all weather, and smart locks eliminate the need to carry keys.

Front headlights

Radar device

Crash sensor

Rear light camera

Smart bike lock

Helmet with built-in lights

Utility equipment

For both touring and commuting, it is inevitable that you will need to carry things with you. Over long distances, transporting gear on the bike is more comfortable. For shorter journeys, a backpack or messenger bag can often be more convenient and easier to use.

⚙ RACKS AND PANNIERS

Pannier racks carry big loads but cannot be attached to all bikes. Longer chainstays are necessary to accommodate large rear panniers, and lightweight forks will not be able to accomodate front racks.

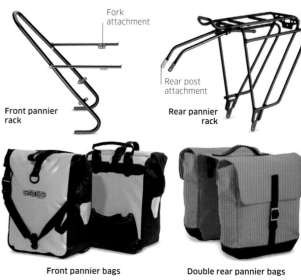

Fork attachment

Front pannier rack

Rear post attachment

Rear pannier rack

⚙ BACKPACKS/MESSENGER BAGS

Backpacks can handle bigger, heavier loads more comfortably than messenger bags, which offer easier access to their contents.

Messenger bag

Roll-top backpack

Mountain bike backpack

Front pannier bags

Double rear pannier bags

⚙ FRAME BAGS

By distributing weight within your bike's frame, these bags affect handling less than traditional panniers, making them particularly suited to off-road riding. They are often lighter and provide a more balanced ride.

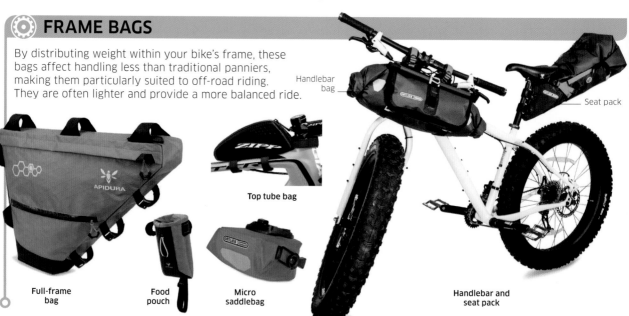

Handlebar bag

Seat pack

Top tube bag

Full-frame bag

Food pouch

Micro saddlebag

Handlebar and seat pack

Tailfin pannier bags attached to rack

OTHER RACK SYSTEMS

A front or rear basket is convenient for carrying groceries. Top-mounted bags often have a quick-release mechanism.

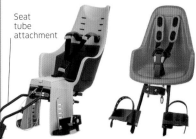

Metal basket

Seatpost-mounted rack

Luggage clip

Tailfin quick-release rear rack

HANDLEBAR BAGS

Handlebar bags provide easy access to important items, while bar-mounted map pockets are useful for navigation.

Map pocket

Clear map case

Handlebar bag

CHILD SEATS AND TRAILERS

A small child can be carried in a child seat. As they get bigger, a trailer or trailer bike may be more appropriate.

Seat tube attachment

Quick-release

Converts to stroller

Seat tube-mounted child seat

Top tube-mounted child seat

Pannier-mounted child seat

Two-seat child trailer

LUGGAGE TRAILERS

Useful on shopping trips or for carrying extra gear, double-wheel trailers offer good stability. Single-wheel versions are better for off-road cycling.

Waterproof cover

Flatbed standing trailer

Frame bars

Cargo trailer

Smaller wheels

Flag for visibility

Standing trailer

Journey trailer

Road riding

Everyday clothes are fine for short trips, but for longer rides or if the weather is bad, you will be a lot more comfortable in the correct gear. Wearing clothing cut for the specific movements your body makes while pedaling will make a huge difference in your ride experience. Fabrics are lightweight and breathable, which enables your sweat to evaporate, extra padding absorbs shock, and water and windproof layers protect you from the elements.

ESSENTIAL LAYERS

Being too hot or too cold is uncomfortable, so adding and removing layers is a useful way to keep your core body temperature consistent. Layers trap heat, and should be easily removed or added to. An all-weather layered outfit might consist of:

- A breathable base layer worn next to your skin. This wicks away moisture on hot days and retains heat on cold ones.
- A middle layer of stretchable jersey that protects from the sun and helps to regulate your body temperature.
- A removable waterproof or windproof shell layer that protects you from the rain and offers your skin ventilation when you sweat.

ROAD CLOTHING

Cycling clothes are designed to fit close to your body, with longer sleeves and backs cut to accommodate a forward-leaning riding position. Breathable fabrics "wick" sweat away from your skin, while bib shorts have comfortable straps in place of restrictive waistbands.

① **Wicking base layer** keeps you dry and warm.

② **Short-sleeved shirt** with high neck to shield you from the sun.

③ **Sleeveless gilet** (padded jacket) for warmth and wind protection.

④ **Bib shorts** are padded for extra comfort in saddle.

⑤ **Thin wicking socks** draw perspiration away from your feet.

⑥ **Fingerless gloves** are padded, while absorbant patches can be used to wipe away your sweat.

⑦ **Road helmet** is lightweight and aerodynamic with good ventilation.

⑧ **Cycling shoes** have rigid soles, ensuring your feet a stable platform.

⑨ **Glasses** protect eyes from sun, as well as insects and stones.

Air vents cool head

Low collar

Shoes with cleats

EXTRAS

From protective glasses and cleat covers to lightweight caps, gloves, and warmers, bike accessories fulfil a range of functions and offer you added comfort.

Cleat covers

Mirrored glasses

Cycling cap   Full-finger gloves   Arm warmers

HI-VIS GEAR

High-visibility clothing is essential if you cycle at night or on cloudy days. Some garments have added reflective areas, and you can customize your gear with stick-on patches.

Helmet   Gloves   Jacket

FOR WET WEATHER

While riding in the rain may be unavoidable, it is still possible for you to stay dry with the right gear. Key items include waterproof jackets and packable capes.

Fleece-lined for warmth

Hood shields face

Overshoes   Helmet rain cover   Waterproof rain jacket   Lightweight, showerproof jacket   Waterproof cape

FOR COLD WEATHER

Warm clothing is a must if you want to keep riding through the winter. Gloves, thermal vests, and bib tights all help to regulate body temperature.

High-visibility strip

Straps lined with fleece

Insulated gloves   Micro-wool socks   Thermal vest   Windproof, full-sleeve jacket   Full-length bib tights

Off-road riding

Looser and less form-fitting than road-bike clothing, off-road clothes prioritize freedom of movement. Baggy mountain bike shorts are hard-wearing, with practical pockets and padded liners for extra comfort on rough, rocky terrain. The loose clothing gives you a greater range of movement. Waterproof options can help you withstand splashes of mud and water on the trail, while full-face helmets and body armor help protect you on more extreme rides.

BEFORE YOU BUY

Comfort and flexibility are crucial to off-road gear, so be sure to shop around and try clothes on before you buy.

- Ensure shorts and pants allow you to move your legs freely.

- When trying on tops and jackets, make sure they allow you room to stretch upward, and that they do not ride up to expose your back.

- Choose clear glasses that can be worn all year round. Some have interchangeable lenses—yellow ones are good for overcast or dull light conditions.

- Helmets should fit properly. Always buy the right-size headgear; check that it comes with the correct certification.

MOUNTAIN BIKE CLOTHING

Off-road clothing is designed to allow you as broad a range of movements as possible. Baggy shorts accommodate protective knee pads and are designed to be worn over padded lycra shorts, or feature an integrated liner, so you do not need underwear. Breathable fabrics keep you insulated as well as dry, and shoes have durable soles with ample tread.

① **Wicking underlayer** moves your sweat away from your skin.

② **Baggy jersey** offers you a full range of movements.

③ **Softshell mountain bike jacket** protects against wind and showers.

④ **Baggy shorts** with a padded liner give you a more comfortable ride.

⑤ **Merino socks** provide warmth.

⑥ **Full-finger, padded gloves** with extra grip protect your hands.

⑦ **Lightweight, vented helmet** fully covers your head.

⑧ **Ankle-height** shoes with off-road cleats allow you to pedal efficiently.

⑨ **Glasses** with orange or yellow interchangable lenses.

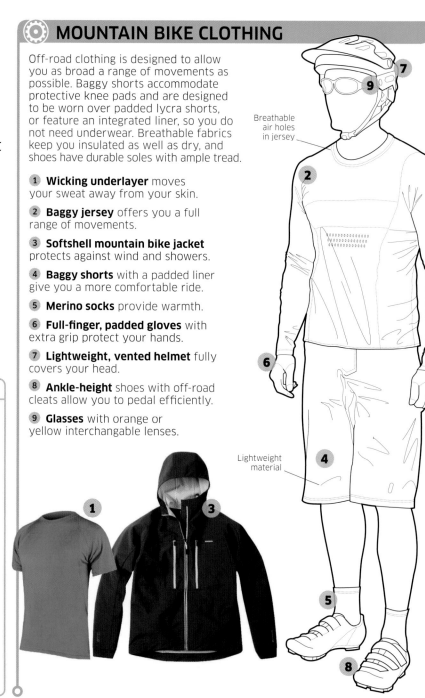

Breathable air holes in jersey

Lightweight material

Buyer's tip: Waterproof jackets can lose their water resistance if they become too dirty and sweaty: the fabric will start to absorb rather than repel water. In-wash products can help with reproofing, and durable water repellent sprays are also available.

EXTRAS

Good-quality accessories will reduce the risk of broken bones and bruises. Full-face helmets are vital for extreme mountain biking, while goggles protect eyes from debris. Knee and elbow pads give you maximum flexibility without compromising your safety.

Lightweight polycarbonate shell

Full-face helmet

Antifogging lenses

Flexible joints

Goggles

Elbow protectors

Knee protectors

FOR WET WEATHER

Taking to the trails in wet weather is a lot more comfortable if you are wearing the right clothing. Overpants protect your legs from wheel spray, and socks may come with waterproof liners.

Elastic waistband

Nonslip soles

Waterproof shoes

Lined socks

Water-resistant overpants

Waterproof hardshell jacket

FOR COLD WEATHER

Jackets with dropped backs and high necks keep the cold out and the heat in. You can wear your neck warmers like scarves, or folded upward to keep ears warm. Full-length bib tights form an insulating layer against your skin.

Windproof layer

Neck warmer (a.k.a. buff)

Insulated winter gloves

Thermal underlayer

Full-sleeve, waterproof thermal jacket

Full-length bib tights

CLOTHING CARE

Off-road clothes can be expensive, so always check the manufacturer's instructions before washing them in case you inadvertently damage them. Avoid household fabric softeners, as they can damage a material's wicking properties.

- Wash any mud off in the shower before putting your clothes in the washing machine.
- Clean your shorts after every ride to avoid bacteria build-up.
- Wash your cycling clothes separately–they need a cool, gentle setting with a low spin speed. Use a detergent that works at low temperatures.
- Zip up your jacket before putting it in the machine to prevent the zipper tearing other clothes.
- Air-dry Lycra-based or other stretchy clothing. Hot tumble driers can wreck expensive gear.

Wide straps for comfort

GETTING STARTED

Workshop tools

Bike tools are a low-cost investment that could save you large amounts of money in the long run. Having a proper tool at hand will allow you to carry out most maintenance tasks and keep your bike at peak performance. Start by purchasing the basics, adding more specialized tools as needed.

⚙ STANDS AND PUMPS

Choose a frame stand that fits your bike and workshop space. A pump with an accurate gauge will help you keep your tires and shocks at the right pressure.

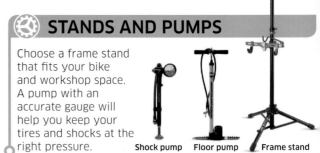

Shock pump   Floor pump   Frame stand

🔍 ESSENTIAL TOOL KIT

There are some basic tools that you cannot do without. These will allow you to perform a range of common tasks in order to keep your bike on the road.

Mechanic tools
- Multi-tool
- Adjustable wrench
- Set of wrenches
- Pliers
- Screwdrivers–flat-head and Phillips

Other equipment
- Puncture repair kit
- Tire levers
- Oil
- Grease
- Degreaser

⚙ PLIERS AND SCREWDRIVERS

A small set of screwdrivers incorporating varying sizes of flat-head and Phillips is useful for making small adjustments. Needle-nose pliers are suitable for tight areas.

Razor-sharp edge

Needle-nose pliers   Pliers   Cable cutters   Phillips and flat-head screwdrivers

⚙ WRENCHES AND KEYS

The number and variety of available wrenches and keys can be intimidating, so start by buying an adjustable wrench that you can use on a range of tasks. Supplement this with a good set of hex keys and then, as you grow in confidence, start buying tools that are designed for specific tasks.

Headset wrenches

Adjustable wrench

Cone wrenches

Set of wrenches

Ring end

Set of hex keys

Pedal wrench

Adjustable torque tool

Torx keys

CLEANING TOOLS AND SPARE PARTS

- Bike-specific brushes
- Bucket and sponges
- Chain keeper
- Alcohol-based cleaner
- Bike polish
- Cable housing (brake/gear)
- Inner tubes (correct size/valve type for your bike)
- Inner cables (brake/gear)
- Brake pads
- Cable end caps

CHAIN AND CASSETTE

Different brands and types of cassette require different tools, so check that the one you buy is compatible with your bike. Chain whips enable cassette removal, and some come in combination with a lockring tool.

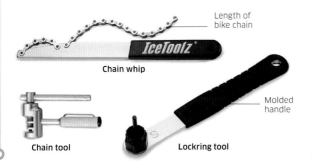

Length of bike chain

Chain whip

Molded handle

Chain tool

Lockring tool

CRANKARMS AND BBS

The bottom bracket (BB) requires specific maintenance tools that may be worth buying if you want to remove or tighten the BB, for example. Crank pullers are useful to ensure you can evenly and efficiently remove the crankarm.

BB ring wrench with preload cap tool

Chainring peg spanner

Splined BB remover tool

Crank puller tool

SPECIALIZED EQUIPMENT

In addition to the essential workshop tools, there are many other pieces of equipment that will make maintenance tasks easier. You may not use them very often, but they could save you time and money in the long run. For example, a chain wear indicator could prevent expensive cassette repairs later.

Internal jaws

Measuring caliper

Tire pressure gauge

Grease gun

Tubeless valve core remover

Caliper arms

Master link pliers

Chain wear indicator

Grips for tension

Cable puller

Trueing stand

BLEED KIT

Hydraulic disc brakes will eventually need bleeding in order to keep them performing at their peak. Kits make it easier and quicker to do a thorough bleed, but make sure you get the appropriate kit for your brakes.

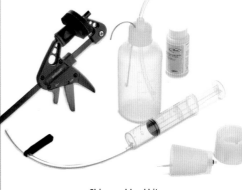

Shimano bleed kit

Bleed blocks and keys

▶ **TOOLS AND TECHNIQUES**
Workshop techniques

From vintage models to cutting-edge superbikes, all bicycles employ the same basic technology of nuts and bolts. Nevertheless, there are a few basic principles–as well as some less obvious workshop hints and tips– that will help to make maintenance more straightforward and precise, and that, if followed correctly, should save you time and money.

PREPPING PARTS

Threaded components should be "prepped"–prepared–prior to assembly. Clean them with degreaser or an alcohol-based cleaner, then apply the appropriate agent to them, as outlined below.

- **Grease** Use for most parts, especially: crank bolts, pedal axles, cable clamp bolts (on derailleurs and brakes).

- **Threadlock** Use for parts that are prone to rattling loose, such as: jockey pulley bolts, brake caliper or disc rotor bolts, stem face plate bolts, and cleat bolts.

- **Antiseize** Use for parts that are prone to binding up, especially those that are made of aluminum or titanium.

- **Carbon assembly paste** Use when either or both parts are carbon (except for stem/ steerer tube contact, which should be left dry).

DIRECTION OF TIGHTENING

Nearly all parts tighten clockwise (to the right) and loosen counter-clockwise (to the left). The exceptions are pedals and some bottom brackets (BB). To check, inspect the threads–they slope upward toward the direction of tightening.

Clockwise
(standard) thread

Counterclockwise
(less common) thread

MECHANICAL ADVANTAGE

When working on parts that require significant force to loosen, such as a cassette lockring, place tools at 90 degrees to each other, the part, or your bracing hand, to increase the derailleuranical advantage–the amount by which the tool amplifies the force you are applying.

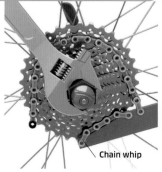

Chain whip

PUSH DOWN

Tighening or loosening parts is easier if you position the tool so that you can push downward. Be aware that this reduces the effort required, so be careful you do not overtighten the part.

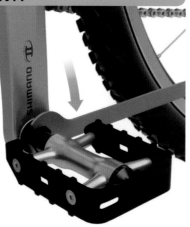

DANGER AREAS

When working near potentially dangerous areas, position tools so that if your hands slip they move away, from sharp parts, such as chainrings, sprockets, and disc brake rotors.

Position tools
away from
danger area

CROSS-THREADING

Occurring when two threaded parts are screwed together without properly aligning the threads, cross-threading can lead to stripped threads. To avoid it, screw the part in by hand so that you can feel when the two threads are "seated" and can tell immediately if the force required to turn the part increases; if it does, then loosen the part and start again. Try screwing the part the other way until you feel a slight click—this is the feeling of the threads engaging. Tighten carefully by hand.

Pedal and crank cross-threading is common

CARING FOR TOOLS

Look after your tools with the same level of care as you would your bike. Keep everything clean—grit, grease, and water can cause your tools to rust or wear out. Keep an eye on the condition of your tools, and throw away any that show signs of wear—rounded hex keys or wrenches with worn-down jaws can damage the bicycle parts you use them on. Store your tools in dry areas, out of sunlight, ideally hanging them up on a pegboard or similar.

HEXAGONAL HEADS

When working on bikes secured with hexagonal-head nuts and bolts (rather than the hex bolts found on most modern bikes), use the ring end of a combination wrench, or a socket wrench. These grip the head on all six faces, rather than just two faces (as an open-ended wrench does).

Ring wrench on a hexagonal-headed bolt

RECESSED BOLTS

If you are working on a recessed hex bolt, you might need to use the long axis of your hex key to reach it. If the bolt is tight, you can increase the leverage by sliding a close-fitting length of tubing over the hex key's shorter axis.

Insert key at right angle to bolt head surface

EXPOSED BOLTS

Hex and torx bolts have a recessed head that can fill with mud or other dirt, especially on pedal cleats. Take care to clean out any dirt or debris before trying to loosen or tighten these bolts, so that the key can fit in easily.

Dig out dirt before inserting hex key

LOOSENING BLOW

Pedal threads, crank bolts, and BB cups can get very tight. Often a short, sharp blow on the wrench with the heel of your hand or a rubber hammer will loosen them. If not, place a length of tubing or a spare seatpost over the handle of the tool to increase leverage.

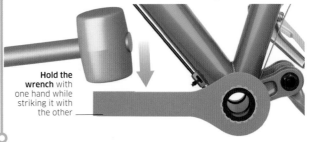

Hold the wrench with one hand while striking it with the other

The M-checks

The M-checks are a series of tests you can use to ensure your bike is functioning safely. You have a duty to pedestrians, motorists, and other cyclists–not to mention yourself–to ensure your bike is safe, so perform M-checks regularly.

Named after the M-shaped path of the checks, M-checks are a thorough series of inspections of a bicycle's frame and components for wear and tear, damage, and poor adjustment. Start at the front wheel, then work up the fork to the handlebar and controls, over the frame and saddle, and finally on to the gears.

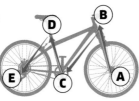

PRERIDE CHECKS

In addition to the periodic M-checks, you should make a series of preride safety checks every time you ride your bike.

① **Pull brake levers** to check adjustment of pads and that wheels can be locked.

② **Inspect brake pads** for wear and alignment with rim.

③ **Twist stem, handlebar, saddle, and seatpost** in turn to check that all clamp bolts are tight. (For carbon parts, do not twist or push– instead, check bolts with a torque wrench.)

④ **Squeeze tires** to check pressure.

⑤ **Grip wheels** to check quick-releases/wheel nuts are secure in dropouts.

A WHEEL AND FRONT HUB

The first area to check is the front of the bike. Start by slowly spinning the wheel, then move on to the hub, fork, and brake.

While spinning the wheel, check that:

① **Tire tread/sidewalls** are not worn, and pressure is correct.

② **Rim brakes** do not rub.

③ **Disc brake rotor** is straight.

④ **Rim** is true, with no cracks, wear in the braking surface, or bulges at the spoke holes.

⑤ **Tire bead** is seated in the rim, with no inner tube visible.

⑥ **Spoke** tension is even.

Push the top of the wheel sideways to check that:

⑦ **Wheel nut/quick-release** is secured tight in the dropout.

⑧ **Hub bearings** are tight.

Visually inspect:

⑨ **Fork** for dents or cracks.

Apply brake to check that:

⑩ **Brake** functions correctly.

⑪ **Suspension bushings** are not worn by pushing forward with the brake applied.

B HEADSET AND HANDLEBAR

Next, check the "cockpit"–the bar, stem, headset, and controls.

① **Apply front brake,** turn handlebar 90 degrees, hold steerer assembly, and push forward. Any play indicates loose headset bearings.

② **Inspect bar** for dents/straightness.

③ **Check end plugs** are inserted.

④ **Grip brake and gear** levers to check they are securely fastened.

⑤ **Check bar** is at 90 degrees to wheel with your legs either side of front wheel.

⑥ **Grip bar** to check all stem bolts are tight.

C BOTTOM BRACKET

Move down to the BB area to begin the drivetrain checks.

① **Wobble crankarms** side-to-side by hand. Movement indicates a loose BB.

② **Spin pedals** to check axles turn.

③ **Twist pedals** on their axles to check bearings are tight and threads are securely tightened on crankarms.

④ **Shift gears** so the chain is in the smallest chainring and middle of cassette, then backpedal to check chainrings are straight, bolts are tight, and chain is free of stiff links.

⑤ **Check front derailleur** is tight, parallel to chainrings, and not worn.

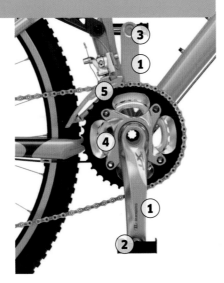

D FRAME, CABLES, SADDLE, AND SUSPENSION

Traveling back up the bike, check the frame, cables, saddle, and suspension.

① **Check each frame tube** for dents/cracks by running your fingers over it. (Clean the bike before doing this.)

② **Inspect cable** housings/hydraulic hoses for wear, especially where they rub on frame.

③ **Check seatpost** is tight in clamp.

④ **Check saddle** is securely clamped on the seatpost, and look down on it to check its alignment with top tube.

⑤ **Check rear suspension's** shock by holding the saddle and pushing on the tire. Check for play in the linkage bushings/bearings.

Ensure shock absorber is moving correctly

E REAR WHEEL

Finish M-checks by inspecting the rear wheel, brakes, and gears.

① **Stand behind wheel** to check rear derailleur and hanger are not bent. Look for loose pivots and worn jockey pulleys.

② **Spin the rear wheel** to check for tire or rim wear, spoke tension, and brake alignment.

③ **Check the rear brake** functions.

④ **Check for hub play** by pushing the wheel's top, then secure axles.

⑤ **Run through gears** to ensure derailleurs are correctly adjusted. Inspect sprockets for worn teeth.

⑥ **Use a chain wear indicator** to check for chain wear.

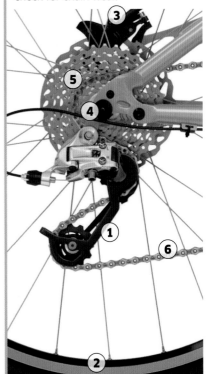

Cleaning your bike

The first line of defense in maintaining your bike is regular cleaning to prevent a build-up of dirt that can wear out parts. Focus on your entire bike, cleaning the dirtiest areas first. Follow every step listed here for a complete wash, or clean each area as it gets dirty.

⊙ CLEANING TIP

Never turn your bike upside-down when cleaning it—dirty water can seep inside the frame and damage the saddle and handlebar. If you do not have a frame stand, lean the frame against the wall vertically.

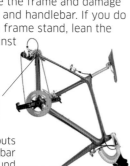

Rest rear dropout against wall

Fork dropouts and handlebar on ground

⊙ MUD AND ROAD GRIME

Before cleaning your bike, remove any accessories. Depending on the riding conditions and the type of cycling you do—off-road riding is notorious for spreading mud—it may require washing all over. Begin by spraying or brushing the dirt away, paying special attention to these areas:

① **Tires**

② **Wheels**

③ **Frame**

④ **Under saddle**

⑤ **Under the down tube**

⑥ **Fork blades**

⑦ **Brace**, crown, inside steerer (mountain bikes)

⑧ **Brake calipers** (road bikes)

Spray your bike all over with a cycling-specific detergent that will not damage the paintwork and brakes, and then rinse with water.

⊙ DRIVETRAIN

For the best results when cleaning the drivetrain, remove the wheel and loop the chain around a chain keeper clamped to the rear dropout.

① **Begin turning the pedals** backward, then brush or spray degreaser onto the chain. Scrape dirt off the jockey pulleys with the plastic bristles of a brush as you backpedal.

② **Apply degreaser** to chainrings. Scrub using a sponge on both sides of the chain and chainrings.

③ **Degrease** the front and rear derailleurs with a small bottlebrush.

④ **Hold a sponge**, brush, or chain bath against the chain while backpedaling to dislodge dirty lubricant.

⑤ **Rinse off degreaser** thoroughly—any left will repel future lubricant.

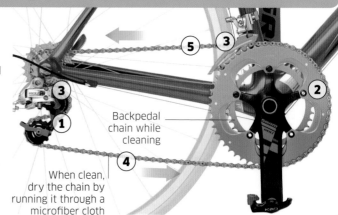

Backpedal chain while cleaning

When clean, dry the chain by running it through a microfiber cloth

Workshop tip: Do not clean your bike with hot water, which can melt the grease that coats threads and bearings. If using a hose, keep the pressure low and do not aim the water at the bearings. Detergents should be specially formulated for cleaning bicycles.

CASSETTE, WHEELS, ROTORS

The most effective way to clean the wheels is by removing them from your bicycle.

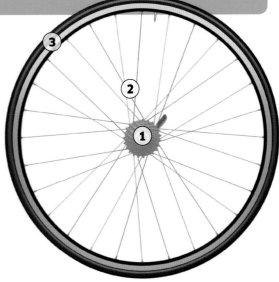

(1) **Scrub the cassette** with a brush and degreaser to remove any dirty lubricant and grime, scrubbing the rear of the cassette (coming at it from the hub side). Use a rag to "floss" back and forth between cogs to remove hard-to-reach grime.

(2) **Wash the tires**, spokes, and hub body with bike detergent.

(3) **Wipe the rim** with a rag soaked in bike detergent, checking the braking surface for wear as you do so. Repeat the process with the front wheel.

(4) **Clean the disc rotors** with disc-cleaning spray, which removes dirt without leaving a residue that can contaminate pads.

FRAME AND FORK

For best results use bike detergent to sponge-wash the frame, fork, and any other dirty areas, such as the brakes, pedals, and inside faces of the crankarms.

(1) **Clean under the saddle**, down tube, bottom bracket, and inside the stays.

(2) **Remove any grit** from the brake calipers and pads.

(3) **Replace the wheels** and allow to drip-dry. Disperse moisture by spraying with a Teflon-based bike polish, then apply lubricant as necessary (see pp.44–45).

Clean dirty bar tape or grips with rag soaked in penetrating oil

Rear stays are prone to dirt build-up

ELECTRONIC GEARS

Although electronic gears and drive systems are designed to work in wet conditions, be careful when cleaning them with water and detergents. To be safe, use a bike detergent or a specialized electronic shifter cleaning spray, which will clean and dry without needing to be wiped or rinsed off.

- Avoid using alcohol-based cleaner, soaking electronic parts in degreaser, or using sprays or brushes that can damage seals.

- If the junction box is dirty, remove it from the bike and cables, and clean it with bike detergent. Carefully wipe any charge ports or battery stations.

- Fit a rubber cover over crankarm-mounted power meters before cleaning them in order to protect them from water.

Lubricating your bike is as important as cleaning it and should be done immediately after every single bike wash. Lubricant and grease reduce friction on moving parts, so it is especially important to keep your chain lubricated. Lubricants also form a seal to protect bike components against water and corrosion, and they create a protective barrier between different materials—such as a steel frame with an aluminum seatpost inside—that prevents parts from seizing up.

CHAIN AND REAR DERAILLEUR

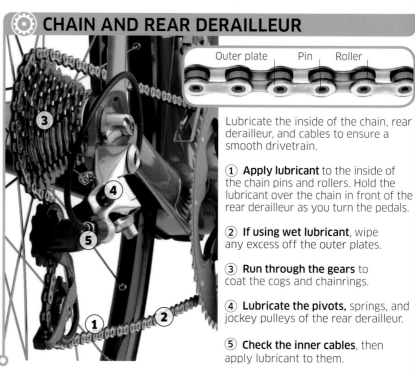

Outer plate   Pin   Roller

Lubricate the inside of the chain, rear derailleur, and cables to ensure a smooth drivetrain.

① **Apply lubricant** to the inside of the chain pins and rollers. Hold the lubricant over the chain in front of the rear derailleur as you turn the pedals.

② **If using wet lubricant**, wipe any excess off the outer plates.

③ **Run through the gears** to coat the cogs and chainrings.

④ **Lubricate the pivots**, springs, and jockey pulleys of the rear derailleur.

⑤ **Check the inner cables**, then apply lubricant to them.

CRANKARMS AND WHEELS

Lubricate the front derailleur and pedals at the same time as the spokes.

① **Lubricate** the front derailleur hangers and the springs.

② **On the wheels**, drip a small drop of lubricant where each spoke enters the nipple to prevent any corrosion.

③ **Lubricate** the retention spring of clipless pedals.

Retention spring

RIM BRAKES

Lubricate the brake pivots and cables to ensure powerful, effective braking.

① **Lubricate the pivots** of the brake calipers.

② **Dribble lubricant** into the cable housing; open the brake quick-release lever and shift the gears to expose the inner cables.

Open quick-release lever tab before lubricating cables

- Lubricants (see Types of Lubricant and Grease box)
- Microfiber cloth or rag
- Cable tie

Workshop tip: When applying lubricant, use the smallest amount possible, and wipe away any excess. This is because lubricants will become contaminated with dirt over time, eventually forming a grinding paste that wears out components.

SUSPENSION PIVOTS, SEATPOST

Grease the suspension to ensure it moves freely and also lubricate the seatpost, as it is the part most likely to seize inside the frame.

(1) Apply grease or carbon-assembly paste to the base of the seatpost and inside the top of the seat tube, to prevent seizing.

(2) Check the full-suspension pivots on mountain bikes, then apply grease to the pivot bearings or lubricant to the bushings.

(3) Dribble specialized suspension lubricant into the rear shock, then push downward on the saddle to distribute it.

Lubricate bushings or bearings

SUSPENSION FORK

Lubricate the front fork to keep it responsive.

(1) Dribble suspension lubricant down the fork stanchion.

(2) Use a cable tie to pry back the seal, allowing the lubricant to penetrate inside the fork sliders. Pump the fork to distribute the lubricant.

Apply lubricant to fork stanchion

TYPES OF LUBRICANT AND GREASE

You should always use bike-specific lubricants; household oils are too thick, and penetrating oil is suitable only for cleaning away lubricant and grease you have applied.

- **Wet lubricants** use a heavy, oil-based formula. They are ideal for wet, muddy conditions, as they are less likely to be washed off. However, they can trap dust and grime.

- **Dry lubricants** use a light formulation with the lubricant suspended in a solvent. The solvent evaporates after application, leaving the lubricant as a dry, waxy film on the chain. These lubricants pick up less dirt than wet lubricants, but must be reapplied more often. They are most useful in dry conditions and sandy, dusty terrain.

- **Basic grease** reduces friction on static parts such as bearings and threads. Some types of grease are waterproof; others are designed specifically to protect high-temperature areas such as disc brake pistons.

- **Antiseize grease** contains particles of copper or aluminum to prevent two surfaces seizing together due to corrosion.

- **Carbon-assembly paste** contains microparticles that improve friction. It is ideal for components that must be tightened to low torque values, such as carbon-fiber parts.

Protecting your frame

Bikes are designed to cope with intensive use. However, you can extend your bike's lifespan by protecting the frame from damage caused by debris, parts rubbing each other, or even wear from your own legs and feet. Protective items for specific areas are shown here.

3 CABLE DONUTS/SPIRALS

Installing rings or spirals of rubber or plastic around the cable housings will help to stop them slapping against your frame.

Donuts | Spirals

2 DOWN TUBE PROTECTORS

Install a down tube protector, or a section of old tire attached with cable ties, to your bike to protect it from impact from rocks and debris.

Cover base of down tube

Some down tube protectors cover bottom bracket

Rider's knees may rub top tube

Chain may "slap" against chainstay

1 TUBE PROTECTORS

Apply tube protectors or tape such as "helicopter tape" (see Workshop tip) to areas vulnerable to scratches, chips, or strikes from debris.

Strips may be shaped to fit curved areas

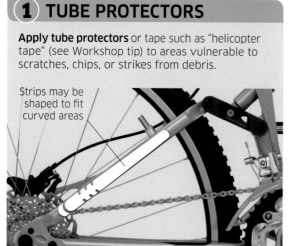

7 CHAINSTAY GUARD

Install a chainstay guard to protect the frame from chain slap, which occurs when the chain bounces repeatedly against the frame. You could buy a neoprene or plastic chainstay protector. Alternatively, you can use "helicopter tape" or even an old inner tire (see box, right).

4 FRAME PATCHES

Apply small stickers or pieces of tape to the frame wherever the cable housings rub.

Cable housings may rub against head tube

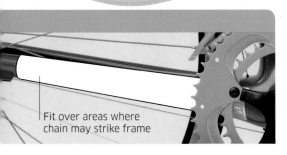

Fit over areas where chain may strike frame

PROTECTION IN TRANSIT

Before transporting your bike, pad the frame and secure the handlebar.

- Fix foam lagging around the frame with tape.
- Pad the delicate front forks and rear derailleur area.

Turn handlebars to lie parallel to frame

5 DOWNHILL BIKE CHAIN GUARD

A chain guard will help to stop the chain falling off the chainrings when you ride over rough terrain. In addition, install a bash guard to protect the chainrings against debris strikes from beneath the bike.

Bash guard

6 ROAD BIKE CHAIN CATCHER

This simple bolt-on device will stop the chain from slipping off the inner (small) chainring and possibly damaging the frame.

End of chain catcher lies beside inner chainring

DIY CHAINSTAY PROTECTION

Cut a section of old inner tube and wrap it around the chainstay to protect the frame against chain slap.

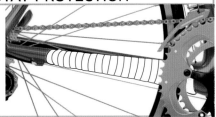

Emergency repairs

It is inevitable that at some point you will need to make road- or trail-side repairs of some kind. Carry basic supplies such as food, water, a phone, and money, and put together a repair kit (see box, right). A preride safety check (see p.40) will reduce the chance of a mechanical problem, and if you learn basic repair skills such as how to fix a puncture and how to use quick fixes (see box, opposite), you should have the knowledge you need to get home safely.

🔍 REPAIR KIT

In addition to the kit you normally carry in a saddlebag (see pp.24–25), take a few extras to help fix problems that could otherwise end your ride. Equipment will depend on your bike set-up, but examples include:

- Chain master link
- Zip ties
- Tire boot (2 in [5 cm] square of old tire)
- Duct tape
- Derailleur hanger
- Presta–Schrader valve converter (for using gas station tire inflators on road bikes)
- Valve extender (for screwing over the valve if a Presta tip breaks)

⚙ PUNCTURE REPAIR

Punctures are the most common problem that cyclists encounter. A puncture may result from a sharp object piercing a tire, or may occur in a sudden impact, if the inner tube gets pinched between the tire and the wheel rim. This damage produces two parallel, slitlike holes, sometimes called a "snakebite" puncture. Always carry tire levers and a puncture repair kit; these kits contain patches to repair an inner tube, plus items such as sandpaper, glue, and chalk.

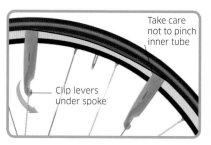

Take care not to pinch inner tube

Clip levers under spoke

1 Remove the wheel and check the tire for the cause of the puncture. Push the lever under the tire bead and lift it off the rim. Do the same with the second lever, and slide it around the rim.

2 Once you have taken off one side of the tire, you can remove the inner tube by sliding it out. Check over the tube to try and find the cause of the puncture.

6 Roughen the hole site with sandpaper to prepare the surface of the rubber for the glue. The roughened area should be slightly larger than the repair patch you will be using.

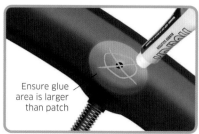

Ensure glue area is larger than patch

7 Apply glue to the whole of the roughened area, centered over the puncture. Leave the glue for about 30–60 seconds until it becomes tacky. Ensure that it is not runny in consistency.

Press for 30–60 seconds

8 Apply the patch in the middle of the tacky area, making sure you have covered all of the hole. Press it from the center outward to push out any air bubbles. Leave the patch to dry.

⚙ QUICK FIXES

Even if you keep your bike well-maintained and carry out regular safety checks (see pp.40–41), mechanical failures can still occur. In such cases, or if you lack spare parts or tools, try these roadside fixes.

Broken spoke	■ Remove the spoke, or if that is not possible wrap it around its neighbor for stability. Open up the brake caliper.
Bent wheel	■ If the wheel is seriously bent, place the bent part of the rim over the front of your knee, then pull the wheel from the side to straighten the rim. As a last resort, hit the rim on the ground to get rid of the bend. Replace the rim when you get home.
Split rim	■ Use zip ties to bind the split together. Ensure that you take great care riding home.
Broken rear derailleur	■ Remove the derailleur, then use a chain tool to shorten the chain. Reconnect it with a master link, then ride home single speed.

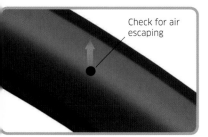

Check for air escaping

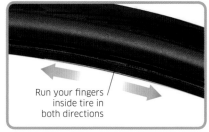

Run your fingers inside tire in both directions

Mark center of hole

3 **If you cannot find** the cause, pump air into the tube and listen for the hiss as air escapes. To find a tiny hole, lift the tube to your lips (where your skin is sensitive) to feel for escaping air.

4 **If you still have not discovered** the cause of the puncture, run your fingers carefully around the inside of the tire to feel for any sharp objects. Once found, check the corresponding area of the tube.

5 **Mark the hole area** with a ballpoint pen or crayon, with the hole at the center. Check the other side of the tube again in case the puncture is a "snakebite" type, with a second hole on the other side.

Dust chalk to cover glue beyond the patch edge

Run fingers under inside tire to check for dirt

9 **Grate chalk dust** against the repair-kit box and spread the dust over the glued area. This chalky dust will help to prevent the inner tube from sticking to the inside of the tire.

10 **Check the inside** of the tire and the rim again. Remove whatever caused the puncture, and any other pieces of grit, dirt, or debris that could puncture your newly repaired inner tube.

11 **Fit one side** of the tire into the rim. Partially inflate the tube so that it is soft but holds its shape. Insert the tube under the tire and fit the valve through the rim. Reseat the tire in the rim.

STEERING AND SADDLE

Headsets

A headset enables the forks to rotate within the head tube as you turn the handlebar. Older, threaded types (see pp.54-55) are fastened to a thread on the fork's steerer tube, which is connected to the handlebar with a quill stem. On modern threadless headsets (see pp.56-57), the stem clamps directly onto the steerer tube of the forks. There are two types of threadless headset–built in (shown right) and external cup. Built-in headsets have cartridge bearings that sit inside the head tube of the frame. To replace a cartridge bearing, simply pull it out and put a new one into place. The external cup system has cups that are pressed into the frame. These need to be installed with a headset press tool.

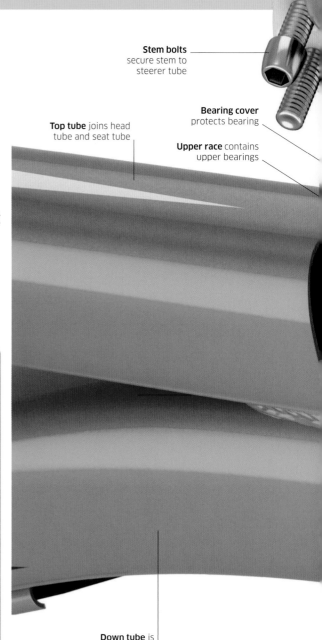

Stem bolts secure stem to steerer tube

Bearing cover protects bearing

Top tube joins head tube and seat tube

Upper race contains upper bearings

Down tube is joined to head tube

⚙ PARTS FOCUS

The headset contains two sets of bearings, contained within races, which enable the handlebar and front wheel to turn.

① The **star nut** is located inside the steerer tube, and pulls the stem and fork together inside the head tube.

② On a modern threadless headset, the **spacers** (as shown here) enable you to adjust the height of the stem and handlebar.

③ **Bearings** ensure that your handlebar and forks can turn smoothly. You need to keep them well maintained (see pp.54-57).

④ The **crown race** is the lowest bearing race on the headset. It sits below the lower head tube race, on the crown at the top of the forks.

Top cap bolt threads into the star nut inside steerer tube

Stem connects handlebar to steerer tube

1

2

Upper bearing contains individual ball bearings

Compression ring holds bearing in place

3

Ball bearings reduce friction, allowing forks to move smoothly

Bearing spacer holds loose bearings in place

Steerer tube connects forks to stem and handlebar

Head tube houses steerer tube

Stem clamp secures handlebar to stem

Handlebar can be turned freely due to bearings in headset

Fork crown joins forks to steerer tube

Lower race sits at base of head tube

3

Lower bearing sits inside lower race

4

Forks turn as handlebar is moved

▶ **SERVICING A HEADSET**
Threaded headsets

Threaded headsets secure the forks using adjustable and locking nuts that screw onto the threaded steerer tube. They feature either ball or cartridge bearings. Notchy or rough steering is a sign that your headset needs maintenance.

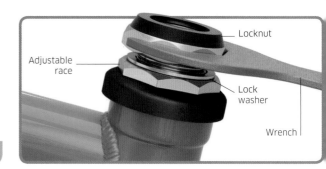

Locknut

Adjustable race

Lock washer

Wrench

 BEFORE YOU START

- Secure your bike in a frame stand, if available
- Prepare a clear space where you can lay out the parts
- Remove the handlebar and stem (see pp.58–59)
- Remove the front wheel (see pp.78–79)

2 **With the forks secured** to the down tube, unscrew the locknut with a wrench. Remove the lock washer, any spacers, and the adjustable race, so that you can access the bearings in the headset.

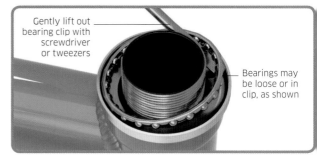

Gently lift out bearing clip with screwdriver or tweezers

Bearings may be loose or in clip, as shown

3 **Remove the bearings** from the top race, and check that the races are smooth and undamaged. Replace any worn bearings. If the races are worn, you will need to source a replacement headset.

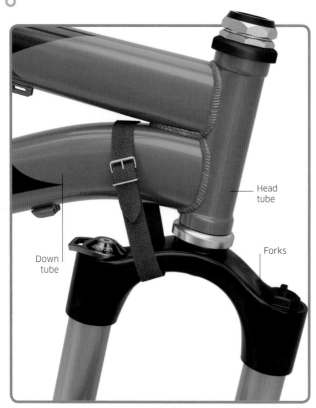

Head tube

Forks

Down tube

Remove strap to release forks

Bearings in a clip

Crown race

Forks

1 **Secure the forks** to the down tube of the frame with an adjustable strap. This will stop them from dropping out of the frame as you loosen the adjustable race and the locknut.

4 **Remove the adjustable strap** and lower the forks from the head tube so that you can access the bearings in the crown race. Remove, check, and clean the bearings. Replace them if they are worn.

TOOLS AND EQUIPMENT

- Frame stand
- Adjustable strap
- Set of wrenches
- Flat-head screwdriver
- Tweezers
- Grease

Workshop tip: Make a note of the order and position of any seals, washers, and spacers removed. If the races contain loose bearings, count how many there are before removing them, and use a magnet to stop them from falling on the floor or rolling away.

Grease crown race

5 **Apply a liberal amount** of grease to the crown race, and reinstall the bearings, or insert new ones if required.

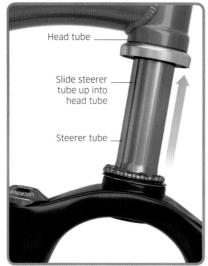

Head tube

Slide steerer tube up into head tube

Steerer tube

6 **Slide the steerer tube** into the head tube. Secure the forks using the strap until the locknut is flush against the down tube.

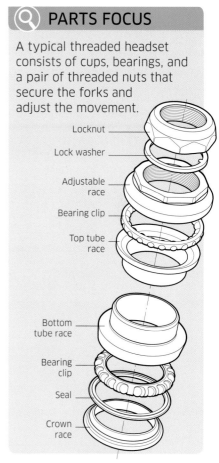

PARTS FOCUS

A typical threaded headset consists of cups, bearings, and a pair of threaded nuts that secure the forks and adjust the movement.

Locknut
Lock washer
Adjustable race
Bearing clip
Top tube race

Bottom tube race
Bearing clip
Seal
Crown race

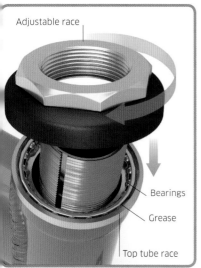

Adjustable race

Bearings

Grease

Top tube race

7 **Grease the inside** of the top tube race and insert the bearings. Screw the adjustable top tube race onto the steerer tube.

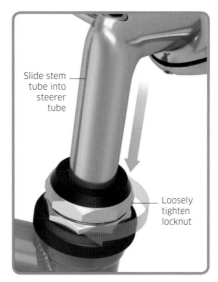

Slide stem tube into steerer tube

Loosely tighten locknut

8 **Fit the lock washer** and nut, then insert the handlebar stem into the steerer tube, tightening the locknut with your fingers.

Hold adjustable race still

Tighten locknut against lock washer

9 **Using two wrenches**, fully tighten the locknut against the lock washer. Position the handlebar, then tighten securely.

Threadless headsets

Threadless headsets secure the forks by allowing the handlebar stem to clamp around the steerer tube. A top cap compresses everything together. As with threaded headsets, a rough feeling when steering is usually an indication that the bearings need maintenance or replacement.

 BEFORE YOU START

- Secure your bike in a frame stand
- Remove the front wheel (see pp.78–79)
- Release the brake and gear cables, if required
- Support the forks with an adjustable strap (see pp.54–55)

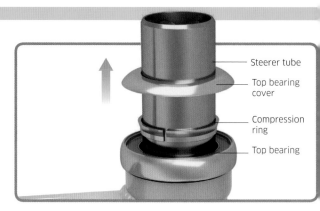

Steerer tube

Top bearing cover

Compression ring

Top bearing

2 **Push the steerer tube** down through the head tube. If it sticks, tap the top of it with a rubber hammer to free the compression ring. Remove the top bearing cover and the compression ring.

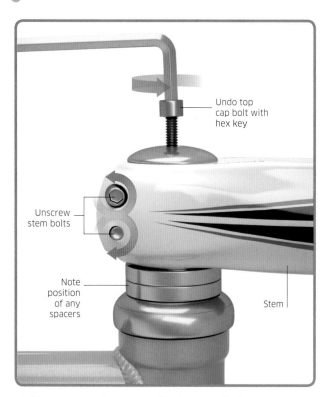

Undo top cap bolt with hex key

Unscrew stem bolts

Note position of any spacers

Stem

1 **Unscrew and remove the top cap bolt**. Loosen the stem bolts and pull the stem off the steerer tube, along with any spacers. Put the stem down carefully, so as not to damage gear or brake cables.

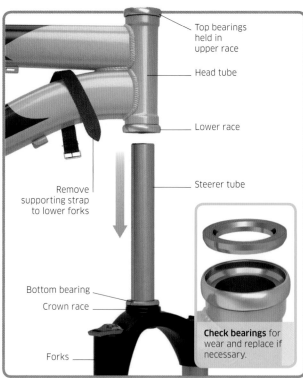

Top bearings held in upper race

Head tube

Lower race

Steerer tube

Remove supporting strap to lower forks

Bottom bearing

Crown race

Forks

Check bearings for wear and replace if necessary.

3 **Lower the forks** out of the head tube. Remove the top bearing from the upper race, and the bottom bearing from the crown race. Clean the bearings, inside of the head tube, and races.

Workshop tip: Use an adjustable strap to prevent the fork from dropping out of the headset when the compression ring is removed. Otherwise, support it with your hand.

Top bearing

Apply fresh grease inside upper race

4 Liberally grease the inside of the bearing races, as well as the bearings, even if new. Place the top bearing into the upper race.

Maintain upwards pressure on forks once inserted.

5 Slide the bottom bearing down the steerer tube, then insert the steerer tube up through the head tube—hold it in place.

Compression ring presses onto top bearing

6 Slide the compression ring down on to the steerer tube, and push it into the upper race, ensuring it is the right way up.

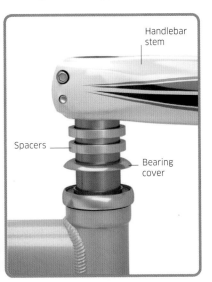

Handlebar stem

Spacers

Bearing cover

7 Replace the bearing cover over the bearings, install any spacers required, and loosely reattach the handlebar stem.

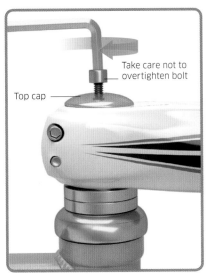

Take care not to overtighten bolt

Top cap

8 Reattach the top cap and bolt, and tighten to remove any slack in the headset. Avoid overtightening, as this will make the steering stiff.

Check for play before tightening stem bolts

9 Reattach the front wheel, ensuring that the handlebar and stem are straight, before securing the bolts on the side of the stem.

Handlebars and stems

Top cap bolt
secures stem to
steerer tube

Stem bolts are loosened
to adjust alignment
of handlebar

Headset
allows handlebars
and forks to
turn smoothly

A handlebar is essential for steering your bike. As you turn the bar, the stem turns the fork, adjusting the direction of the front wheel. The bar also holds the brake levers and gear-shift levers. There are two forms of handlebar: "drop" types for road bikes, and straight for mountain bikes. Handlebars and stems also come in a range of sizes. Wider bars will suit you best if you have broad shoulders, while longer stems enable you to adopt an aerodynamic position for racing. When replacing your handlebar, you should note the diameter of the exisiting one, as the replacement will have fit your stem clamp.

Electrical tape
holds gear and brake
cables to handlebar

PARTS FOCUS

The handlebar is a relatively simple component on a bike but has a crucial role, so ensure that it is secure and fitted correctly.

① The **stem** joins the handlebar and steerer tube.

② The **stem clamp** has a face plate that bolts over the handlebar, holding it to the stem. The diameter of the stem clamp must match that of the bar.

③ The **handlebar** holds the brake levers and shifters. Most handlebars are made of aluminum; top-end versions may be carbon.

④ **Handlebar tape and grips** improve grip and comfort for the rider. Handlebar tapes are used to cover gear and brake cables.

⑤ **Bar end plugs** cover each end of a drop handlebar and secure the bar tape.

Brake and gear cables are routed from handlebar to frame mounts

Bar end plugs
push into ends
of drop handlebar

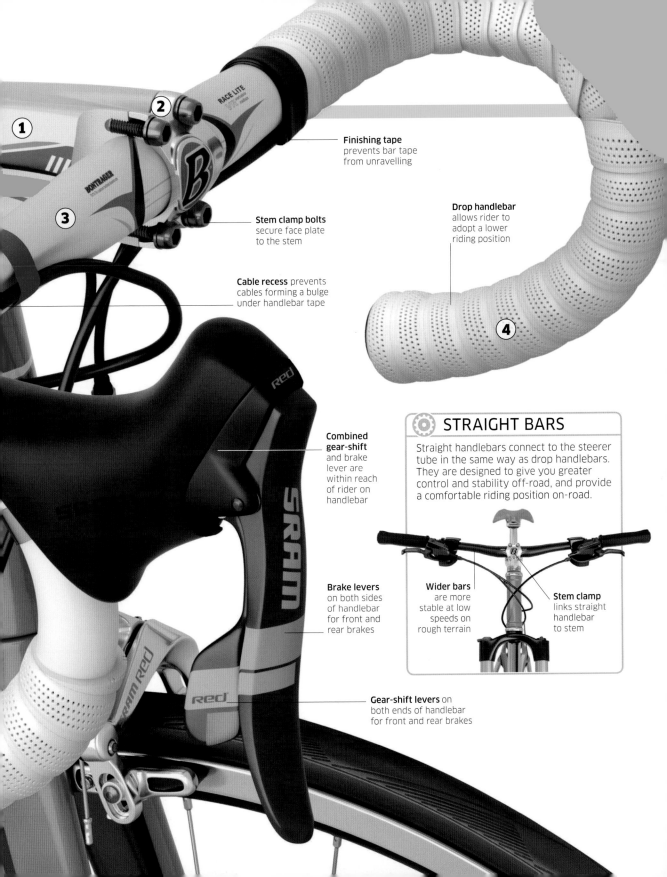

(1)

(2)

RACE LITE

Finishing tape
prevents bar tape
from unravelling

Drop handlebar
allows rider to
adopt a lower
riding position

(3)

BONTRAGER

Stem clamp bolts
secure face plate
to the stem

Cable recess prevents
cables forming a bulge
under handlebar tape

(4)

**Combined
gear-shift**
and brake
lever are
within reach
of rider on
handlebar

RED

SRAM

Brake levers
on both sides
of handlebar
for front and
rear brakes

SRAM RED

Red

Gear-shift levers on
both ends of handlebar
for front and rear brakes

STRAIGHT BARS

Straight handlebars connect to the steerer
tube in the same way as drop handlebars.
They are designed to give you greater
control and stability off-road, and provide
a comfortable riding position on-road.

Wider bars
are more
stable at low
speeds on
rough terrain

Stem clamp
links straight
handlebar
to stem

▶ REMOVING AND REPLACING
Drop and straight handlebars

A handlebar does not need to be replaced routinely, but it is something you may need to do after an accident, if you want to upgrade them, or to improve the look or comfort of your bike. It is a simple task, and the steps are similar for straight and drop handlebars (shown here).

🔧 BEFORE YOU START

- Make sure that your stem and new handlebar are compatible with your bike
- Take note of the angle and position of the old handlebar
- Measure the existing position of the brake and gear levers
- Secure your bike in a frame stand

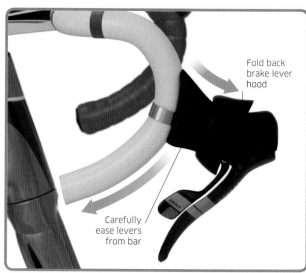

Fold back brake lever hood

Carefully ease levers from bar

2 Expose the clamp bolts on the gear and brake levers. Using an hex key or wrench, loosen the first lever clip and slide the lever from the bar. Repeat for the second lever. Let the levers hang by the cables.

Unwrap bar tape

Cables remain attached

If existing grips on flat handlebars are stuck, carefully cut through them with craft knife to access brake or gear levers.

1 Remove the bar tape or grips (see pp.62–65). If required, fold back the brake-lever hoods to give you better access to the handlebar, and cut away any tape holding the brake and gear cables in place.

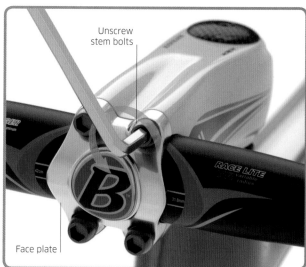

Unscrew stem bolts

Face plate

3 Undo the stem bolts on the face plate and remove the plate. If you are replacing like for like, note the bar angle. Lift out and clean the bar with cleaning fluid, checking the stem for damage.

TOOLS AND EQUIPMENT

- Tape measure
- Frame stand
- Craft knife

- Set of hex keys
  or wrenches
- Cleaning fluid

- Cloth
- Grease or fiber grip

Workshop tip: Adjust the position and angle of your brake and gear levers until they are comfortable for your riding style. Readjust as necessary.

Secure handlebar, leaving bolts just loose enough so small adjustments can be made later.

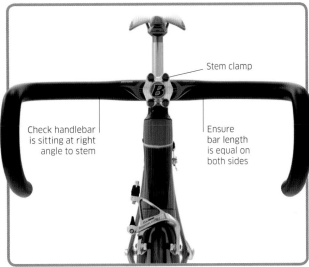

Stem clamp

Check handlebar is sitting at right angle to stem

Ensure bar length is equal on both sides

4 Apply a little grease to the new bar, face plate, and stem bolts. If you are installing carbon fiber bars, apply grease or fiber grip to increase friction. Tighten the bolts just enough to hold the new bar in place.

5 Center the handlebar to ensure that it sits straight in the stem clamp—most bars have markings to help you do this. Adjust the angle to your preference, then tighten the bolts all the way, working diagonally.

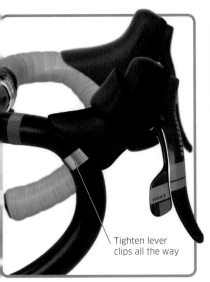

Tighten lever clips all the way

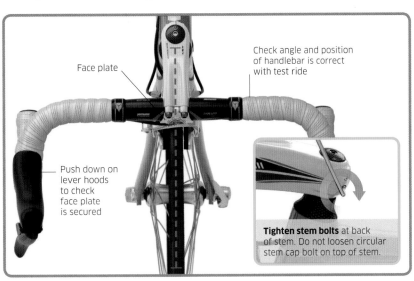

Face plate

Check angle and position of handlebar is correct with test ride

Push down on lever hoods to check face plate is secured

Tighten stem bolts at back of stem. Do not loosen circular stem cap bolt on top of stem.

6 Reattach the levers, adjusting the angle. Tighten the bolts and tape up the cables. Replace the bar tape or grips (see pp.62-65).

7 Ensure the stem is aligned with the front wheel, then loosen the two stem bolts by a quarter of a turn. Holding the front wheel between your knees, twist the handlebar to align the stem. Tighten the bolts incrementally, alternating between the left and right bolt.

Replacing handlebar tape

Handlebar tape provides comfort and grip for your hands, as well as protection for your cables. Sweat, poor weather, and regular use can all make the tape dirty, or cause it to loosen, wear thin, and tear. Worn tape is easy to change.

 BEFORE YOU START

- Source a handlebar tape suitable for your handlebar
- Wash your hands so you do not soil the new handlebar tape
- Unravel the handlebar tape and lay it out
- Cut 8in (20cm) strips of electrical tape with scissors

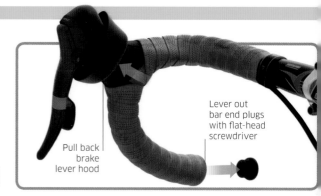

Lever out bar end plugs with flat-head screwdriver

Pull back brake lever hood

1 **Pull back each brake lever hood** from the body of the brake levers to expose the handlebar tape beneath. Lever out the bar end plugs from both ends of the handlebar with a flat-head screwdriver.

Cut away old electrical tape with craft knife

2 **Beginning at the stem**, carefully unwind the old handlebar tape. If your bike has concealed brake or gear cables, remove any electrical tape holding them in place, as it is likely to be worn down or loose.

Secure cables with electrical tape

3 **Clean the handlebar** using an alcohol-based cleaner to remove any dirt or leftover glue residue. Replace the electrical tape, ensuring that the cables follow their original routes along the bar.

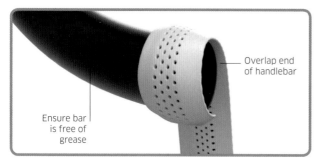

Overlap end of handlebar

Ensure bar is free of grease

4 **Attach the end** of the handlebar tape to the bottom of the handlebar, overlapping the end of the bar by half of the width of the tape. Wind the tape around the bar in a clockwise direction.

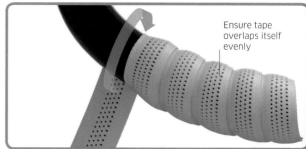

Ensure tape overlaps itself evenly

5 **Maintain an even tension** on the tape as you apply it. The tape should evenly overlap up to half the width of the previous turn. If present, ensure the glue strip sticks to the handlebar only.

Workshop tip: Always wrap replacement handlebar tape in a clockwise direction—from the inside of the bar outward. The tape will tighten as your hands naturally twist outward when cycling, keeping it in position.

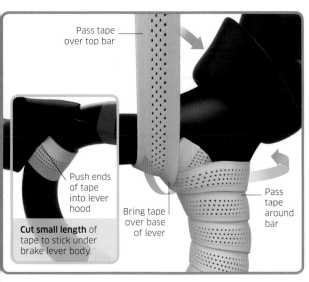

Pass tape over top bar

Push ends of tape into lever hood

Cut small length of tape to stick under brake lever body.

Bring tape over base of lever

Pass tape around bar

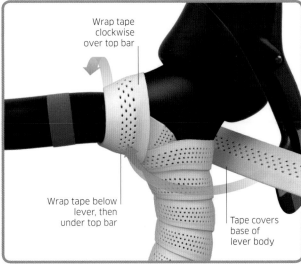

Wrap tape clockwise over top bar

Wrap tape below lever, then under top bar

Tape covers base of lever body

6 **At the brake levers,** pass the tape around the bar and below the base of the lever body. Bring it under and over the bar on the other side of the lever. Be sure to maintain an even tension.

7 **Wrap the tape** back over the bar and beneath the lever body in the opposite direction as before, then pass it back over the top bar. Continue covering the top bar in a clockwise direction.

Stick electrical tape half on handlebar tape and half on bar, securing the ends.

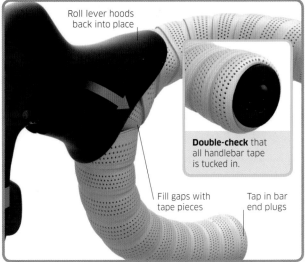

Roll lever hoods back into place

Double-check that all handlebar tape is tucked in.

Fill gaps with tape pieces

Tap in bar end plugs

8 **When the tape reaches** the handlebar stem, cut the last 3–4 in (8–10 cm) at a shallow angle toward the bar. Wrap the remaining tape around the bar, then secure it in place using electrical tape.

9 **Roll the lever hoods** back into place and check there are no gaps. Push the ends of the tape into the ends of the handlebar, and secure them by tapping in the bar end plugs with a rubber hammer.

Replacing handlebar grips

Grips have a big influence on bike handling and will need replacement when they fade, rip, or twist out of position. You may also want to upgrade your grips to improve your bike's performance. Standard grips are held in place by friction, while lock-on grips are secured to the bars with small bolts. Replacing both types is a simple task.

 BEFORE YOU START

- Secure your bike in a frame stand
- If you are using lock-on grips, assemble them in advance
- Loosen the brake and gear levers, and slide them into the middle of the handlebar to give you better access

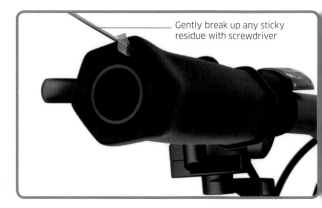

Gently break up any sticky residue with screwdriver

2 **Insert a small flat-head screwdriver** under the grip, pushing it inward about 1 in (2.5 cm) to loosen and break the seal. If the grip is sealed shut, push the screwdriver in from the opposite end.

Plastic bar end plug

Remove lock-on grip from handlebar by unscrewing retaining bolt using hex key, then slide grip off bar.

1 **Pull the bar end plugs** out of the bar with your fingertips. If they are tight and hard to remove, use a small, flat-head screwdriver to lever out the plug. Avoid damaging the plugs if you are reusing them.

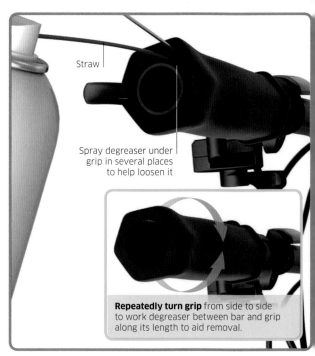

Straw

Spray degreaser under grip in several places to help loosen it

Repeatedly turn grip from side to side to work degreaser between bar and grip along its length to aid removal.

3 **Lift up the grip** with the screwdriver to create a gap. Insert the degreaser straw into the cavity and spray degreaser on all sides. The grip should now be loose enough to pull from the bar. Twist it off.

Workshop tip: If the grips are hard to fit, thread cable ties inside them. Slide each grip onto the handlebar, and when it is in place, pull out the ties.

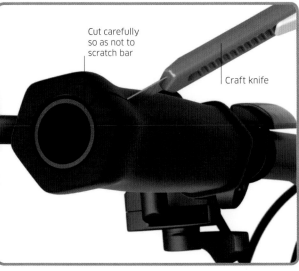

Cut carefully so as not to scratch bar

Craft knife

Spray directly onto bar using straw

4 **If the grip remains stuck** to the bar, run a sharp craft knife along its length, taking care not to cut or scratch the metal underneath. Carefully peel the grip away from the bar and discard it.

5 **Clean the handlebar thoroughly** with degreaser to remove any oil, dirt, or residue left by the old grip. Wipe away any remaining fluid and rub dry. If the bar is open, check that the inside of it is dry, too.

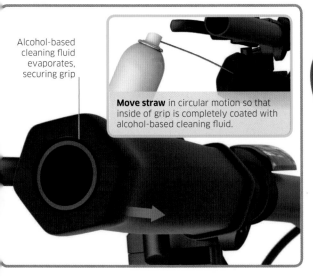

Alcohol-based cleaning fluid evaporates, securing grip

Move straw in circular motion so that inside of grip is completely coated with alcohol-based cleaning fluid.

Bar end plugs have expansion mechanism to ensure secure fit

If reattaching lock-on grips, tighten bolt-on end cap with hex key, turning it clockwise.

6 **Spray the bar** and the inside of the grip with an alcohol-based cleaning fluid. Slide the grip onto the bar and twist it into position, making sure that the edge is flush. Leave the grip to set for 10 minutes.

7 **Push in the bar end plug** so that it is aligned with the end of the grip and does not stick out from the end of the bar. If the bar end plugs are tight, tap them in gently with a rubber hammer.

Seatposts and saddles

Choosing a saddle is a personal decision, as you need to be comfortable. Saddles are available in a range of widths and shapes, with padding and cutouts for comfort. Road bike saddles are longer and narrower than mountain bike ones, while those for touring bikes are wider to provide a greater contact area for longer rides. The saddle has rails on the underside to fix it to the seatpost. The rails allow you to adjust the saddle position and angle, and they connect to the seatpost. Seatposts are available in different lengths and diameters, and their height can be adjusted (see pp.68-69). They are commonly made from aluminum or carbon fiber.

Saddle skin
may be synthetic fiber or leather

Nose may be reinforced with Kevlar to protect against damage

Saddle flexes on rails to provide cushioning for rider

Top tube forms top of bike frame

Brake cable port

⚙ PARTS FOCUS

The **saddle** is secured to the seatpost by a pair of rails, and the seatpost slides into the seat tube on the frame.

① Steel, titanium, or carbon **rails** under the saddle allow you to attach the saddle to the seatpost and to adjust its position forward or backward.

② The **saddle rail clamp** attaches the saddle to the seatpost by clamping over the rails. Most designs allow the angle of the saddle to be adjusted.

③ The **seatpost** connects the saddle to the seat tube. You adjust the saddle height by raising or lowering the seatpost—ensure the minimum insertion mark is inside the frame (see pp.68-69).

④ The **seatpost clamp** secures the seatpost inside the seat tube.

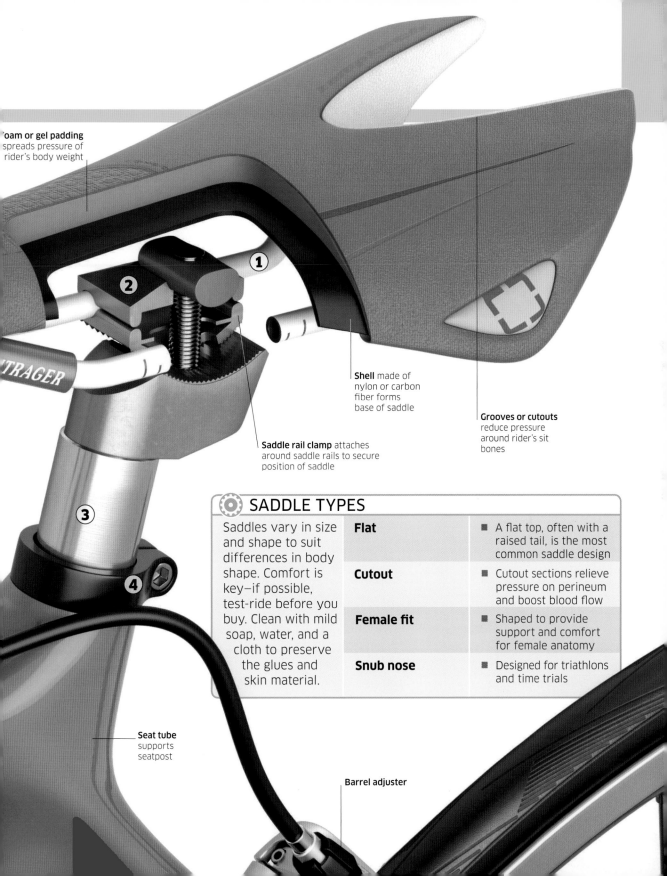

Foam or gel padding spreads pressure of rider's body weight

Shell made of nylon or carbon fiber forms base of saddle

Grooves or cutouts reduce pressure around rider's sit bones

Saddle rail clamp attaches around saddle rails to secure position of saddle

TRAGER

① ② ③ ④

Seat tube supports seatpost

Barrel adjuster

⚙ SADDLE TYPES

Saddles vary in size and shape to suit differences in body shape. Comfort is key—if possible, test-ride before you buy. Clean with mild soap, water, and a cloth to preserve the glues and skin material.

Flat	■ A flat top, often with a raised tail, is the most common saddle design
Cutout	■ Cutout sections relieve pressure on perineum and boost blood flow
Female fit	■ Shaped to provide support and comfort for female anatomy
Snub nose	■ Designed for triathlons and time trials

Seatpost maintenance

Ensuring that your saddle is at the right height is essential for riding efficiency and comfort, and helps you prevent knee and hip injuries. Adjusting the height is a simple task, although your seatpost can become stuck over time.

BEFORE YOU START

- Secure your bike in a frame stand
- Clean the seatpost and clamp using a cloth and cleaning fluid
- Ensure that the saddle is firmly installed

ADJUSTING THE SEATPOST HEIGHT

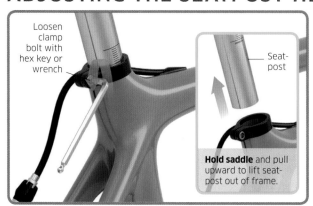

Loosen clamp bolt with hex key or wrench

Seat-post

Hold saddle and pull upward to lift seatpost out of frame.

1 Loosen the seatpost clamp bolt or quick-release lever just enough for you to pull the post out easily. Do not force it. If there is resistance, twist the saddle in both directions as you pull.

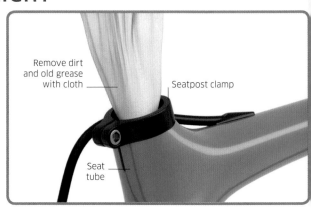

Remove dirt and old grease with cloth

Seatpost clamp

Seat tube

2 Clean the seatpost, seatpost clamp, and top of the seat tube with a cloth to wipe away dirt and surface corrosion. If the clamp bolt is rusty or the clamp shows signs of damage, replace the clamp.

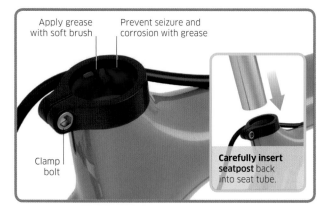

Apply grease with soft brush

Prevent seizure and corrosion with grease

Clamp bolt

Carefully insert seatpost back into seat tube.

3 Grease the upper part of the seat tube, the area just inside the frame, and the clamp bolt thread. Apply antislip compound to carbon frames and seatposts instead of grease, so the seatpost will not slip.

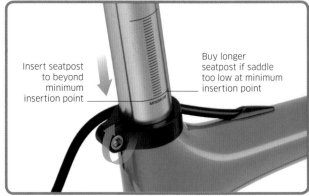

Insert seatpost to beyond minimum insertion point

Buy longer seatpost if saddle too low at minimum insertion point

MINIMUM

4 Set the saddle to your preferred ride height (see pp.20–23), and check that it is straight. Tighten the seatpost clamp bolt or quick-release lever. Ensure you do not overtighten the bolt or lever.

FREEING A STUCK METAL SEATPOST

Wipe any penetrating oil from paintwork

Distribute oil by moving saddle

Loosen and slide clamp up seatpost. Spray penetrating oil where seatpost enters seat tube.

1 Loosen the seatpost clamp bolt or quick-release lever. If the bolt is difficult to move, spray it with penetrating oil and let soak in. Slide the clamp up the seatpost and spray penetrating oil onto the seatpost where it enters the seat tube. Twist the saddle to distribute the oil.

🔍 LOOSE SEATPOSTS

If your seatpost is slipping or squeaks, check that the clamp is properly tightened, and that you have the correct post for your frame.

- If your seatpost is still slipping, the likely causes are dirt or rust on the seatpost and clamp.

- Remove and clean the seatpost and clamp, wiping off any dirt or rust. Regrease the seatpost and clamp, and reattach to bike.

- If the seatpost still slips or squeaks, it may be worn down and in need of replacement.

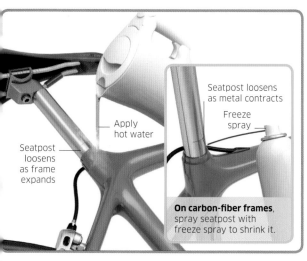

Seatpost loosens as frame expands

Apply hot water

Seatpost loosens as metal contracts

Freeze spray

On carbon-fiber frames, spray seatpost with freeze spray to shrink it.

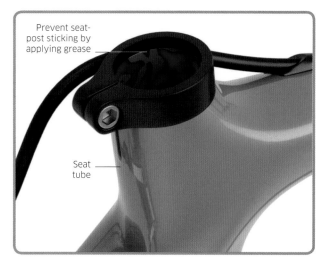

Prevent seat-post sticking by applying grease

Seat tube

2 If your frame is made of metal and the seatpost remains stuck, pour hot water around the top of the seat tube. This will cause the metal to expand, loosening it against the seatpost. Repeat as required.

3 After removing the seatpost, clean inside the seat tube with a cloth to get rid of any dirt, then apply plenty of grease. Clean and regrease the seatpost and clamp to prevent them seizing again.

Dropper seatposts

Dropper seatposts enable you to lower the height of your saddle while you are riding the bike, either by pressing a remote lever on the handlebar or by pulling a lever under the saddle. They are a popular upgrade for mountain bikes, and can be mechanical (as shown here) or hydraulic.

BEFORE YOU START

- Remove the existing seatpost (see pp.68-69)
- Secure your bike in a frame stand
- Clean the inside of the seat tube with cleaning fluid
- Plan how the cable will be routed—internally or externally

Ensure lever is easy to reach

1 Attach the remote lever to your handlebar, following the manufacturer's instructions. Position it within easy reach.

Route cable internally or externally

2 Depending on your frame, feed the cable housing from the top of the seat tube to the exit point near the head tube.

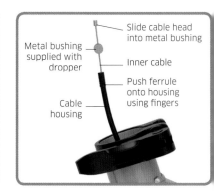

Slide cable head into metal bushing

Metal bushing supplied with dropper

Inner cable

Push ferrule onto housing using fingers

Cable housing

3 Slot the metal bushing onto the cable; slide the cable head into it. Push a ferrule onto the housing, and thread the cable along it.

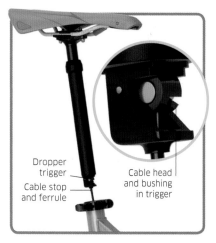

Dropper trigger

Cable stop and ferrule

Cable head and bushing in trigger

4 Fit the bushing and cable head into the trigger mechanism. Insert the ferrule on the housing into the cable stop on the trigger.

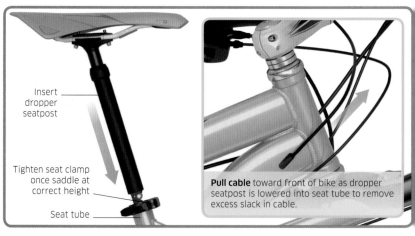

Insert dropper seatpost

Tighten seat clamp once saddle at correct height

Seat tube

Pull cable toward front of bike as dropper seatpost is lowered into seat tube to remove excess slack in cable.

5 Insert the dropper seatpost into the seat tube, while pulling the control cable and housing through from the front of the frame toward the handlebar. Set the saddle to the correct ride height, with the dropper post extended all the way.

Workshop tip: If your dropper post and frame have internal routing, you may need to remove the bottom bracket (BB) so that the cable can travel around the base of the seat tube (see pp.176–181).

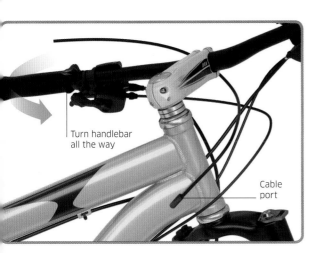

Turn handlebar all the way

Cable port

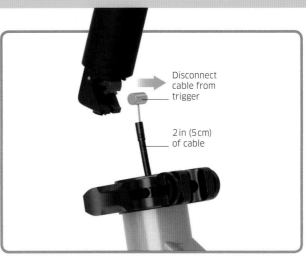

Disconnect cable from trigger

2 in (5 cm) of cable

6 **Ensure you have enough cable** and housing for the handlebar to turn all the way. Turn the handlebar as far as possible from the cable port, and use a tape measure to see how much cable you need.

7 **Remove the dropper post** and disconnect the cable from the mechanism. Pull both the cable and housing up through the seatpost until about 2 in (5 cm) protrudes from the top of it.

Cut housing to length

Push ferrule on to housing

Lower dropper into seat tube

Reconnect cable to trigger

Pull cable through frame toward front to remove slack.

Adjust position of lever if required

Tension cable by pressing lever 10-12 times to bed it in, and remove slack and movement.

8 **Pull enough cable** through the housing at the seatpost end, so the empty housing at the remote lever can be cut to length.

9 **Reconnect the cable** to the dropper mechanism and lower the dropper post into the seat tube. Set the saddle to the right height.

10 **Fasten the cable** to the remote lever according to the manufacturer's instructions, and adjust the cable accordingly.

WHEELS

Wheels

There are multiple types of bicycle wheel available, each with different capabilities and advantages. You may want just one type of wheel, or several to use at different times, depending on the kind of riding you are doing. Take care when upgrading your wheels, as they are front- and rear-specific and some are only compatible with 11-speed drivetrains.

TYPE	SUITABILITY	SPOKES
UTILITY/TOURING For everyday riding and adventure cycling, wheels need to be strong and built of durable materials. Low weight and "pro bike" looks are of secondary importance.	■ **Commuting**, or long-distance riding with luggage. ■ **Light off-road riding** on a road or hybrid bike.	■ **Stainless steel**, plain gauge, attached with hooks through flange holes and with nipples through rim eyelets. ■ **Up to 36 spokes**, with more on hybrid or touring bikes.
FAST ROAD These wheels, often made with aero parts, are fitted to high-end road and race bikes. Made of carbon or aluminum alloy, they blend lightness, stiffness, and strength to enable fast, smooth road riding.	■ **Road racing,** triahlon, and cyclo-cross bikes, or to complement a light bike. ■ **Hill riding,** where having lighter, faster wheels offers a serious performance advantage.	■ **Usually stainless steel,** but can be aluminum or even composite. They are aero or bladed on some models. ■ **Typically** 20–32 spokes. Radial lacing is popular on front wheels.
TRAINING ROAD Fitted as standard to many mid-price road bikes, training wheels are suitable for all types of road riding apart from racing and can be used for winter training.	■ **General road riding** and training. ■ **Regular, longer**, noncompetitive, rides, as the wheels are sturdy enough for heavy usage.	■ **Stainless steel**, plain gauge, attached with hooks through flange holes and with nipples through rim eyelets. ■ **More spokes** than a lightweight wheel–usually 28–36.
MOUNTAIN BIKE These wheels are designed for tough, off-road riding conditions, but some wheel types provide lightness and stiffness as well, especially when used on mountain bikes with suspension.	■ **Off-road cross-country** and downhill racing on mountain bikes with suspension on forks and/or the back end. ■ **Muddy** and slippery off-road conditions.	■ **Stainless steel** or aluminum, depending on quality and lightness of the build. ■ **Typically 28–32 spokes** on a standard mountain bike wheel, but can be as few as 24 on a lightweight type.

In addition, the axle attachments (skewer or quick-release) need to be compatible with the bike frame. Be aware that the various components of a bicycle wheel are measured in several different ways, with rim width, tire width, and wheel diameter all affecting a tire's performance. For simplicity, measurements here are given in the most common denomination.

RIMS

- **Aluminum,** with braking track for use with caliper brakes.
- **Mostly clincher design,** with internal reinforcement on heavy-duty versions.
- **Wider variants** will take heavy-duty and mountain bike tires.

- **Alloy or carbon fiber** with eyelets for spokes.
- **Hardened brake surface** (for caliper brakes only).
- **Sections vary** from box to V.
- **Rim bed** must match the tire: clincher, tubular, or tubeless.

- **Heavier and stronger** than lightweight versions, often with a box or shallow V section.
- **Lighter rim** with no braking track on disc-enabled wheels.
- **Mostly designed** for use with clincher tires, but can also be used with tubeless tires.

- **Commonly aluminum,** with no braking track on disc-braked bikes.
- **Can be carbon** on high-performance versions.
- **All mountain bike rims** are designed for use with either clincher or tubeless tires.

HUBS

- **Usually** made of alloy.
- **The flange is small,** with sealed or cup-and-cone bearings and a quick-release or through-axle fixing.
- **There is often a heavy-duty axle** on load-carrying bikes, especially on the rear wheel.

- **These are normally small flange** with annular bearings and a spindle with quick-release.
- **Disc-enabled designs** have a threaded disc carrier or boss and a through-axle closure of the wheel.

- **Usually made of alloy** with a spindle and quick-release skewer or a through-axle secure to bike.
- **These may have cup-and-cone** bearings, which require greasing and correct adjustment.

- **Usually** made of alloy, with competition wheels built in carbon.
- **The flange is small** with holes or straight pull slots for spokes.
- **The axle** has a closure to secure the wheels in the bike.
- **Sealed bearings** protect against dirt.

VARIATIONS

- **Popular** in standard 700c size.
- **Also popular** in smaller 26 in size, which can take larger-volume tires with heavier tread patterns. These wheels are more suitable for rough tracks and paths.

- **Industry standard is 700c,** with rim widths of 13–25 mm (the most popular being 18/19 mm).
- **Wider rims are suitable** for tires with larger volumes ranging from 25–40 mm.

- **Industry standard is 700c,** with rim widths from 13–25 mm (the most popular being 18/19 mm).
- **Wider rims can be used** for tires with larger volumes ranging from 25–40 mm.

- **The three most common sizes** are 29 in, 26 in, and 27.5 in (also termed 650b).
- **The latest types** include the slightly smaller 584 mm+ and 622 mm+ options, some of which are interchangeable on the same bike.

Wire-spoke wheels

Wheels are your bike's contact point with the ground. When you ride over rough terrain or bumps, the tire and rim absorb impacts and transmit these to the spokes, which flex to cushion the shock at the rim. Spokes brace the rim in relation to the hub. Some performance racing wheels feature bonded composite spokes, but most bikes have wire ones. Most spokes are made of stainless steel; the latest aero, flat, or bladed profiles can streamline and improve a bike's performance. Spokes are attached to the rim by nipples. Turning the nipple alters the spoke tension and the alignment of the rim.

⚙ PARTS FOCUS

A wheel comprises a hub, spokes, a rim, and a tire. Rear wheels have more spokes than front wheels, as they power the drivetrain.

① The **wheel hub** supports the spokes. It transmits motion through the spokes to the rim, so it's under significant load when moving.

② **Wheel rims** are made of alloy or carbon, and have a recess to hold the tire. There are several depths and designs for different riding styles.

③ The side edge of the rim provides a **braking surface** for bikes with rim brakes. If it is worn, you should replace the wheel (see pp.78–83).

④ The **spokes** may be "laced" in various patterns, such as radial, crossed, or mixed, for strength and to absorb braking and acceleration forces.

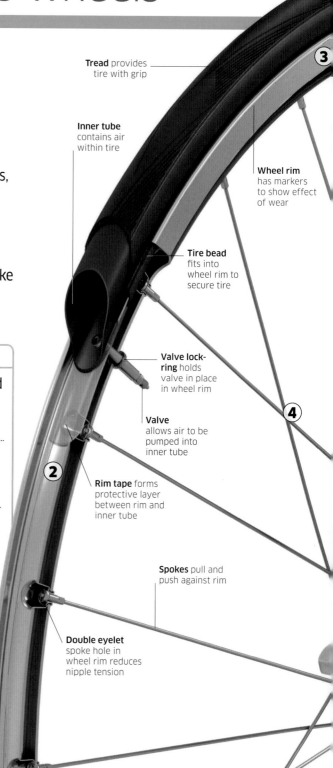

Tread provides tire with grip

Inner tube contains air within tire

Wheel rim has markers to show effect of wear

Tire bead fits into wheel rim to secure tire

Valve lock-ring holds valve in place in wheel rim

Valve allows air to be pumped into inner tube

Rim tape forms protective layer between rim and inner tube

Spokes pull and push against rim

Double eyelet spoke hole in wheel rim reduces nipple tension

Spoke nipple connects spoke to rim and allows spoke tension to be adjusted

Front forks connect wheel to frame

Tire provides contact point between wheel and road or track

Quick-release lever enables wheel to be removed without tools

Flange is point where spokes attach to hub

①

▶ REMOVING AND REINSTALLING A WHEEL
Quick-release front wheels

It is often necessary to detach a front wheel to transport a bike or repair a puncture. Most modern bikes have quick-release wheels, which can be removed without tools. Wheels on older bikes sometimes have conventional bolts, undone using a wrench.

 BEFORE YOU START

- Secure your bike in a frame stand
- Check whether there is any rust or corrosion on the quick-release lever; if so, spray around the area with oil

Quick-release lever

Hold quick-release nut firmly on right-hand side of wheel, then turn lever.

2 **Locate the quick-release lever** on the wheel hub, if attached. Open the lever and gradually unscrew it, but do not remove the nut. If bolts are attached, unscrew on both sides using a wrench.

Brake caliper

1 **Loosen the front brake** using the quick-release tab on the brake caliper. This widens the gap between the pads, so the tire can pass through. (Campagnolo calipers are released via a button on the gear-shift lever.)

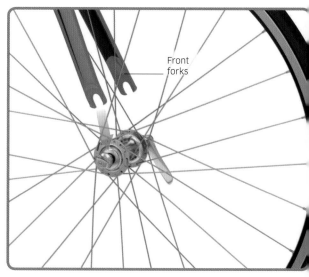

Front forks

3 **Lift up the frame** and push the wheel out and away from the front forks. If the wheel does not drop out, undo the quick-release lever or bolts a little more without loosening all the way.

Workshop tip: If you need to remove both wheels from your bike, remove the front one first. This will help you avoid dragging the chain or bashing the rear derailleur on the ground.

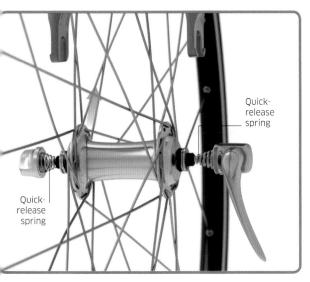

Quick-
release
spring

Quick-
release
spring

Press firmly
to close
lever tightly

4 **To reattach your front wheel**, check that the springs are in place on both sides of the quick-release mechanism, and that the lever is on the left-hand side of the bike. Lower the forks onto the wheel.

5 **Place the wheel** on the floor, using the weight of the bike to keep it straight. Hold the nut, and tighten the quick-release mechanism, if attached. For older bikes, tighten both wheel bolts.

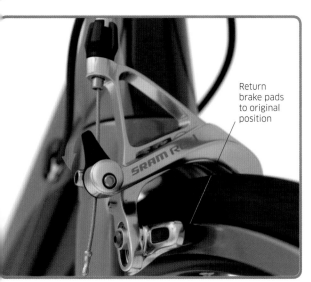

Return
brake pads
to original
position

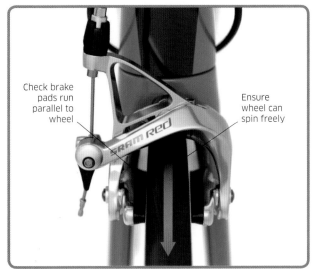

Check brake
pads run
parallel to
wheel

Ensure
wheel can
spin freely

6 **Close the quick-release tab** (or press the button on the lever if you have Campagnolo brakes). Ensure that the brake pads are correctly positioned on the rim.

7 **Stand in front of your bike** with the front wheel between your knees and check that it is centered between the brake pads. If it is not, undo the quick-release and repeat steps 3–7 to reattach the wheel.

Wheels with a cassette

Removing and reattaching a rear wheel involves releasing and reattaching the chain from the rear hub. This task requires more care on bikes with a cassette and rear derailleur (mech), as these are vital components of the drivetrain. It is a simple process, only taking a few minutes, especially if the wheel has a quick-release mechanism.

BEFORE YOU START

- Spray the lever with oil if there is rust or corrosion
- Shift the chain into the largest chainring at the front
- Shift the chain onto the smallest rear sprocket
- Secure your bike in a frame stand

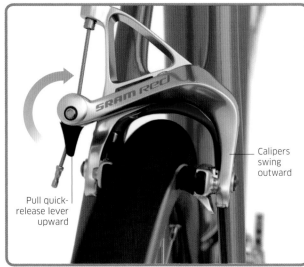

Calipers swing outward

Pull quick-release lever upward

2 **Locate the quick-release lever** on the rear brake caliper or on the lever hood, and pull it upward to open it. Once released, the calipers will widen, letting the wheel pass easily between the brake pads.

Push quick-release lever downward

1 **Loosen the rear wheel**, holding the quick-release nut on the nondrive (left) side with one hand. With your other hand, rotate the quick-release lever 180 degrees, opening the mechanism.

3 **Hold the rear derailleur** in your hand, and pull it backward and upward. The wheel should come free from the dropouts. If not, turn the quick-release lever one more turn and repeat until it does.

TOOLS AND EQUIPMENT

- Oil
- Frame stand

Workshop tip: Some quick-release systems have a locking mechanism for security reasons. Both sides tighten together and connect through a hollow axle. Always keep the appropriate keys packed with your puncture repair kit in case of a puncture, .

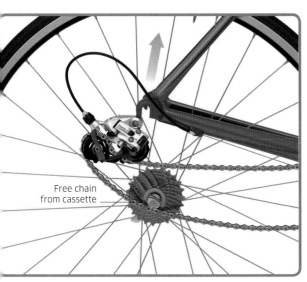

4 **Lift the frame** up by the saddle or the top tube, allowing the rear wheel to move forward slightly. Carefully guide the cassette away from the chain. If the chain sticks to the cassette, lift it away by hand.

Free chain from cassette

5 **To reattach the rear wheel**, ensure the rear derailleur is shifted into the highest gear. Guide the wheel into position, allowing the chain to sit on top of the smallest sprocket, and lower the frame.

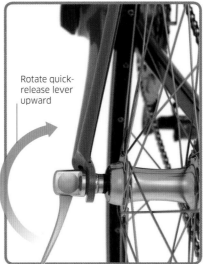

Rotate quick-release lever upward

Close quick-release lever

Wheel should spin freely

6 **Pull the wheel** upward and backward, slotting it into the dropouts. Make sure the wheel is centered in the frame.

7 **Close the quick-release lever** to secure the rear wheel. The tension should be the same as before—firm but not too tight.

8 **Close up the brake pads** using the lever on the caliper or the button on the lever hood. Spin the wheel to check the pads align.

Wheels with a hub gear

Hub gears mainly feature on hybrid and utility bikes, and also on some mountain bikes. In order to remove the rear wheel with the hub gear from the frame, you will first need to disconnect the hub from the brake cable.

 BEFORE YOU START

- Clean any dirt from around the hub gear
- Make a note of any washers
- Ensure that the gear cables are in good condition
- Secure your bike in a frame stand

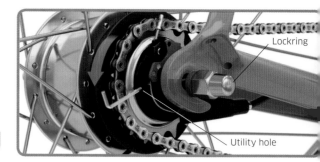

Lockring

Utility hole

1 **Using the gear-shift lever**, set the hub into first gear. Locate the utility hole on the cable carrier or the hub and insert a hex key. Use the hex key to rotate the carrier, so that the gear cables become slack.

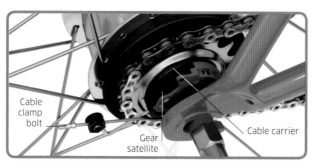

Cable clamp bolt

Gear satellite

Cable carrier

2 **Holding the cable carrier** in position with the hex key, use your free hand to remove the cable clamp bolt from the gear satellite on the cable carrier. If it is tight, ease it out using pliers.

Hub gear

Housing stop

Cable housing

3 **Pull the cable** around to the front of the hub, then free the end of the cable housing from the housing stop on the hub gear. Move the cable away from the rear wheel.

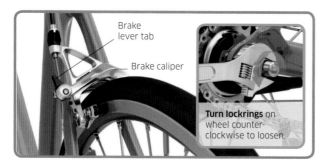

Brake lever tab

Brake caliper

Turn lockrings on wheel counter-clockwise to loosen.

4 **Open the rear brake calipers** according to the type equipped on your bike (see pp.112–117). Loosen the lockrings on the wheel using a wrench, but do not remove them from the wheel entirely.

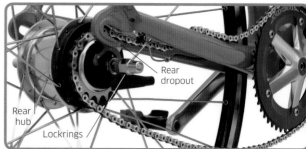

Rear dropout

Rear hub

Lockrings

5 **Ease the wheel** out of the rear dropouts, and lift the chain from the rear hub. Rest the chain on the frame. Holding the wheel with one hand, lift the frame away from it.

Workshop tip: When retightening the wheel lockrings, use a tool that you can take with you out on the road. You will then be able to adjust the wheel if necessary when cycling.

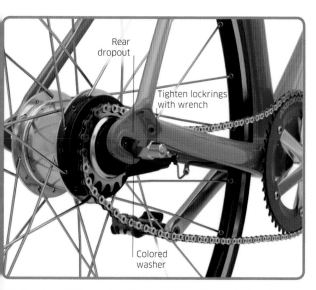

Rear dropout

Tighten lockrings with wrench

Colored washer

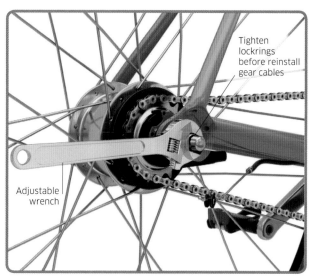

Tighten lockrings before reinstall gear cables

Adjustable wrench

6 **Reattach the wheel** by guiding the axle back into the rear dropouts, ensuring that the colored washers sit outside the frame. Lift the chain back onto the hub, then half-tighten the wheel lockrings.

7 **Align the wheel** so that it rotates centrally within the frame, and position it so that the chain is engaged all the way on the hub. Secure the lockrings using a wrench, making them as tight as possible.

Rotate cable carrier with hex key

Engage brake calipers once wheel is in place

8 **Reinstall the gear cables** by securing the housing into the housing stop. Rotate the cable carrier toward the housing stop, then insert the cable clamp bolt into the gear satellite (reversing steps 1–3).

9 **Ensure the wheel spins** evenly and re-engage the brake calipers according to the type you have. Test the gears to check they shift cleanly. If they do not, you will need to adjust them (see pp.152–53).

▶ REPLACING A TIRE
Clincher tires

Flat tires are caused by air leaking from the inner tube, either because of "pinch flat"–the tube being pinched–or because a sharp object has pierced the tube. You should also replace your tires if the top section is worn down or if threads appear on the sidewall.

BEFORE YOU START

- Remove the wheel from your bike (see pp.78-83)
- Remove the old tire (see pp.48-49)
- Unfold the new tire and push it into shape
- Check that the inner tube is in good condition and the valve is not bent
- Ensure that rim tape is in good condition; replace it if not
- Ensure that the tire is the right width and size for the wheel

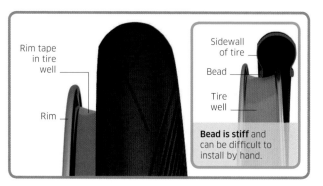

Rim tape in tire well

Sidewall of tire

Bead

Tire well

Rim

Bead is stiff and can be difficult to install by hand.

1 **Fit the first side** of the tire onto the wheel, placing the bead over the first half of the rim and working it around the wheel with your hands. If it feels tight, use a tire lever to hook the bead onto the rim.

Ensure tire is fitted all way around

Rim

Bead against rim

Installing one side of tire creates a void for inner tube.

2 **Ease the tire** across the well, pushing the bead to the far edge of the rim in order to create space for the inner tube. Rotate the tire, pushing the tire across all the way around the wheel.

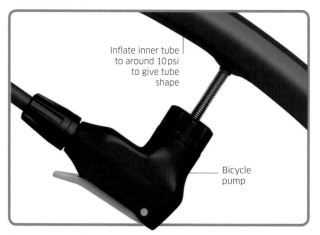

Inflate inner tube to around 10psi to give tube shape

Bicycle pump

3 **Remove the valve cap** and retaining nut from the inner tube, and partially inflate it just enough so that it takes its shape. Do not overinflate the tube, as you will struggle to feed it into the tire.

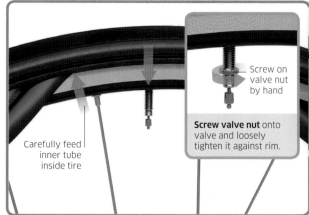

Screw on valve nut by hand

Carefully feed inner tube inside tire

Screw valve nut onto valve and loosely tighten it against rim.

4 **Insert the inner tube valve** through the valve hole in the rim, so that it sits straight. Working away from the valve on both sides, ease a small section of tube into the tire, then fit the valve nut.

Workshop tip: Try to finish installing the tire opposite the valve, as this provides more tire material to help lever the bead over the wheel rim edge.

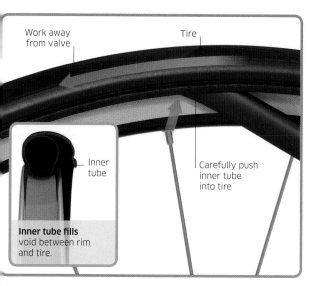

Work away from valve

Tire

Inner tube

Carefully push inner tube into tire

Inner tube fills void between rim and tire.

Work all the way around wheel

Last section will be hardest to fit

5 **Keep working from the valve** in both directions, tucking the inner tube inside the tire, so that it fits in the well between the tire and the rim. Ensure the inner tube is not twisted or kinked at any point.

6 **Roll the second bead** of the tire over the rim, making sure it does not pinch or twist the inner tube. If the tire is too tight to fit by hand, carefully use tire levers. Deflate the inner tube.

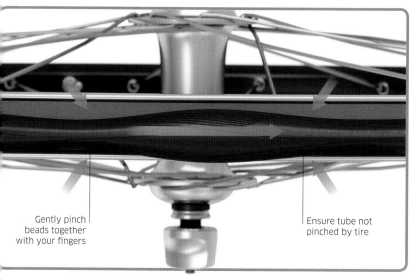

Gently pinch beads together with your fingers

Ensure tube not pinched by tire

7 **Once the tire is fitted**, squeeze the tire beads together to expose the rim tape, and check that the inner tube is not pinched between the rim and the bead—which could cause a "pinch flat." If the tube is pinched anywhere, carefully wiggle the tire to release the pinched tube.

8 **Inflate the tire** to the correct pressure—which is usually printed on the tire—and refit the wheel to the bike (see pp.78-83).

▶ **REPLACING A TIRE**

Tubeless tires

Tubeless tires, often installed on mountain bikes, fit firmly against the wheel rim without an inner tube, reducing the risk of punctures. If the tire is cut, sealant in the tire instantly dries around the hole, which prevents the tire from deflating.

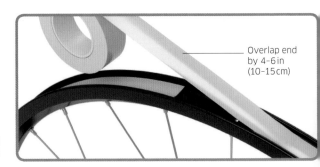

Overlap end by 4–6 in (10–15 cm)

🔧 BEFORE YOU START

- Ensure that the wheel and tires are tubeless-compatible
- Unfold the new tire and push it into shape
- Remove the wheel from the bike (see pp.78–83)
- Remove the tire from the wheel (see pp.48–49)

2 Apply tubeless rim tape to the well of the wheel, covering the spoke holes and the valve hole. Apply even tension to the tape, ensuring that it comes up to the edges and is free of wrinkles.

Clean thoroughly with alcohol-based cleaner

Locate position of valve hole

Valve hole

3 Locate the valve hole and carefully pierce the tape with a craft knife or similar sharp object, so that the valve can be pushed through. Make sure that you do not make the hole too large.

Rubber valve end

Valve collar

1 If the wheel is tubeless-compatible, move directly on to step 5. If not, remove any existing rim tape, and clean away any sticky residue and grease on the rim using an alcohol-based cleaner.

4 Remove the valve collar, push the valve through the hole, and secure the rubber end to the rim tape. Refit and tighten the valve collar on the inside of the wheel until it is secure against the rim.

TOOLS AND EQUIPMENT

- Cloth and alcohol-based cleaner
- Tubeless rim tape
- Craft knife
- Bicycle pump or air compressor
- Soapy water
- Tire sealant

Workshop tip: After adding sealant and inflating the tire, cover the wheel and valve stem area in soapy water. Wait 10-20 seconds, then check the tire for any places where the soapy water bubbles. Bubbling means that the tire is leaking.

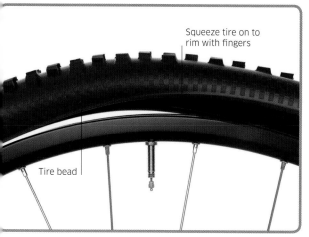

Squeeze tire on to rim with fingers

Tire bead

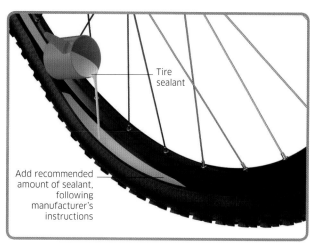

Tire sealant

Add recommended amount of sealant, following manufacturer's instructions

5 **Mount the tubeless tire** to the rim by hand—using tire levers may damage the tape. Once fitted, inflate the tire to 100 psi, and soak the rim with warm, soapy water to help identify any leaks.

6 **To seal the tire**, first deflate it all the way by releasing the air valve. Then, using your fingers, pry a small section of the tire from the rim on one side. Pour tire sealant into the gap.

Rotate tire once closed

Squeeze tire closed

Use pump or air compressor to inflate tire

Tire will snap into rim as it inflates

7 **Close the tire** up again using your fingers, then rotate the wheel several times to spread the sealant inside.

8 **Inflate the tire** to 90 psi using a pump or compressor, then hang up the wheel with the valve in the eight o'clock position to set.

VARIATIONS

Certain brands of sealant can be injected directly into the tire via the valve using a syringe.

- Follow steps 1-5 to fit the tire, then deflate it all the way.

- Following the instructions provided, fill the syringe with the recommended amount of sealant.

- Attach the end of the syringe to the opened tire valve and inject the sealant into the tire. Rotate the tire to spread the sealant.

- Detach the syringe and inflate the tire (see step 8).

Tightening loose spokes

Over time, the spokes on your bike's wheels can become slack, causing the wheels to lose shape. "Trueing," or straightening wheels, is achieved by adjusting the tension of the spokes on either side of the rim. Even spoke tension is key to the strength and integrity of a wheel. You can adjust spoke tension by tightening or loosening the spoke nipples adjacent to the wheel rim.

⚙ BEFORE YOU START

- Secure your bike in a frame stand, so that you can spin the wheel freely
- Ensure that you have the correct-size spoke wrench

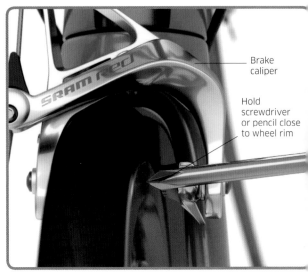

Brake caliper

Hold screwdriver or pencil close to wheel rim

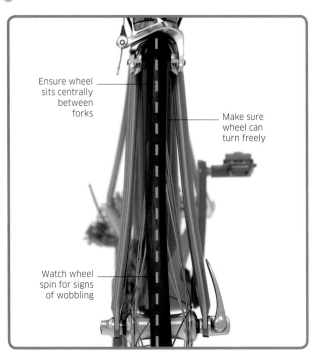

Ensure wheel sits centrally between forks

Make sure wheel can turn freely

Watch wheel spin for signs of wobbling

1 **Stand in front** of the wheel and check that it is centered between the forks. Adjust, if necessary (see pp.78–79). Spin the wheel and, watching from the front, check if it wobbles from side to side.

2 **Rest a screwdriver** or pencil against the brake caliper and spin the wheel. Note the areas where the rim touches the tool and mark the rim using a piece of chalk. Repeat on the other side of the rim.

Loose spokes flex easily

3 **Press the spokes** nearest to the chalk marks to identify any that feel more slack than the others. Spokes on opposing sides of the rim counter the pull of each other, so you will need to adjust both sides.

Workshop tip: If you find some of the nipples on the spokes are hard to turn, do not force them, as the spoke could snap. Spray them with penetrating oil, wait for a few minutes, then try again. Repeat if necessary.

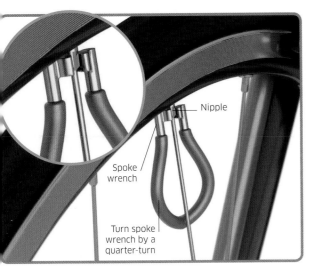

Nipple

Spoke wrench

Turn spoke wrench by a quarter-turn

Spin wheel

4 **If the wheel wobbles** to one side when spun, loosen the spoke nipple on that side by turning it clockwise, and tighten the loose spoke on the opposite side of the rim by turning the nipple counterclockwise.

5 **Using the screwdriver** or pencil, spin the wheel to check for any further wobble. Adjust 2–3 spokes at a time to avoid uneven tension. Work around the wheel, loosening and tightening.

Turn nipple with spoke wrench

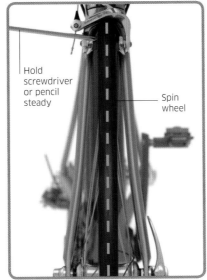

Hold screwdriver or pencil steady

Spin wheel

6 **Turn the spoke wrench** in very small increments. Any adjustment, however slight, will affect the rest of the wheel.

7 **With your screwdriver** or pencil in place, check to ensure that the wheel is running straight. Readjust as required.

CHECK THE WHEEL

It is important that you hold the screwdriver or pencil still when checking the accuracy of a wheel. If it moves while the wheel is turning, you will not be able to assess where it deviates from true. If you cannot hold it steady, try the following:

- Securely attach the screwdriver or pencil to the brake caliper using a rubber band. You will have to reattach it each time you retest the wheel.

- Attach a wire tie to the caliper, pulling it tight. Cut the end so it just avoids the rim. This, too, will need reattaching later.

Wheel hubs

The hub, at the center of your bike's wheel, consists of an axle, shell, and flange. The axle is secured to the frame at the dropouts. The hub shell contains bearings, which allow it to rotate around the axle. The flange at each end of the axle has holes drilled to hold the spokes. The number of spoke holes on the hub corresponds with the number of them on the wheel rim. Hubs traditionally have 28, 32, or 36 spoke holes. The higher the number of spokes, the stronger the wheel is, although it will also be heavier. Hubs may be made from steel, machined alloy, or carbon fiber. High-quality hubs use cartridge bearings and additional seals to keep them running more smoothly for longer.

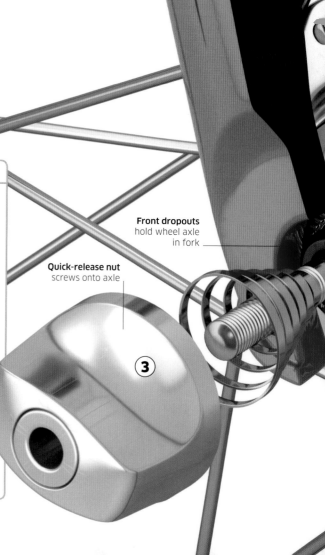

Front fork holds front wheel

Front dropouts hold wheel axle in fork

Quick-release nut screws onto axle

③

⚙ PARTS FOCUS

The wheel hub enables the wheel to turn. It is fixed to the frame at the axle, and connects to the rim via the spokes.

① The **axle** passes through the wheel hub. It has threaded ends onto which the cone nut and lockrings are screwed to hold it in place.

② The **bearings** inside the hub shell allow the wheel to rotate freely. They may sit inside a sealed cartridge or be loose within the bearing races. You should perform maintenance on hub bearings regularly (see pp.92–95).

③ The **quick-release mechanism**, passing through the center of the axle, allows you to remove the wheel quickly without tools.

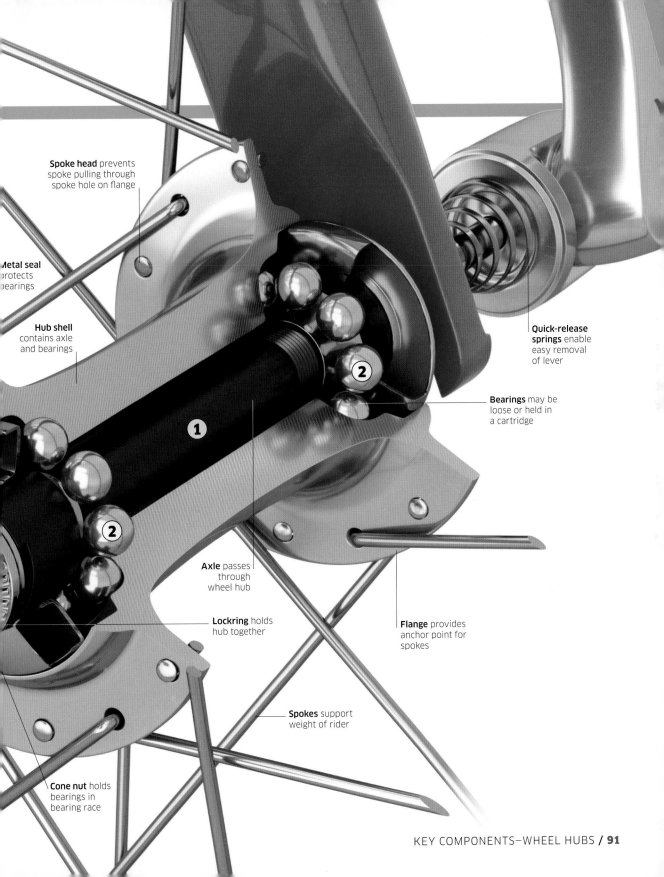

Spoke head prevents spoke pulling through spoke hole on flange

Metal seal protects bearings

Hub shell contains axle and bearings

Quick-release springs enable easy removal of lever

Bearings may be loose or held in a cartridge

1

2

2

Axle passes through wheel hub

Lockring holds hub together

Flange provides anchor point for spokes

Spokes support weight of rider

Cone nut holds bearings in bearing race

Press-fit cartridge types

The wheel bearings are often contained within cartridges that need specialty tools to replace. The bearings can be maintained, however, and you should do this regularly to prevent wear and prolong their life. Maintaining a hub cartridge involves cleaning and regreasing the bearings. A press-fit hub is simply held closed by the forks, and should pop open when removed. The telltale sign that your bearings need attention is when your bike's wheels feel rough when cycling, or make a rumbling or grinding noise.

 BEFORE YOU START

- Prepare a clear space where you can lay out the parts
- Secure your bike in a frame stand

Quick-release mechanism

1 **Remove the wheel** from your bike (see pp.78–83) by opening the quick-release lever or loosening the retaining bolts. Relax the brake calipers and ease the wheel from the frame.

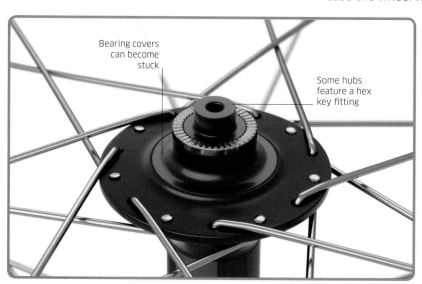

Bearing covers can become stuck

Some hubs feature a hex key fitting

2 **When the wheel is** clear of the forks, pop off the press-fit bearing cover. If it is stuck, carefully pry it away with a flat-head screwdriver. (Some bearing covers have a hex key fitting–for these, use a hex key to twist the covers off, rather than unscrew them.)

3 **Lift off the bearing cover** to reveal the protective dust seal over the cartridge bearing. Clean the cover before replacing it later.

Workshop tip: If you are unsure whether the bearings in your wheel hubs need maintaining, spin each wheel while resting your ear on the saddle, as any noise from the wheel hub will be amplified through the bike frame.

Dust seal

Bearings will be easily visible once duct seal is removed.

4 **Use a thin-bladed tool,** such as a screwdriver, to pry off the seal to expose the bearings. Take care not to damage the edge of the seal, as this could make it less effective when reattached.

PARTS FOCUS

A typical press-fit hub with cartridge bearings has a cassette at each end, held in place by compression.

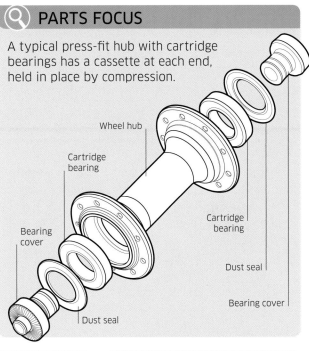

Wheel hub

Cartridge bearing

Bearing cover

Dust seal

Cartridge bearing

Dust seal

Bearing cover

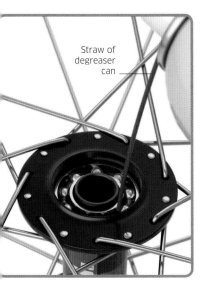

Straw of degreaser can

Grease gun

5 **Flush the bearings** with degreaser, rotating them as you do so. Clean away any old grease and dirt with a cloth.

6 **Once the cartridge is** dry, lightly coat the bearings with fresh grease. Replace the protective dust seal.

7 **Replace the bearing cover,** and repeat steps 2–6 on the other side of the hub. Reattach the wheel, checking that it spins freely.

SERVICING A WHEEL BEARING
Cup and cone types

A rumbling or slow spinning wheel, and play in the axle, are signs that the bearings are worn down. Replacing your hub bearings once a year will ensure a longer life for your hub and wheel. There are many brands of bearings, all of which are installed in similar ways.

BEFORE YOU START

- Refer to your owner's manual to check which type of hub your bike has
- Select the correct size of cone wrench for the hub
- Source the right size of replacement bearings
- Release the front brake calipers (see pp.112–117)

Unscrew quick-release nut

Open quick-release lever

1 **Remove the front wheel** from the bike by either opening the quick-release mechanism (see pp.78–79) or by loosening the retaining nuts with a wrench. Lay the wheel on a flat surface.

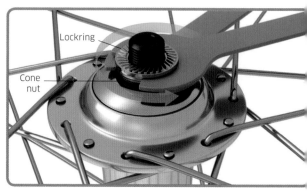

Lockring

Cone nut

2 **Holding the cone nut** in place with one cone wrench, unscrew the lockring with a second. Remove the lockring, and any washers and spacers, noting the order in which they were removed.

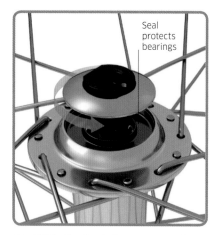

Seal protects bearings

3 **With the lockring removed**, fully unscrew the cone nut to expose the bearing seal that protects the bearings inside.

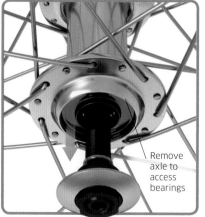

Remove axle to access bearings

4 **Leaving the cone** on the other end of the axle in place, draw the axle through the hub and remove it completely.

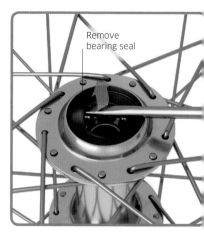

Remove bearing seal

5 **Check if the bearing seal** can be pried out to access the bearings. If so, carefully ease it out with a flat-head screwdriver.

PARTS FOCUS

Wheel bearings consist of similar components, regardless of brand.

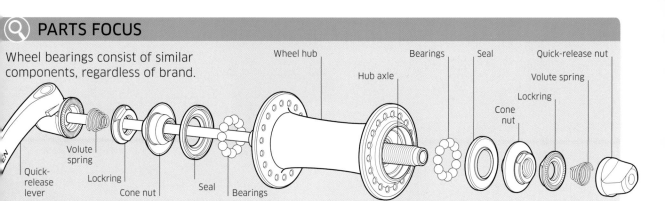

Quick-release lever | Volute spring | Lockring | Cone nut | Seal | Bearings | Wheel hub | Hub axle | Bearings | Seal | Cone nut | Lockring | Volute spring | Quick-release nut

Clean inside hub with a cloth and degreaser. Check for wear and damage.

6 If the bearing seal cannot be removed, lift out the bearings using a magnet. Count how many there are and place them in a container. Repeat this for the bearings on the other side of the hub axle.

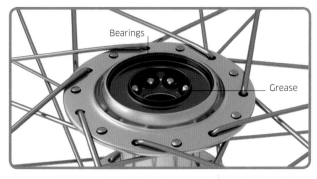

Bearings

Grease

7 Grease one of the bearing surfaces, then replace the bearings using tweezers—using the same number as you removed. Turn the wheel over and repeat the process on the other end of the axle.

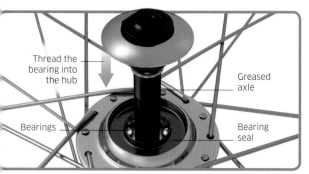

Thread the bearing into the hub

Greased axle

Bearings

Bearing seal

8 Rethread the axle through the hub and reinstall any spacers or washers in the correct order—take care not to dislodge any of the bearings. Replace the cone nut, tightening it with your fingers.

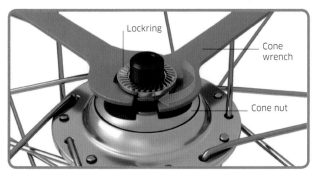

Lockring

Cone wrench

Cone nut

9 Using two wrenches, reverse the process in step 2, tightening the lockring against the cone nut. Do not tighten the cone nut itself again—this will prevent the wheel from turning freely and can crush the bearings.

BRAKES

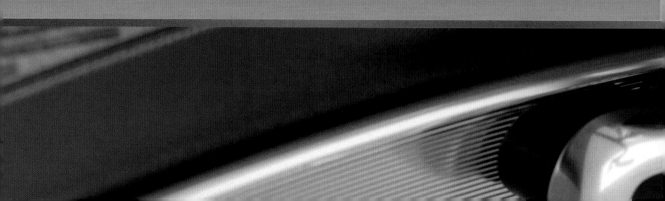

Brakes

All brake systems work in generally the same way: when activated, brake pads push against part of the wheel surface to create friction and slow the bike. The pressure is applied either at the rim of the wheel (dual-pivot, cantilever, center-pull, V-brake) or at the hub (disc brake). Although their basic function is the same, the various brake systems have different strengths

TYPE	SUITABILITY	OPERATION
DUAL-PIVOT The most popular cable-operated brake, dual-pivot brakes have been in use for over 45 years. Dual-pivot systems are reliable and lightweight; in particular, they are lighter than disc brakes.	■ **Road cycling**, from racing to triathlon and training. ■ **Lightweight** road bikes. ■ **Use in warm, dry** conditions. ■ **Limited tire clearance** rules out use on off-road bikes.	■ **The cable pulls up** on the arm of the caliper to bring the brake pads into contact with the rim of the wheel. ■ **Modern dual-pivot brakes** exert more pressure than traditional single-pivot designs.
DISC Universally adopted for mountain biking, disc brakes are increasingly popular on road bikes. High-quality systems often have hydraulically operated brakes, while budget disc brakes use simpler cable operation.	■ **Both off-road and road bikes**, especially in wet or muddy conditions or for use in carrying loads. ■ **Cyclo-cross** or gravel riding. ■ **Use in winter** or poor weather.	■ **At the wheel hub**, pistons on one or both sides of the wheel push the brake pads onto a disc. ■ **Activation is either** by cable (mechanical systems) or by hydraulic pressure from fluid in a hose connected to the brake lever.
V-BRAKE Often installed on hybrids, utility bikes, tandems, and older mountain bikes, V- or linear-pull brakes give lots of power. Specialized versions are also used on road and time trial bikes.	■ **A wide range of uses**, including on shopper and utility bikes, mountain bikes, and tandems, as the long caliper arms produce considerable leverage and stopping power, and good feel. ■ **Off-road riding,** as the long arms allow installation of fat tires.	■ **The two long, spring-loaded** caliper arms are mounted on the metal bosses on the fork, and act on the rim. ■ **When the brake is applied**, the cable housing pushes one arm while the inner cable, running above the tire, pulls the other.
CANTILEVER/CENTER-PULL Cantilever systems are derived from a brake design that has been in use for nearly 100 years. They are popular with cyclo-cross riders due to their simplicity and low weight, and because they allow large tire clearances.	■ **Cyclo-cross racing bikes**, where they remain popular despite the increasing availability and effectiveness of disc brakes. ■ **Touring bikes**, as they allow for the use of large tires.	■ **Cantilever and center-pull brakes** operate on the same principle of a transverse "straddle" wire pulling upward on a pair of caliper arms. ■ **Both types operate via cables** running to brake levers on the handlebar.

nd weaknesses. A disc brake provides almost immediate stopping power, but will weight your bike down more than a dual-pivot. Similarly, V-brakes can be very powerful, but there is a risk you might flip the bike if used too suddenly when riding at a very high speed. Also consider that some systems, like hydraulic disc brakes, may require maintenance more regularly.

KEY COMPONENTS

Dual-pivots consist of calipers, brake pads, barrel adjusters, and a quick-release lever.
Cables connect to brake levers attached to the handlebar.

Discs or rotors that attach to the wheel hubs.
Calipers, which operate the discs.
Cables or hydraulic hoses that run back to the brake levers.

Caliper arms that are fixed to the upper forks at the front and to the rear stays at the back.
Cables, which are activated by flat bar levers.
A quick-release lever for the "noodle" over the arms.

Cantilever brakes that have arms fixed to bosses on the fork, and a "yoke" or link wire.
Center-pull brakes that have crossed arms connecting to a central mount above the wheel.

POSITION

- **The front brake** is normally attached to the fork crown and the rear to a brake bridge in the rear stays.
- **A threaded stud** in the back of the brake is secured with a flush-fit hex bolt.

- **Discs are located** in the center of one side of the wheel.
- **The calipers are fixed** to the lower end of one fork blade on the front wheel, and to the rear triangle of the seat and chainstays on the rear wheel.

- **V-brakes are normally** located at the top of the forks in front, and high on the seat stays at the rear.
- **"Aero" types** lie flush with the fork blades at the front. On rear brakes, they lie behind the bottom bracket.

- **Cantilever brakes** can only be fitted to bikes with permanently attached threaded bosses on the top of the front fork blades and high up on the rear stays.
- **Center-pull brakes** are attached using a center bolt on the fork crown and seat stay bridge.

ADJUSTMENTS

- **Brake pads can be moved in or out** with the barrel adjuster.
- **Dual-pivot brakes** can be centered using a recessed screw in the caliper.
- **The angle of the pads** can be adjusted on a dished washer.

- **Hydraulic disc brakes** do not normally need adjusting; the pistons in the caliper will automatically keep the pads close to the disc.
- **Mechanical disc brake pads** may need to be moved closer to the rotor as they wear down.

- **The lever arms** can be moved in and out using a small adjustment screw on the spring, where the lever arm is attached to the boss.
- **The quick-release lever** on top of the cable disengages one lever arm completely.

- **The brakes are adjusted** either at the bolts holding the arms or (on center-pull brakes) at the stirrup linking the brake cable to the straddle wire.
- **Fine-tuning** is offered on some cantilevers via a grub screw on the arm itself.

Rim brakes

Rim brakes engage rubber pads against the sides of the wheel rim to create friction and slow your bike. When you pull the brake lever, the brake cable comes under tension, pulling the brake arms into position, while a powerful spring returns the brake arms to the open position when you release the brake lever. Most modern road bikes use dual-pivot calipers, which exert higher pressure than single-pivot calipers. Cantilever and V-brake calipers have pairs of independent arms. You will see them on mountain, cyclo-cross, and touring bikes, as they offer greater stopping power and tire clearance.

PARTS FOCUS

Rim brakes may be twin-armed calipers that rotate around a dual or single pivot, or may have brake arms mounted on the fork blades.

(1) The **brake pads** press onto the rim to slow the wheel. They are made of rubber-based compounds; specific types are used for carbon or ceramic rims.

(2) Brake calipers are mounted on **pivot points** that allow the arms to move and provide leverage. Modern systems feature two pivots.

(3) The **brake arms** press the brake pads onto the braking surface. There are different types of mechanisms to suit road and off-road bikes.

(4) Single- and dual-pivot brakes have a single caliper **mounting bolt** on the frame. Cantilever and V-brakes have one bolt for each caliper arm.

Barrel adjuster can be turned to give minor cable adjustments

Braking surface on wheel rim

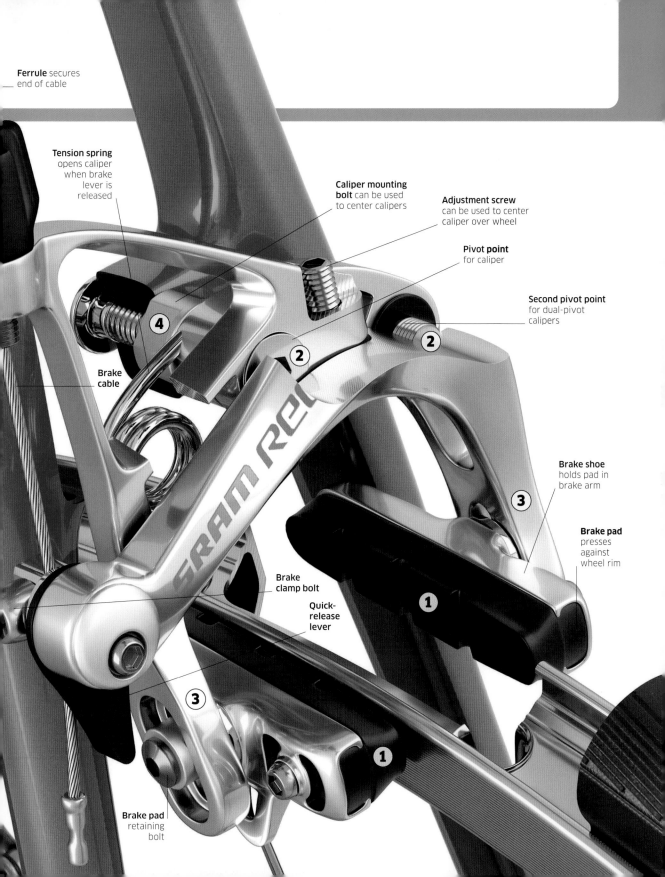

Ferrule secures end of cable

Tension spring opens caliper when brake lever is released

Caliper mounting bolt can be used to center calipers

Adjustment screw can be used to center caliper over wheel

Pivot point for caliper

Second pivot point for dual-pivot calipers

Brake cable

Brake shoe holds pad in brake arm

Brake pad presses against wheel rim

Brake clamp bolt

Quick-release lever

Brake pad retaining bolt

SRAM RE

④ ② ② ③ ① ③ ①

Drop handlebars

Brake cables wear down and stretch over time, reducing the power of your brakes. When correctly installed, the cables should allow you to turn your handlebar all the way in each direction, and to brake firmly with no looseness or shake as you pull the lever.

BEFORE YOU START

- Refer to your owner's manual to check the correct torque settings of your bike's cable clamp bolts
- Check the existing cable routing for incorrectly sized sections
- Make a note of the existing cable routing
- Source the correct cables for your bike

Cable clamp bolt

Cable end cap

1 **Using cable cutters,** cleanly snip the end cap off the existing cable, so the cut end pulls through the cable clamp easily.

2 **Undo the quick-release** lever and unscrew the cable clamp on the brake caliper with a hex key. Pull the cable free.

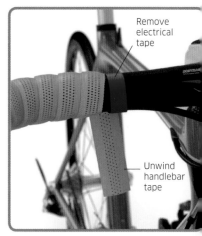

Remove electrical tape

Unwind handlebar tape

3 **Unwrap the bar tape** to expose the cable housing. Release the cables from the bar by cutting the cable tape with a craft knife.

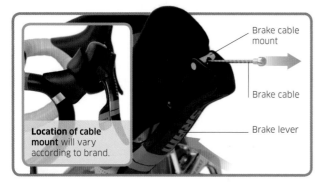

Brake cable mount

Brake cable

Brake lever

Location of cable mount will vary according to brand.

4 **Squeeze the brake lever** to expose the cable mount, and pull the end of the cable out using pliers. You may need to fold the rear hood of the brake levers forward to access the cable.

Free housing from frame mounts

5 **Pull the cable** completely free from the bike, working toward the levers. Remove each length of housing, making a note of where each piece came from, and where each end was located.

Workshop tip: Lubricating cable inners during installation protects them from water and rust, and keeps them running smoothly for longer. Dab some dry lube between your finger and thumb, and gently pull the cable through your fingers to coat it.

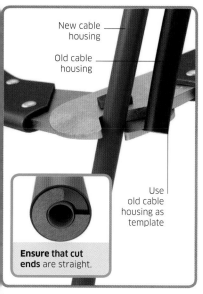

New cable housing

Old cable housing

Use old cable housing as template

Ensure that cut ends are straight.

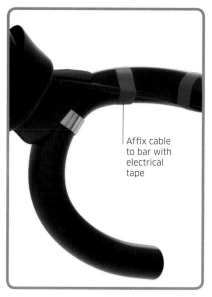

Affix cable to bar with electrical tape

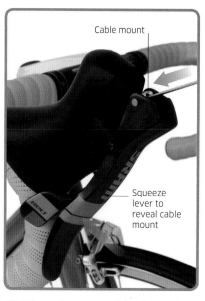

Cable mount

Squeeze lever to reveal cable mount

6 **Cut new lengths** of cable housing, using the existing sections as a template. To ensure a clean cut, do not cut at an angle.

7 **Attach the new housing** to the bar with tape, following the original route, then place handlebar tape over it (see pp.62-63).

8 **Thread a new cable** through the brake cable mount in the lever mechanism, then feed it inside and along the new housing.

Cable end caps fit into mounting points

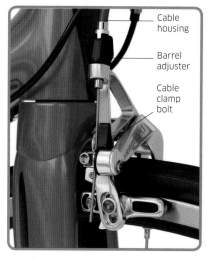

Cable housing

Barrel adjuster

Cable clamp bolt

9 **Continue to feed the cable** along the bike, toward the brake, threading it through the housing. Fit ferrules where required. If the cable gets jammed, do not force it. Ensure there is sufficient slack in the cable to allow the handlebar to turn freely.

10 **Secure the end** of the cable to the brakes, according to the type you have, then adjust them (see pp.112-117).

▶ INSTALLING BRAKE CABLES
Straight handlebars

It is simpler to fit new brake cables to bikes with a straight handlebar than it is to fit them to bikes with a drop bar (see pp.102–03), as the cables are easier to access. Wear and damage to cables are more frequent on mountain bikes, so you will need to replace them more often.

BEFORE YOU START

- Source new cables that are suitable for your bike
- Secure your bike in a frame stand
- Prepare a space where you can lay out the new cables, so they are tension-free and unwound when you need them
- Check that the brake pads are in good condition

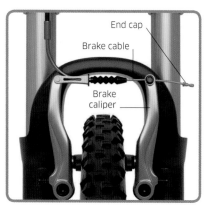

End cap
Brake cable
Brake caliper

1 Detach the brake cable from the caliper, according to the type you have (see pp.112–17). Cut the end cap off the cable.

Cable slot
Turn barrel adjuster

2 Loosen the barrel adjuster on the brake lever. Align the cable slots in the adjuster and the lever body to release the cable.

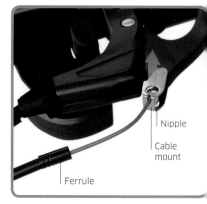

Nipple
Cable mount
Ferrule

3 Squeeze the lever to expose the cable mount. Ease the cable out of the cable slots and free the nipple from the mount.

Remove cable ties and clips from frame
Remove cable and housing

4 Make a note of the original routing before removing the cable. Working from the brake levers, pull the cable through the housing, and unclip each section of housing from the frame mounts in turn. Remove any cable ties, and keep any clips that you want to reuse.

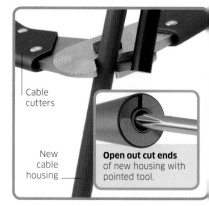

Cable cutters
New cable housing

Open out cut ends of new housing with pointed tool.

5 Cut the new cable housing, using the old pieces as a template. Push ferrules onto the ends of each new piece of housing

Workshop tip: Before buying a new brake cable, check which type is recommended for your bike. Make sure the cable has the correct nipple at the end that fits into the brake lever–in general, barrel nipples are used on mountain bikes and pear nipples on road bikes.

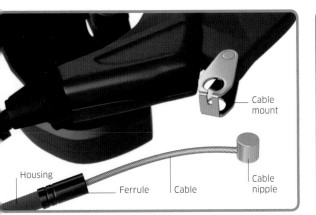

Housing
Ferrule   Cable   Cable nipple
Cable mount

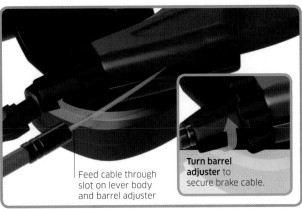

Feed cable through slot on lever body and barrel adjuster

Turn barrel adjuster to secure brake cable.

5 Squeeze the brake lever, and hook the nipple of the new cable into the cable mount. Reversing step 3, release the lever to secure the nipple; feed the free end of the new cable into the cable housing.

7 Feed the cable into the cable slot in the brake lever body and barrel adjuster. Push the ferrule on the cable housing into the barrel adjuster, then rotate the barrel adjuster to lock the cable in place.

Ensure housing curves smoothly, with no sharp bends

Slide housing into cable frame mounts

Noodle

Trim excess cable with cable cutters

Tighten cable clamp with hex key

Crimp end cap over cut end of brake cable using pair of pincers.

8 Working toward the brakes, thread the new cable along the frame, following the original route, and threading it through lengths of housing where required. Reattach any clips and cable ties.

9 At the brake caliper, thread the cable through the noodle and rubber cover, reversing step 1. Feed the cable into the cable clamp, and tighten the bolt. To adjust the brake, see pp.112–17.

Replacing hoses

Hydraulic brake systems usually come correctly installed and ready for use. In some cases, however, it may be necessary to change or shorten one of the hoses. Brake hoses also need to be replaced if they are damaged or start to leak, which will cause the brakes to fail.

Rear brake caliper

Brake lever

Front brake caliper

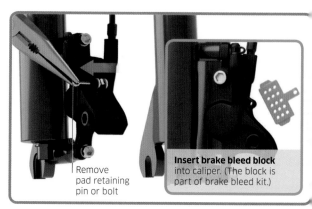

Remove pad retaining pin or bolt

Insert brake bleed block into caliper. (The block is part of brake bleed kit.)

1 **Following the route** of the existing hose, measure the amount of new hose you need by running it along the frame from the brake lever to the caliper. Use a hose cutter to cut the new hose to length.

2 **Remove the brake pads** (see pp.120–21) to prevent them being contaminated with brake fluid. Insert a brake bleed block between the pistons to stop them closing when the system is refilled with fluid.

Compression nut

Rubber cover

Brake lever

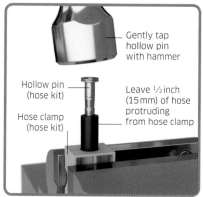

Gently tap hollow pin with hammer

Hollow pin (hose kit)

Hose clamp (hose kit)

Leave ½ inch (15mm) of hose protruding from hose clamp

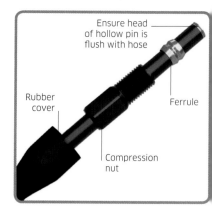

Ensure head of hollow pin is flush with hose

Rubber cover

Ferrule

Compression nut

3 **Remove the existing hose** by sliding back the rubber cover at both ends and unscrewing the compression nuts with a wrench.

4 **Insert each end** of the new hose into the hose clamp, and hold it in a bench vise. Tap a hollow pin into the ends with a hammer.

5 **Prepare the lever end** of the hose by threading the rubber cover, compression nut, and ferrule onto the hose, in that order.

- Frame stand
- Cleaning kit
- Brake hose kit
- Brake fluid
- Brake bleed kit
- Plastic sheet
- Goggles and gloves
- Hose cutter
- Set of wrenches
- Bench vise
- Hammer

CAUTION! Some brake systems use "DOT" fluid, which is corrosive. When applying it, always wear safety gloves and goggles, protect your frame with plastic sheets, and wipe up spills.

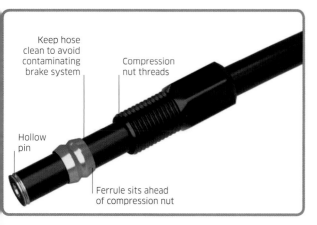

Keep hose clean to avoid contaminating brake system

Compression nut threads

Hollow pin

Ferrule sits ahead of compression nut

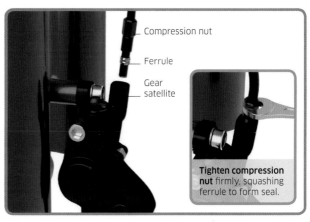

Compression nut

Ferrule

Gear satellite

Tighten compression nut firmly, squashing ferrule to form seal.

6 **Prepare the caliper end** of the new hose in the same way as for the lever end (see step 5). Place the hose down carefully on a clean surface until you need it to prevent losing any of the fittings.

7 **Insert the new hose** into the gear satellite on the caliper and push it in firmly. Slide the ferrule and compression nut down the hose. Using a wrench, screw the compression nut into the caliper.

Reattach hose clips where required

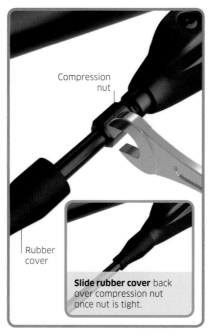

Compression nut

Rubber cover

Slide rubber cover back over compression nut once nut is tight.

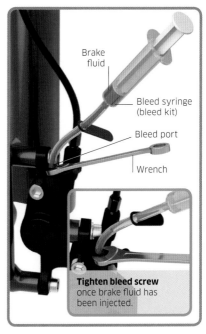

Brake fluid

Bleed syringe (bleed kit)

Bleed port

Wrench

Tighten bleed screw once brake fluid has been injected.

8 **Secure the new hose** along the frame. Ensure the handlebar can turn each way completely without the hose kinking.

9 **Firmly insert the end** of the hose into the brake lever. Tighten the compression nut using a wrench, as shown in step 7.

10 **Inject brake fluid** into the bleed port of the caliper until the system is full, and then bleed the brakes (see pp.108–09).

Bleeding the system

Hydraulic brake systems require bleeding to eliminate any air in the system, normally as a result of maintaining, installing, or reinstalling a brake hose, or because of moisture seeping in. Air in your brakes will make them feel spongy and they will function less effectively.

BEFORE YOU START

- Source the recommended brake fluid and brake bleed kit for your bike (see pp.36–37)
- Secure your bike in a frame stand and cover the floor
- Remove the wheels (see pp.78–81)
- Remove the brake pads; attach a bleed block (see pp.120–21)
- Put on safety goggles and gloves, and keep a cloth handy

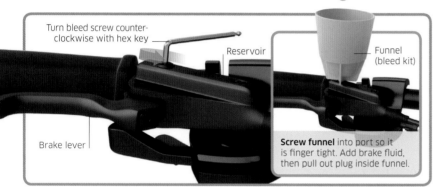

Turn bleed screw counter-clockwise with hex key

Reservoir

Funnel (bleed kit)

Brake lever

Screw funnel into port so it is finger tight. Add brake fluid, then pull out plug inside funnel.

Unscrew mounting bolts with hex key

Brake bleed block (bleed kit)

Brake caliper

1 **Loosen and rotate the brake lever**, so the reservoir is horizontal. Remove the bleed screw from the bleed port on the reservoir. Screw the bleed funnel into the port. Wearing safety gloves and goggles if using "DOT" brake fluid, add a little fluid to the funnel.

2 **Remove the brake caliper** from the fork by unscrewing the mounting bolts. Allow the caliper to hang freely.

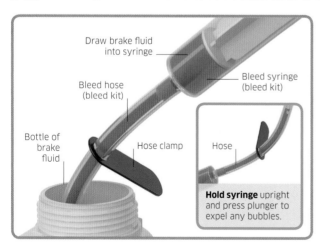

Draw brake fluid into syringe

Bleed syringe (bleed kit)

Bleed hose (bleed kit)

Bottle of brake fluid

Hose clamp

Hose

Hold syringe upright and press plunger to expel any bubbles.

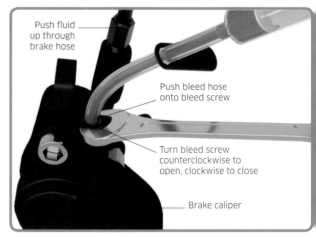

Push fluid up through brake hose

Push bleed hose onto bleed screw

Turn bleed screw counterclockwise to open, clockwise to close

Brake caliper

3 **Push the bleed hose** onto the syringe, then draw brake fluid into the syringe by pulling on the plunger. Once filled, hold the syringe upright to allow any bubbles to float toward the end of the hose.

4 **On the brake caliper**, push the bleed hose onto the bleed screw. Open the screw with a wrench, then inject brake fluid into the caliper, and up to the bleed funnel on the lever. Retighten the bleed screw.

CAUTION! Some brake systems need "DOT" fluid, which is corrosive. When using it, always wear safety gloves and goggles, protect your frame with plastic sheets, and wipe up any spills.

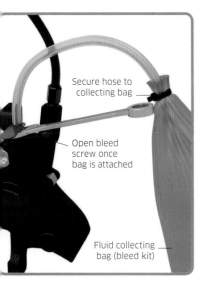

Secure hose to collecting bag

Open bleed screw once bag is attached

Fluid collecting bag (bleed kit)

Tap hose and caliper to dislodge air bubbles

Check hose for bubbles in fluid

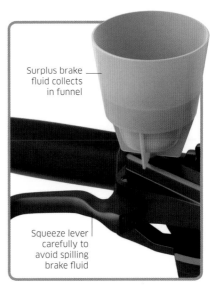

Surplus brake fluid collects in funnel

Squeeze lever carefully to avoid spilling brake fluid

5 **Leave the hose** attached to the bleed screw and replace the syringe with a fluid collecting bag. Half-fill the funnel with brake fluid.

6 **Press the brake lever** to drive fluid through the system to the bag. Once the fluid in the hose is bubble-free, close the bleed screw.

7 **Carefully squeeze** the brake lever a few times. If the action feels firm, you have successfully bled all of the air from the system.

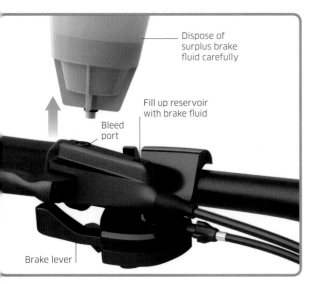

Dispose of surplus brake fluid carefully

Bleed port

Fill up reservoir with brake fluid

Brake lever

Secure brake lever with strap

8 **Insert the plug** inside the bleed funnel and unscrew it from the port. Fill the reservoir to the top with fluid, then reinstall the bleed screw. Reattach the brake caliper, and return the lever to its original position.

9 **If the brakes seem** spongy, squeeze the lever and secure it to the grip. Stand the bike upright and leave overnight to encourage any air to rise to the top of the system, then repeat steps 1–8.

Replacing brake pads

Cold and wet weather can be hard on brake pads. When grit and water mix, they form a paste that gradually wears down the rubber. Brake pads worn down to the shoe can cause brake failure and damage to the rim. A scratching sound when you brake indicates that your pads are worn down.

 BEFORE YOU START

- Secure your bike in a frame stand
- Remove the wheel (see pp.78–83)
- Replace the wheel if the "wear dots" have worn off the rim
- Loosen the brake pad bolt with penetrating oil

DUAL-PIVOT BRAKES

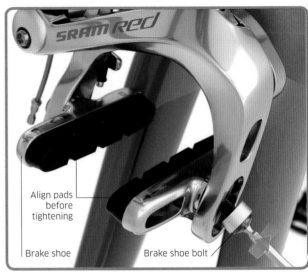

Align pads before tightening

Brake shoe   Brake shoe bolt

2 **Undo the brake shoe bolts** on the caliper arms with a hex key, and remove the old pads. Put the new pads in place. (They will be marked "left" and "right.") Replace the bolts, and tighten.

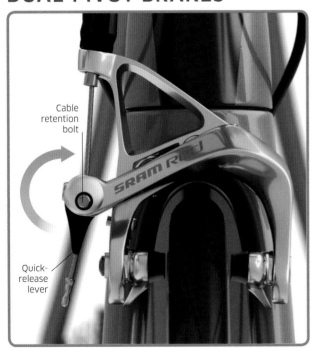

Cable retention bolt

Quick-release lever

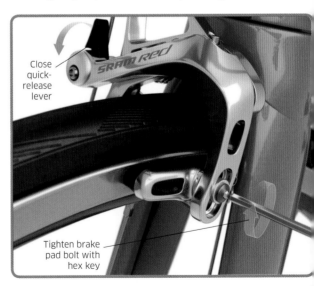

Close quick-release lever

Tighten brake pad bolt with hex key

1 **Open the quick-release lever** on the brake caliper, if attached. If the brake caliper does not have a quick-release lever, undo the cable retention bolt with a wrench or a hex key.

3 **Reattach the wheel** (see pp.78–83). Raise or lower the pads until they strike the rim at its outermost edge. Holding them in place, tighten the brake pad bolts, then adjust the caliper (see pp.112–117).

Workshop tip: Brake pads are left- and right-specific, and each brake shoe is marked with an "L" or "R" to help identify it. Look for the word "TOP" on the pad or shoe so you do not attach it upside down. Wipe down the pads after riding in wet weather to reduce wear.

V-BRAKES AND CANTILEVER BRAKES

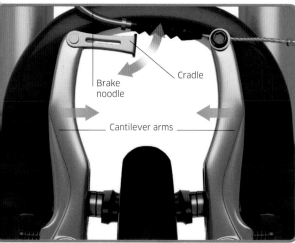

Brake noodle — Cradle

Cantilever arms

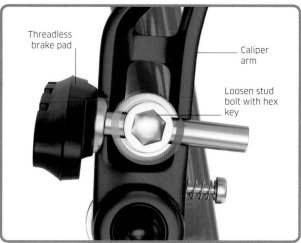

Threadless brake pad

Caliper arm

Loosen stud bolt with hex key

1 Squeeze the arms of the V-brake caliper and release the brake noodle from the cradle. Cantilever brakes have a straddle wire that unhitches from the left cantilever arm (see pp.114–15).

2 If you are replacing a threadless brake pad, loosen the stud bolt on the caliper, slide out the pad, and replace it with the new one. Align the brake pad and loosely tighten the stud bolt.

Replace spacers in same order

Unscrew end nut with hex key

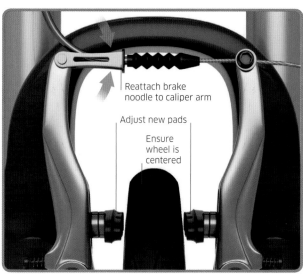

Reattach brake noodle to caliper arm

Adjust new pads

Ensure wheel is centered

3 If you are replacing threaded pads, loosen the end nut on the stud bolt. Remove the brake pad and spacers. Install the new pad by inserting the stud through the caliper arm. Retighten the end nut.

4 Replace the wheel and reattach the brake noodle to the caliper arm. Adjust the position of the brake pads so that they are aligned, ensuring that they do not touch the tire. Tighten the end nut.

▶ ADJUSTING MECHANICAL BRAKES
V-brakes

V-brakes are common on both mountain and hybrid bikes, and are designed to accommodate fatter off-road tires. Like all brake systems, the pads gradually become poorly aligned as they wear down, meaning that your brakes feel spongy, and become less powerful. Due to their quick-release mechanism and simple design, V-brakes are considered to be one of the easiest of all brake systems to install and to adjust. Using some simple tools, the pads can be realigned correctly in a matter of minutes.

BEFORE YOU START

- Check the wear indicator on your brake pads
- Source suitable replacement pads if required
- Secure your bike in a frame stand, so that you can spin the wheel

Wheel must be fully centered before adjusting brakes

1 **Check your wheel** to ensure that it is centered (turning freely and at an equal distance from each fork arm). Make sure the quick release is not overtightened on one side.

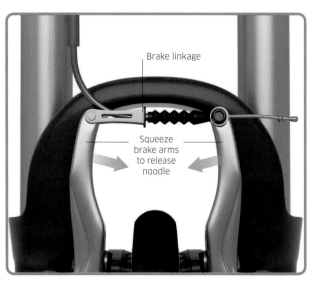

Brake linkage

Squeeze brake arms to release noodle

2 **Squeeze the spring-loaded brake arms** together with one hand, so that the pads touch the wheel rim. This will release the tension in the brake linkage, allowing it to be disconnected.

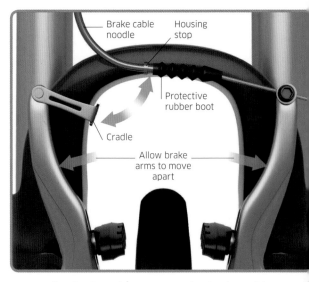

Brake cable noodle   Housing stop

Protective rubber boot

Cradle

Allow brake arms to move apart

3 **Unclip the housing stop** on the brake cable noodle from the cradle, to separate the brake linkage. Release the brake arms, allowing them to open away from the wheel, giving you access to the pads.

- Frame stand
- Set of hex keys
- Phillips screwdriver

Workshop tip: When adjusting the spring tensioner screws, any changes you make to the tension on one side will also affect the other. Avoid tightening the springs as a means to balance the pads too often, as it can increase cable stretch. Adjust them fully as shown.

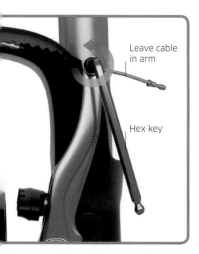

Leave cable in arm

Hex key

Barrel adjuster and lockring

Tighten then slack off lockring and adjustment barrel

4 Loosen the cable retention bolt with a hex key, to allow the cable to slide freely within the bolt.

5 On the brake lever, wind out the barrel adjuster 2–3 full turns to provide slack in the cable. At the brake arm, take up this slack by pulling up to 5 mm of cable through the retention bolt, and hold the cable in place with your fingers.

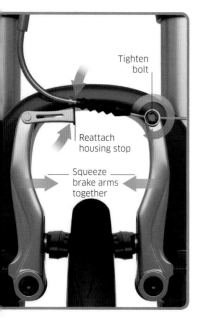

Tighten bolt

Reattach housing stop

Squeeze brake arms together

Check brake pads–do not rub wheel

Barrel adjuster

Use barrel adjuster to fine-tune brakes by turning it inward or outward.

Spring adjustment screw

Screwdriver

6 Reattach the brake linkage and hold the pads close to the rim. Pull the brake cable taut, and tighten the retaining bolt.

7 Squeeze the brake lever 10–12 times to bed in the cable. Rotate the wheel several times to ensure brake pads are not rubbing.

8 Check that brake pads sit evenly, around 1.5 mm from the wheel rim. Adjust the spring tensioner screws on both arms.

Cantilever brakes

Developed for mountain bikes, cantilever brakes feature outward-facing lever arms to provide adequate space for wide or knobby tires. The pads swing in an arc when the lever is pulled, and move down- and inward. Pad alignment to the rim is critical to braking performance.

BEFORE YOU START

- Remove the tire if you need to get a better view
- Check that the wheel is centered in the forks
- Wipe away any dirt or rubber build-up around the pad
- Source replacement brake pads if the existing ones are worn

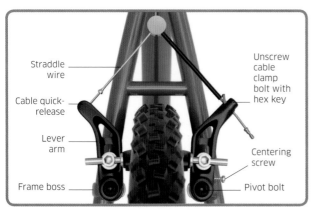

Straddle wire

Cable quick-release

Lever arm

Frame boss

Unscrew cable clamp bolt with hex key

Centering screw

Pivot bolt

1 **Squeeze the lever arms inward** and disconnect the straddle wire from the quick-release on the left brake arm. Unscrew the clamp bolt on the right arm, and release the cable. The arms will hang loose.

Pivot bolt

Clean frame bosses to remove dirt and old grease, then regrease.

2 **Using a hex key**, undo the pivot bolts and ease the arms off the frame bosses. Check the spring tension pins on the back of the arms. Note which hole on the bosses the springs are inserted into.

3 **Slide the brake arms** back onto the frame bosses, ensuring that you return the spring-tension pins on each one to their original hole on the bosses. Tighten the pivot bolts, ensuring the arms move freely.

Slot end of straddle wire into quick-release

Squeeze brake arms together

4 **Squeeze the brake arms** together with one hand and use your other to reinsert the straddle wire into the quick-release slot on the left-hand brake arm. Push it in all the way so it is secure.

Workshop tip: Before adjusting your brakes, ensure the wheels are correctly seated in the dropouts, with all of the nuts or quick-release levers tightened. Check the pads are not set too low on the rim, as a lip will form on the lowest edge, making alignment impossible.

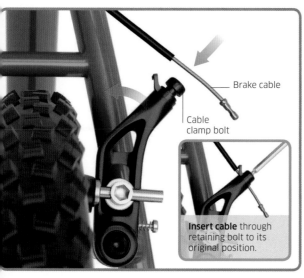

Brake cable

Cable clamp bolt

Insert cable through retaining bolt to its original position.

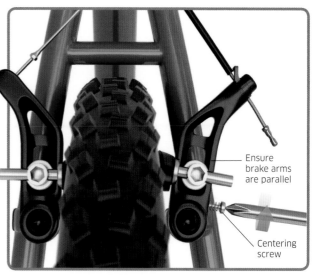

Ensure brake arms are parallel

Centering screw

5 **Still squeezing the brake arms** together, use your free hand to feed the brake cable into the cable clamp bolt on the right-hand brake arm. Once in place, secure the cable by tightening the bolt.

6 **To ensure both brake arms are** at an equal distance from the wheel rim, providing even stopping power, turn the centering screw on each brake arm. The arms should be parallel to the rim.

Barrel adjuster

Ensure pads are evenly spaced

7 **Loosen and adjust the** brake pads so they are parallel to the rim, and strike it squarely. Retighten the bolts all the way.

8 **Turn the barrel adjuster** on the brake lever counterclockwise by up to three turns, until the pads sit 2-3mm from the rim.

9 **Make final fine adjustments** to the position of the brake pads and arms. Ensure the pads are aligned, and the arms centered.

Dual-pivot brakes

On a dual-pivot brake, the caliper has two arms that push the pads into the wheel rim at slightly different angles. Over time, the brake pads wear down and move with use, and will need to be adjusted so that they remain effective. You may also need to recenter the caliper and adjust the tension on the brake cable to relieve any slack.

 BEFORE YOU START

- Secure your bicycle in a frame stand
- Brush off any corrosion from the caliper bolt heads
- Wipe any dirt or residue build-up from the brake pads
- Source new brake pads if yours are worn down

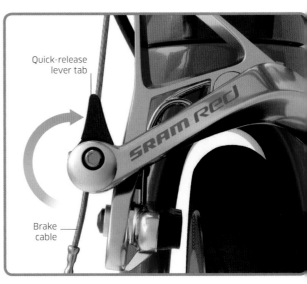

Quick-release lever tab

Brake cable

2 **Release the brake cable** by opening the quick-release lever, if included, or by unscrewing the cable clamp bolt. The brake caliper arms will move outward, well clear of the wheel rim.

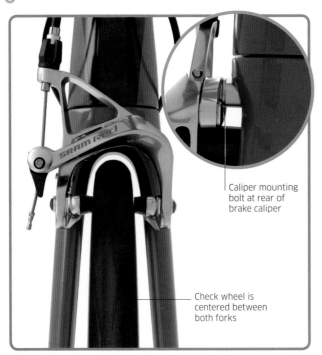

Caliper mounting bolt at rear of brake caliper

Check wheel is centered between both forks

1 **Spin the wheel** to check that it is fully centered between the forks. The center of the tire should also be directly aligned with the caliper mounting bolt. Adjust the wheel, if required (see pp.78–83).

Loosen bolt by half a turn

Retaining bolt

3 **Loosen the retaining bolt** on each brake pad. Move the left pad so that the top of it aligns with the top of the rim. Align the base of the right pad with the base of the rim. Tighten both pad bolts.

TOOLS AND EQUIPMENT

- Frame stand
- Brush and cloth
- Set of hex keys
- Cone wrench

Workshop tip: Squealing brakes are caused by vibrations between the pads and rim. To stop this, "toe-in" each brake pad toward the rim. Loosen the brake-pad-retaining bolt, and rotate the washer behind the pad until the pad surface is parallel to the rim.

Turn barrel adjuster

Open caliper arms all the way

Cable clamp bolt on quick-release lever

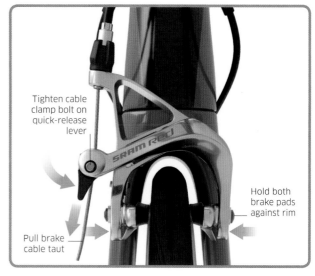

Tighten cable clamp bolt on quick-release lever

Hold both brake pads against rim

Pull brake cable taut

4 Open the barrel adjuster with 3–4 clockwise turns with your hand. Loosen the cable clamp bolt on the back of the quick-release lever with a hex key. This will allow the brake cable to move freely.

5 Squeeze the pads against the rim with one hand. Pull the cable taut with the other. Retighten the cable clamp bolt on the quick-release lever. Squeeze the brake lever several times to bed in the cable.

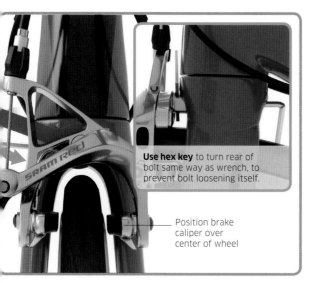

Use hex key to turn rear of bolt same way as wrench, to prevent bolt loosening itself.

Position brake caliper over center of wheel

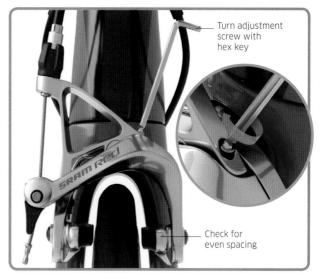

Turn adjustment screw with hex key

Check for even spacing

6 Check that the brake caliper is centered. To adjust it, loosen the mounting bolt (see step 1) with a cone wrench. Insert a hex key behind the bolt, then adjust the caliper. Retighten the mounting bolt.

7 Some calipers have an adjustment screw used for centering. In these cases, turn the adjustment screw in the direction required until the calipers are centered and the pads are evenly spaced from the rim.

Hydraulic disc brakes

In a disc brake system, a pair of brake pads mounted on a caliper act on a metal disc rotor at the wheel hub. Disc brakes are activated by cable or hydraulically. In a hydraulic system, mineral oil or DOT fluid contained in sealed hoses provides the pressure. The brake lever houses a "master cylinder" at the handlebar. When you pull the lever, the master cylinder pushes the fluid to pistons at the caliper, which press the brake pads against the disc rotor. On a cable-operated system, the brake lever pulls the brake cable, which acts on the pistons at the caliper to close the pads. The disc rotor mounts to a hub within the wheel.

Quick-release lever
allows wheel to be removed without using tools

Front fork
supports brake caliper

 PARTS FOCUS

Disc brakes are mounted on the wheel hubs. Both hydraulic and mechanical systems use pads fixed to calipers fixed to the frame.

① Each **piston** in the brake caliper is forced by hydraulic fluid or mechanical tension onto the brake pads as the brake lever is pressed.

② The **brake pads** in the caliper are held clear of the disc rotor by a spring when not in use. They are pressed against the rotor by pistons.

③ The **disc rotor** is fixed to the wheel hub. It turns with the wheel, between the caliper arms, until the brake lever is pressed.

④ The **caliper body** contains the pistons and brake pads. In a hydraulic system it is sealed to maintain the fluid pressure.

Bleed valve used to bleed system

Hydraulic hose carries brake fluid to caliper

Compression nut joins hose to caliper

Brake fluid channel

④

①

②

Return spring holds brake pads clear of rotor when brake lever released

Retaining pin secures brake pads in caliper

Piston chamber contains piston

Caliper mounting bolt holds caliper to fork

③

Brake boss mounts caliper on fork tube upward

Disc brakes

Disc brake pads wear down over time, especially during the winter months, when they pick up more grit from wet roads and muddy trails. A harsh grinding noise when braking indicates that they need urgent replacement to avoid damaging the disc rotor. Pads should be replaced when there is 1.5 mm of material remaining.

🔧 BEFORE YOU START

- Secure your bike in a frame stand
- Remove the wheel (see pp.78–83)
- Remove old disc rotor
- Put on clean gloves before handling the new brake surface
- Wipe away any dust or dirt from the new disc rotor

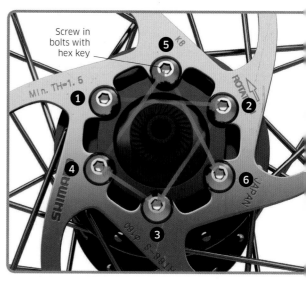

Screw in bolts with hex key

2 **Screw in the rotor mounting bolts**, fastening each in place loosely, before tightening them all the way to the recommended torque settings. Work in a star formation (from 1–6) to avoid distorting the disc

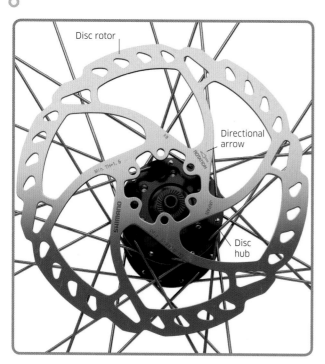

Disc rotor

Directional arrow

Disc hub

1 **Locate the directional arrow** etched on the surface of the new disc rotor, then align the disc rotor with the hub, installing it according to the manufacturer's instructions.

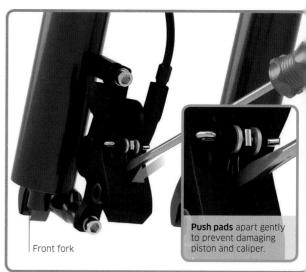

Front fork

Push pads apart gently to prevent damaging piston and caliper.

3 **Using a large flat-head screwdriver**, tire lever, or pad spreader, ease the pads apart and reset the pistons. Then remove the old pads to allow sufficient space for the new, thicker pads.

TOOLS AND EQUIPMENT

- Frame stand
- Cloth and gloves
- Set of hex keys

- Flat-head screwdriver, tire lever, or pad spreader
- Needle-nose pliers

- Degreaser or brake cleaner and cloth

Pads retained by a split pin or bolt

Carefully extract brake pads to avoid damaging caliper.

4 **Remove the pad retainer**— either a bolt or split pin (as above)—and ease the brake pads and spring from the caliper.

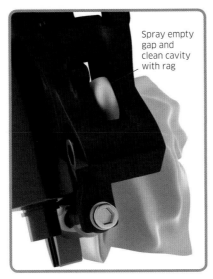

Spray empty gap and clean cavity with rag

5 **Clean inside the brake caliper** by spraying it with degreaser or brake cleaner. Remove any dirt, grease, or brake dust with a cloth.

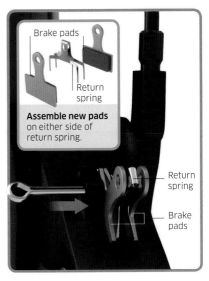

Brake pads

Return spring

Assemble new pads on either side of return spring.

Return spring

Brake pads

6 **Assemble the pads** and spring (inset), then insert them into the caliper. Attach the replacement pad retaining pin or bolt.

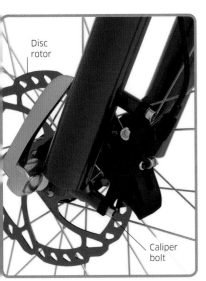

Disc rotor

Caliper bolt

7 **Reattach the wheel** and check that the rotor is centered between the pads, and that it spins freely without rubbing.

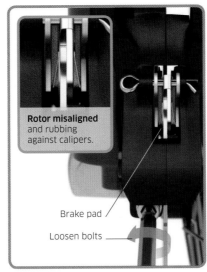

Rotor misaligned and rubbing against calipers.

Brake pad

Loosen bolts

8 **If the wheel does rub**, loosen the caliper bolts and adjust the position of the caliper so that the rotor can spin freely.

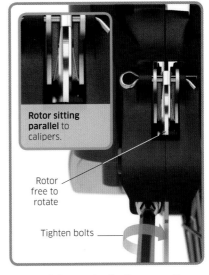

Rotor sitting parallel to calipers.

Rotor free to rotate

Tighten bolts

9 **Retighten the bolts** once the caliper is aligned. Squeeze the brake lever several times to bed in the new pads.

Roller brakes

Commonly used on utility bikes, where their extra weight is offset by extreme longevity, roller brakes are housed inside a specialized hub. Pulling the brake lever activates a brake arm on the outside of the hub, which pushes the internal brake pads against the brake liner on the inside of the hub, slowing the wheel. Since the braking assembly is sealed inside the hub, roller brakes deliver the same braking power in dry, wet, icy, or muddy conditions, and the parts wear down slowly. Most roller brakes, such as the Sturmey Archer XL-FD (shown here), are simple in construction but cannot be easily maintained at home. However, cable tension can be adjusted (see pp.124–25).

BRAKE ACTION

The brake cable pulls the brake hub arm, pushing the internal pads against the brake liner until the lever is released.

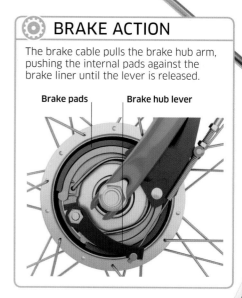

Brake pads   Brake hub lever

Flange oversized for
extra rigidity

Spokes lace rim
onto flange

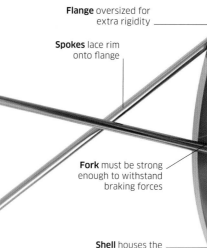

Fork must be strong
enough to withstand
braking forces

Shell houses the
roller unit

PARTS FOCUS

Roller brakes require a specialized hub and a fork or frame that can accept the torque arm, so retro-fitting is possible only on some bikes.

① The **brake pads** are made from a durable metal composite and wear down very slowly. Once worn, they can't be replaced—a new roller unit is required.

② The **brake liner** is the surface within the roller that the brake pads come into contact with. It wears down slowly and can't be replaced.

③ The **hub brake arm** is pulled by the cable and activates the brake pads. Press the arm inward when adjusting the cable.

④ The **barrel adjuster** allows you to make minor adjustments to the brake cable, which will stretch over time (see pp.124–25).

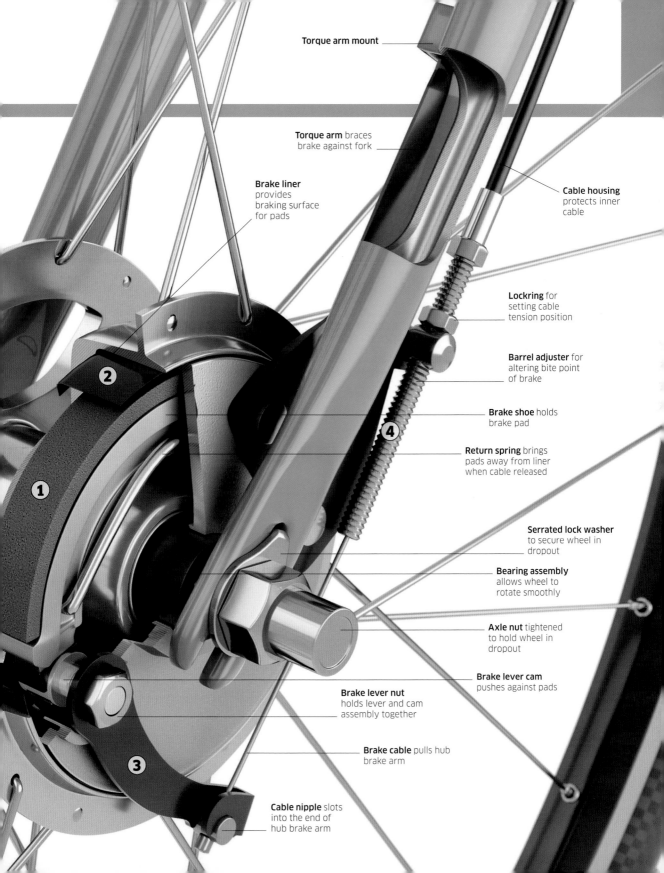

Torque arm mount

Torque arm braces
brake against fork

Brake liner
provides
braking surface
for pads

Cable housing
protects inner
cable

Lockring for
setting cable
tension position

Barrel adjuster for
altering bite point
of brake

Brake shoe holds
brake pad

Return spring brings
pads away from liner
when cable released

Serrated lock washer
to secure wheel in
dropout

Bearing assembly
allows wheel to
rotate smoothly

Axle nut tightened
to hold wheel in
dropout

Brake lever cam
pushes against pads

Brake lever nut
holds lever and cam
assembly together

Brake cable pulls hub
brake arm

Cable nipple slots
into the end of
hub brake arm

Roller brake cables

Roller brakes are installed mainly on commuter and utility bikes, and are largely maintenance-free. If the internal brake pads are worn down, you must replace the entire unit. If the brake cables need to be adjusted or replaced; however, this is a fairly straightforward task.

Ⓠ **BEFORE YOU START**

■ Secure your bike in a frame stand
■ Make a note of the existing cable routing
■ Remove the old cable by following steps 1–5, shown below, in reverse

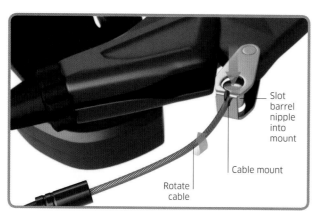

Slot barrel nipple into mount

Cable mount

Rotate cable

1 **To install a new cable**, pull the brake lever to expose the cable mount. Push the barrel nipple of the cable into the mount, and rotate the cable counterclockwise so that the nipple locks into it.

Ferrule

Rotate adjuster to hold cable secure once it has slotted into place.

2 **Align the slots** in the brake lever and the barrel adjuster, and thread the cable through the slots. Seat the ferrule of the cable housing into the barrel adjuster. Turn the adjuster to secure the cable.

Check you can turn handlebar all the way

3 **Route the cable** along the frame from the brake lever to the hub, following the original routing. Secure the cable to the frame, ensuring that you leave sufficient slack so the handlebar turns all the way.

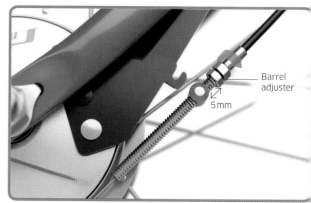

Barrel adjuster

5 mm

4 **At the roller end** of the cable, rotate the barrel adjuster so that there is around 5 mm of thread showing below the lockring. (This will allow for fine adjustments later.)

Workshop tip: Some roller brakes need a brake cable with a factory-installed nipple on each end: a barrel nipple for the brake lever and a pear nipple for the hub brake arm. To remove this type of cable, you will have to cut off one of the nipples.

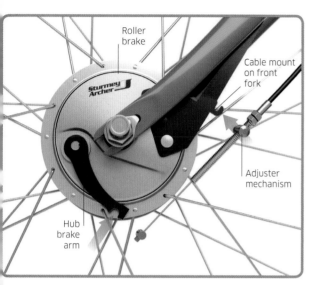

Roller brake

Cable mount on front fork

Hub brake arm

Adjuster mechanism

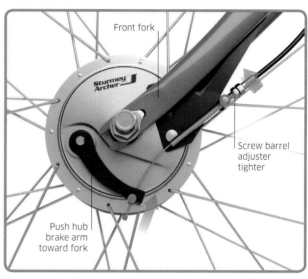

Front fork

Screw barrel adjuster tighter

Push hub brake arm toward fork

5 **Secure the adjuster mechanism** onto the hooked cable mount on the fork (for a front brake) or the chainstay (for a rear brake). Push the hub brake arm toward the fork. Attach the cable nipple into the end.

6 **Push the hub brake arm** toward the fork again, then tighten the barrel adjuster to take up the slack in the cable. Tighten it until the brake engages when the wheel is turned.

Barrel adjuster

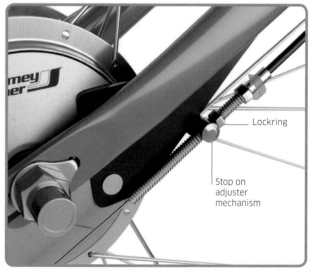

Lockring

Stop on adjuster mechanism

7 **Release the hub brake arm**, and slacken the barrel adjuster off until the brake disengages when you turn the wheel by hand. Pull the brake lever to ensure the brake engages, stopping the wheel.

8 **Pull the brake lever** 10-12 times to remove any slack. Once you are happy with the bite point of the brake, tighten the lockring against the stop on the adjuster mechanism to set the cable tension.

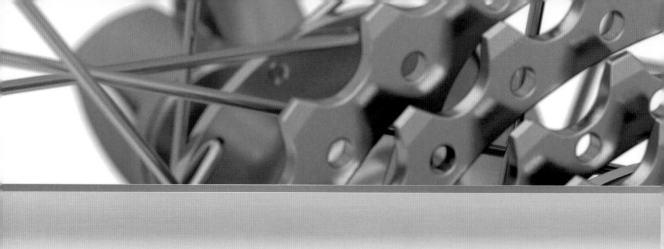

DRIVETRAIN

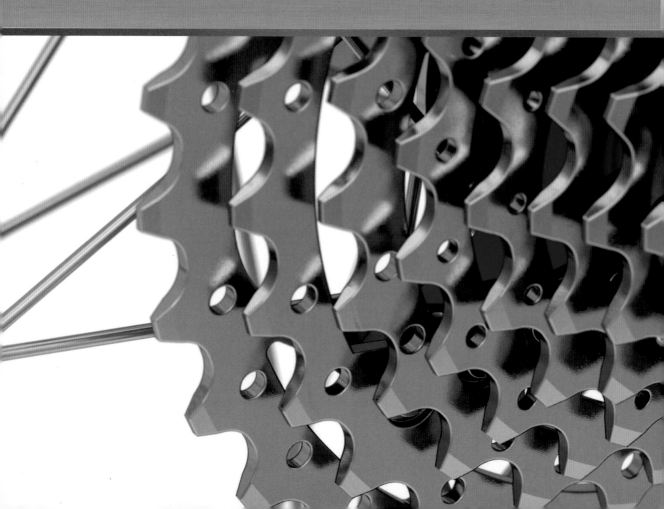

► **CHOOSER GUIDE**

Drivetrain systems

Gears make slow cycling uphill and fast downhill easier if you push harder. There are multiple drivetrain systems that make changing gear possible. The fragile-looking but surprisingly effective and generally reliable derailleur is most popular and still the device of choice on road bikes and utility bikes. Changing gears on a derailleur has undergone significant evolution

TYPE	SUITABILITY	OPERATION
HUB GEARS In a hub gear system, the gears are enclosed within the rear wheel hub. As the gears are shielded from the road, they are less vulnerable to the general wear and tear of riding.	■ **Low-maintenance** utility bikes, hybrid bikes, folding bikes, and city bikes (such as those used in bike-sharing schemes).	■ **Hub gears** are operated with a single gear-shift lever on the handlebar that moves cables around the central "sun gear."
DERAILLEURS In a derailleur system, a lever on the handlebar is connected by a cable to the derailleur, which moves the chain between cogs (on a rear derailleur) or chainrings (on a front derailleur).	■ **All types of road riding,** from racing to touring and utility bikes.	■ **On a rear derailleur,** the cable from the brake lever pulls the mechanism to move the chain to a cog. Two jockey pulleys maintain tension in the chain. ■ **Front derailleurs** have a cage to guide the chain as it is moved.
FIXED GEARS Fixed wheel is the original single-gear system. There is no freewheel; the pedals will keep turning even if you stop pedaling.	■ **Track cycling**, basic city bikes, and training rides to hone pedaling skills.	■ **The cog** is fixed to the rear hub, and turns with the wheel. Some types have a "flip-flop" hub, with a fixed gear on one side and a freewheel on the other.
E-GEARS In an e-gear (electronic gear) system, the gears are changed with switches rather than mechanical levers. A switch on the handlebar is connected by a wire to a battery pack and a small electric motor that drives the derailleur.	■ **Racing** and competitive road events such as triathlons (though e-gears are becoming available to a wide range of cyclists). ■ **Not advisable** for touring or trekking, as use is limited by the need to charge the batteries.	■ **Buttons** and paddle-operated switches secured to the brake levers, or secured remotely on the bar, operate small motors in the front and rear derailleurs. ■ **Battery power is supplied** either by a single cell for wired units or individual cells on wireless types.

with combined brake and gear-shift levers now being overtaken by buttons operating electronic gear mechanisms. Hub gears provide a reliable alternative to derailleurs, requiring minimal, if any, maintenance. Fixed-gear or single-speed bikes are simple to ride and need little maintenance but offer no assistance on steep climbs or extra speed on downhill straights.

KEY COMPONENTS

- **The set of small gears** that turns around a "sun gear" fixed to the axle, all within a larger "ring gear."

- **Rear derailleurs** are made up of a body, screws to limit the range of movement, a barrel adjuster to fine-tune cable tension, and a gear hanger.
- **Front derailleurs** have a body, with no extra parts.

- **The cog that sits** on the rear hub.
- **Some hubs** also have a freewheel.

- **E-gears still use** conventional front and rear mechanisms.
- **Wires are routed** through the frame to the mechanism.
- **A charger is required** for the batteries.

VARIATIONS

- **Hub gears** can have 3–14 gears and are normally run with a single front chainwheel.

- **The latest rear derailleurs** for road bikes work with a wide range of cogs; older types with indexing may work with only a limited number.
- **Front derailleurs** are used with double or triple cranksets.

- **Fixed-wheel systems** for track and road differ in their gearing, with track bikes geared more highly.

- **E-gears work** with both 10– and 11–speed drivetrains.
- **The top-end brands** are made for professional riding, but e-gears are now also supplied for mid-priced road bikes.

ADJUSTMENTS

- **Turn the barrel adjuster** at the hub to alter the cable tension.

- **Turn the rear derailleur** screws to fix the range of movement and the position under the largest cog.
- **Turn the front derailleur** screws to fix the position and the range of movement.

- **Slide the rear wheel** back and forth in the dropout ends to maintain tension in the chain.

- **After installing** by a trained mechanic, both derailleurs automatically self-adjust after each change.
- **Batteries need charging** every quarter; cells in wireless systems require more frequent charging.

Manual shifters

Gear-shift levers allow you to change gear when pedaling. The right-hand shifter controls the rear derailleur, and the left-hand shifter moves the front derailleur. Road bike shifters are integrated within a unit inside the hood of the brake lever. Mountain bike and hybrid shifters clamp separately around the handlebar. There are two main types: trigger and grip shifters. Trigger shifters, unlike grip ones, can be set to different positions, allowing riders to tailor the handlebar set-up to fit their individual preferences. Shimano also makes an integrated brake and gear-shift lever, known as an STI lever.

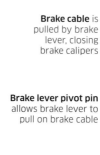

Cable anchor pin secures brake cable

Brake cable is pulled by brake lever, closing brake calipers

Brake lever pivot pin allows brake lever to pull on brake cable

Pivot enables gear lever to move

Shifter lever rotates ratchet wheel, pulling gear cable

Brake lever is pulled to activate brakes

⚙ PARTS FOCUS

Gear-shift levers are "indexed" by a ratchet mechanism, which is activated by pressing the trigger or twisting the grip.

① The **ratchet wheel** pulls the gear cable in set increments, causing the derailleur to move and pull the chain into a new position.

② The **cable anchors** secure the end of the gear cable within the shifter mechanism. The cable must be seated all the way in the anchor to provide tension.

③ **Pivot pins** inside the lever body provide leverage for the shifter lever, allowing it to pull on the tensioned gear cable.

④ The **lever body and hood** contain the internal mechanism of the shifter, holding it in place and protecting it from wear and damage.

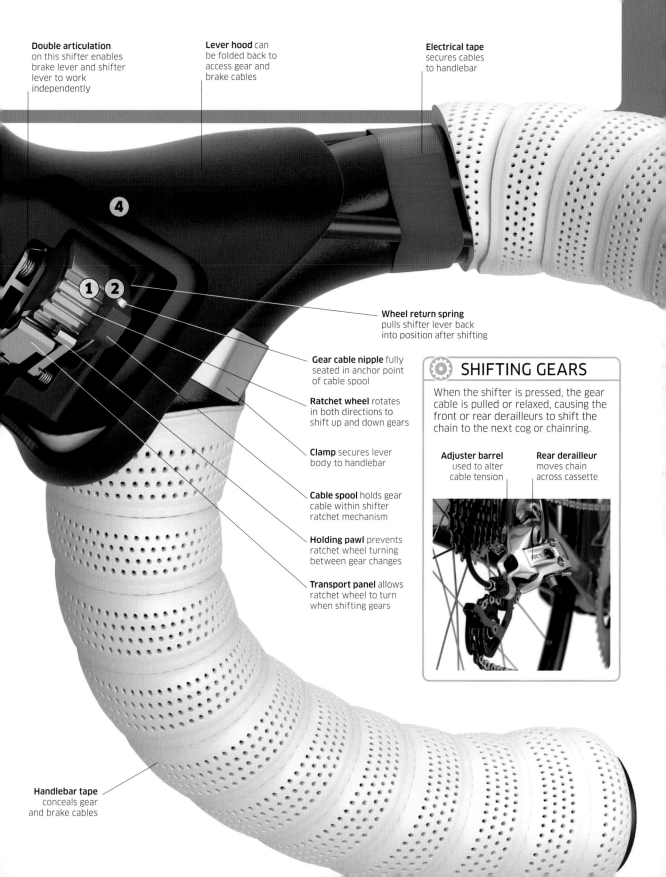

Double articulation
on this shifter enables
brake lever and shifter
lever to work
independently

Lever hood can
be folded back to
access gear and
brake cables

Electrical tape
secures cables
to handlebar

④

① ②

Wheel return spring
pulls shifter lever back
into position after shifting

Gear cable nipple fully
seated in anchor point
of cable spool

Ratchet wheel rotates
in both directions to
shift up and down gears

Clamp secures lever
body to handlebar

Cable spool holds gear
cable within shifter
ratchet mechanism

Holding pawl prevents
ratchet wheel turning
between gear changes

Transport panel allows
ratchet wheel to turn
when shifting gears

Handlebar tape
conceals gear
and brake cables

⚙ SHIFTING GEARS

When the shifter is pressed, the gear
cable is pulled or relaxed, causing the
front or rear derailleurs to shift the
chain to the next cog or chainring.

Adjuster barrel
used to alter
cable tension

Rear derailleur
moves chain
across cassette

External gear cables

Over time cables will stretch through use and affect the tension. Frame-mounted gear cables can develop rust within the cable housing, causing friction that impedes gear-shifting. The solution is to fit new cables and housing.

BEFORE YOU START

- Secure your bike in a frame stand
- Unfold the new cables and cable housing
- Locate the gear-shift lever housing the cable you want to change

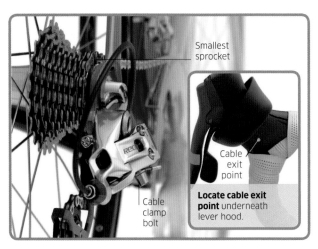

Smallest sprocket

Cable exit point

Locate cable exit point underneath lever hood.

Cable clamp bolt

Inner gear cable

Snip off cable end cap cleanly

1 **To reduce tension** in the chain, set it to the highest gear on the cassette using the gear-shift lever. This will ensure that the gear cable engages with the shifter mechanism correctly when installed.

2 **Using a hex key**, loosen the cable clamp bolt on the rear derailleur (mech), and cut off the inner cable end cap. Doing this will release the inner cable and allow it to travel back through the housing.

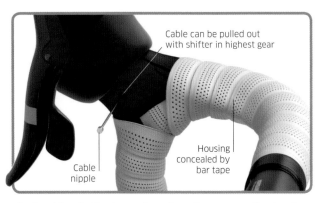

Cable can be pulled out with shifter in highest gear

Housing concealed by bar tape

Cable nipple

3 **Peel back the lever hood** and squeeze the brake lever. Give the cable housing a push where it exits the handlebar, then pull the inner cable from the shifter mechanism at the lever.

4 **Working from the rear** to the front of the bike, remove all of the cable housing from the frame. (Housing concealed by handlebar tape can usually be reused, as it is less exposed to the elements.)

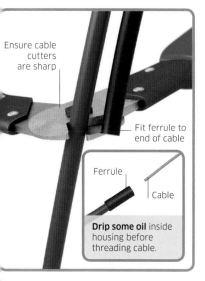

Ensure cable cutters are sharp

Fit ferrule to end of cable

Ferrule

Cable

Drip some oil inside housing before threading cable.

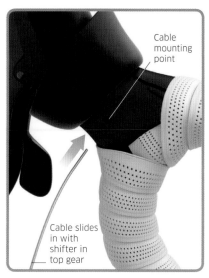

Cable mounting point

Cable slides in with shifter in top gear

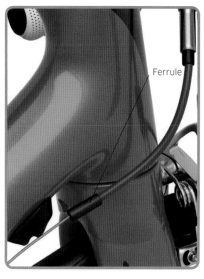

Ferrule

5 **Using the existing housing** as a guide, trim the replacements to length and fit ferrules on the ends. Oil the new inner cable.

6 **Thread the cable** all the way into the shifter and housing, locking the cable nipple into the shifter. Fully test all of the gears.

7 **Ease the cable** along the cable housing mounted on the handlebar, then out toward the first external frame mount.

Ferrule

Cable frame mount

8 **Thread the cable** through each piece of housing, fitting ferrules to the end of each length and into the frame mounts. Pass the cable long the bike and through the bottom bracket guide. Fit the remaining able housing, securing it into the rear frame mounts.

9 **Feed the cable** through the cable clamp, pull it taut, then tighten the bolt. Squeeze the gear-shift lever to pull the cable into place.

Internal gear cables

If your bike becomes sluggish shifting gears, or the gear levers slow to return to position, your gear cables are corroded, and you will need to install new ones. The method shown here is for installing new cabling for the rear derailleur (mech), but it also applies for the front one.

BEFORE YOU START

- Secure your bike in a frame stand
- Unfold the new cables to remove any tension
- Pull back the gear-shift lever hood for the cable you wish to change

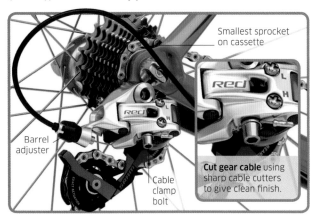

Smallest sprocket on cassette

Barrel adjuster

Cable clamp bolt

Cut gear cable using sharp cable cutters to give clean finish.

1 **Set the gears** to the smallest sprockets on the chainring and the cassette, and cut the existing gear cable cleanly ahead of the cable clamp. Using a hex key, loosen the cable clamp bolt and free the cable.

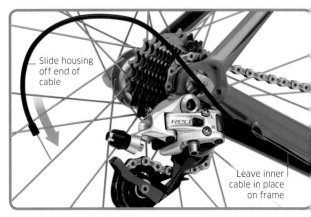

Slide housing off end of cable

Leave inner cable in place on frame

2 **Leaving the existing cable** in place, slide the rearmost piece of cable housing off the free end. Detach the housing from the frame mounts, and set aside the ferrules if you plan to reuse them.

3 **To guide the new cable** through the frame, thread a long, thin tube over the free end of the existing cable. Carefully slide it along the length of the cable, through the entry and exit ports of the frame.

Plastic tube

Tape

Secure ends of tube where they enter and exit frame.

4 **Secure the ends** of the tube at both ends of the frame with tape. Pull the old cable through the frame from the front. Once it is free, disconnect the cable from the gear-shift lever (see pp.132–33).

TOOLS AND EQUIPMENT

- Frame stand
- Sharp cable cutters
- Set of hex keys
- Thin plastic tubing
- Tape
- Ferrules
- Pointed tool
- Oil
- Magnet

Workshop tip: The thin tube should be long enough to reach from the entry point to the exit point of the frame. If you still lose the end of a cable within the frame, you can use a magnet to guide the cable to the exit point.

New housing

Clean cut will help inner cable slide through

Old housing

Ferrule | Housing

Attach ferrules to ends of housing (to secure housing into frame mounts and components.)

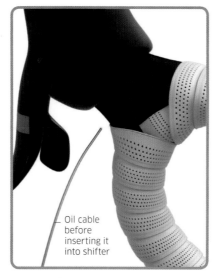

Oil cable before inserting it into shifter

Ease cable into guide tube at frame entry point; push it through.

5 Using the existing housing as a guide, cut new pieces to length. Use sharp cable cutters to ensure the cut ends are clear.

6 Holding the cable in one hand and the shifter in the other, feed the cable into the shifter until the whole cable is through.

7 Feed the cable through the concealed housing on the handlebar. Thread the cable into the tube on the frame (see step 4).

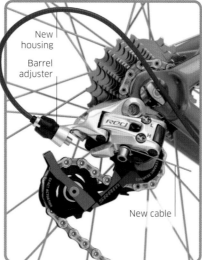

New housing

Barrel adjuster

New cable

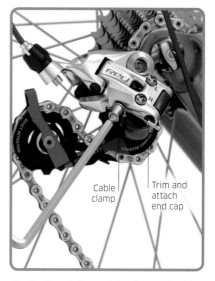

Cable clamp

Trim and attach end cap

8 Once the new cable is routed through the frame, pull the guide tube free by sliding it off the end of the cable at the rear.

9 Attach ferrules to both ends of a piece of housing, and pass the cable through. Secure the housing in the frame mount and derailleur.

10 Feed the cable through the cable clamp, pull it taut, and tighten the bolt. Trim the cable end. To index the gears, see pp.148-49.

Electronic shifting

A recent innovation once reserved for professional cyclists, electronic gear-shifting is increasingly found on many road, mountain, and utility bikes. Electronic derailleurs work just like mechanical ones, but are moved by an electric motor on the derailleur rather than a metal cable. The motor is powered by a rechargeable battery, and is activated when the shifter is pressed. Once set up (see pp.138–39), electronic shifting is quick and precise—reducing chain wear—and the lack of cable stretch means that the derailleurs should never need adjusting. While Shimano and Campagnolo use electric cables to connect the shifters and derailleurs, SRAM's system is wireless.

⚙ PARTS FOCUS

An **electronic rear derailleur** is the same as a mechanical derailleur, other than the motor. SRAM units also include a detachable battery.

① A **motor** inside the derailleur precisely shifts the derailleur arm. Unlike manual systems, every shift moves the derailleur exactly the same distance.

② The **derailleur arm** moves the chain across the cassette, inward or outward, according to the gear selected. It also retains tension in the chain.

③ The **jockey pulleys** perform two essential tasks: the top wheel guides the chain when shifting gear and the lower wheel keeps the chain tensioned.

④ **Pivots** on the derailleur allow the arm to move vertically—keeping the chain under tension—and laterally—across the cassette to change gear.

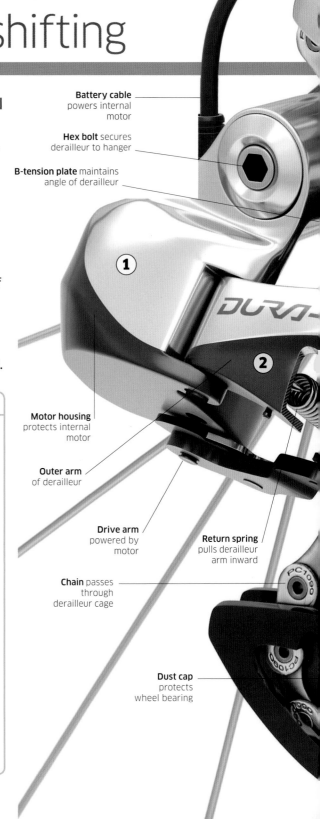

Battery cable powers internal motor

Hex bolt secures derailleur to hanger

B-tension plate maintains angle of derailleur

Motor housing protects internal motor

Outer arm of derailleur

Drive arm powered by motor

Return spring pulls derailleur arm inward

Chain passes through derailleur cage

Dust cap protects wheel bearing

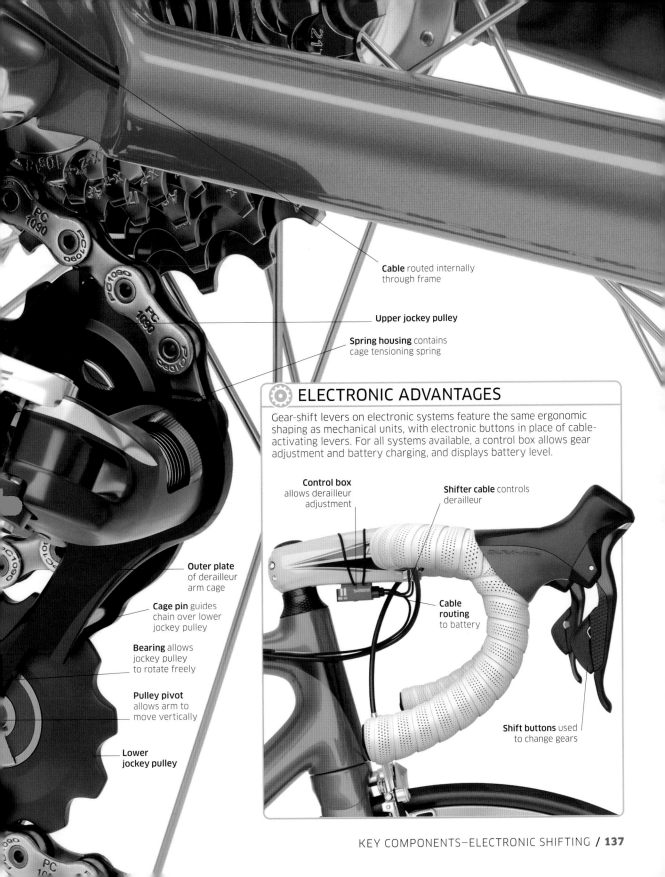

Cable routed internally
through frame

Upper jockey pulley

Spring housing contains
cage tensioning spring

⚙ ELECTRONIC ADVANTAGES

Gear-shift levers on electronic systems feature the same ergonomic
shaping as mechanical units, with electronic buttons in place of cable-
activating levers. For all systems available, a control box allows gear
adjustment and battery charging, and displays battery level.

Control box
allows derailleur
adjustment

Shifter cable controls
derailleur

Cable
routing
to battery

Shift buttons used
to change gears

Outer plate
of derailleur
arm cage

Cage pin guides
chain over lower
jockey pulley

Bearing allows
jockey pulley
to rotate freely

Pulley pivot
allows arm to
move vertically

Lower
jockey pulley

Shimano Di2 systems

An electronic drivetrain, such as the Shimano Di2 system, offers precise reliability—a motor shifts the chain at the same speed and distance every time. Electronic wiring means there is no cable stretch to worry about either. If the shifting has become sluggish or you have installed a new cassette, you may need to fine-tune the system.

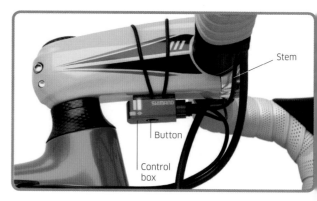

Stem

Button

Control box

🔧 BEFORE YOU START

- Ensure that the battery is fully charged
- Secure your bike in a frame stand
- Check for wear on the cassette and chain

2 **Locate the control box**, which can be found on the stem or beneath the saddle, depending on your bike. Press and hold the button until the "adjustment mode" light comes on.

Chain on middle cog of cassette

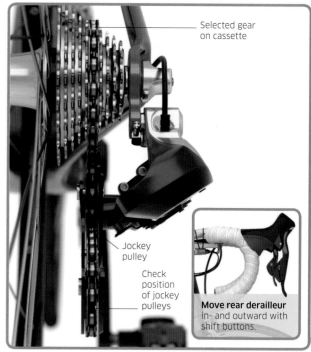

Selected gear on cassette

Jockey pulley

Check position of jockey pulleys

Move rear derailleur in- and outward with shift buttons.

1 **Use the buttons** on the gear-shift lever to move the chain to one of the middle cogs on the rear cassette, such as fourth or fifth gear. The chain can be set on any position on the chainring.

3 **Use the shift buttons** to adjust the position of the rear derailleur (mech) relative to the cassette. The teeth of the jockey pulleys should vertically align with the teeth of the cog of the selected gear.

Workshop tip: The Di2 derailleur has a built-in protection feature. If the bike falls over, the system will need to be reset. Press and hold the button on the control box until the red light flashes, and pedal through the gears—the derailleur will shift and reset.

Hold button until light goes off

Check chain shifts gear quietly

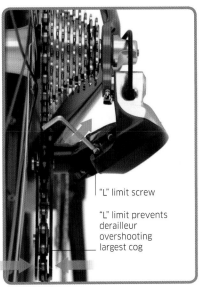

"L" limit screw

"L" limit prevents derailleur overshooting largest cog

4 **Switch the control box** back to "normal mode." The light will turn off. You can use the shifter buttons to change gear again.

5 **Turn the pedals** and shift up and down the gears. If the chain rattles, the derailleur is not in line. Make further adjustments.

6 **Shift to the lowest gear** on the cassette. Turn the "L" (low) limit screw so the teeth of the jockey pulleys align with those of the cog.

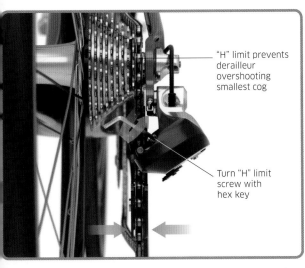

"H" limit prevents derailleur overshooting smallest cog

Turn "H" limit screw with hex key

7 **Shift to the highest gear** on the cassette. Turn the "H" (high) limit screw on the derailleur to align the teeth of the jockey pulleys vertically with those of the smallest cog. The derailleur will move inward.

8 **Pedal the bike** to ensure that everything is working correctly. Shift through the gears from highest to lowest, then back, to test for quick, smooth shifting. Readjust the derailleur, if required.

Front derailleurs

The front derailleur moves the top of the chain sideways between the chainrings. When a new gear is selected, the gear cable comes under tension and pulls on the arm of the derailleur to move the cage on the mechanism. The cage pushes the chain sideways; this causes the chain to run at an angle and fall onto the teeth of a smaller chainring or engage with the pick-up ramps of a larger chainring. The front derailleur is attached to the frame either via a clamp around the seat tube or directly ("braze on"). Derailleur parts may be made of aluminum alloy, steel, plastic, or carbon fiber.

⚙ SHIFTING GEARS

When the gear-shift lever is pressed, the gear cable is pulled or relaxed, causing the front derailleur to move sideways, guiding the chain across the chainrings.

Chain moves between chainrings

Derailleur controlled by gear cable

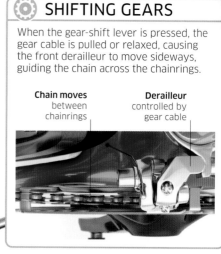

⚙ PARTS FOCUS

A front derailleur has a sprung arm moving on pivots, a cage to shift the chain, and a mount to secure the mechanism to the frame.

① **The cage** consists of two plates between which the chain passes. The inner plate pushes the chain outward; the outer plate pushes it inward.

② **Shifting pins** on the inside of the larger chainrings catch the chain and lift it so that the links engage on the larger chainring.

③ **The derailleur mount** may consist of a clamp, as shown, or a "braze-on" fitting that is bolted to lugs welded to the frame. Both types are common.

④ **Limit screws** stop the derailleur from moving too far and pushing the chain off the chainrings. They may require adjusting (see pp.142–43).

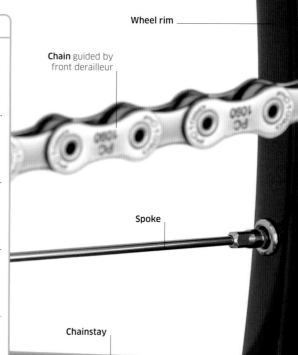

Wheel rim

Chain guided by front derailleur

Spoke

Chainstay

Arm supports and moves cage mechanism

Gear cable may enter derailleur from above or below

Pivots at top and bottom of arm enable it to move

Seat tube is usual location for "braze-on" derailleur

Bolt anchors free end of gear cable

Return spring pulls derailleur inward

Outer plate of derailleur cage

Inner plate of derailleur cage

③

④

④

①

②

Front derailleurs

The front derailleur (mech) moves the chain from one chainring to another. If the chain rattles or slips off when shifted onto the largest gears, then the spring mechanism may have seized, and you will need to adjust or replace the derailleur.

 BEFORE YOU START

- Secure your bike in a frame stand
- Remove the chain (see pp.158–59) and the gear cable
- Detach the cable from the derailleur by reversing step 8
- Remove the existing derailleur by reversing step 1

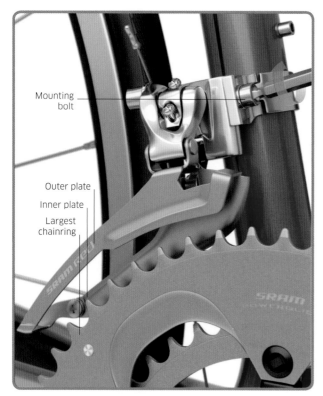

Mounting bolt

Outer plate

Inner plate

Largest chainring

1 **Position the derailleur** so that the outer plate is just above and parallel to the largest chainring. Use a hex key to tighten the mounting bolt, so that it is held in place but can still be moved by hand.

Outer plate of front derailleur

1–3mm gap required

2 **Set the height** of the front derailleur above the chainrings. Check the manufacturer's instructions for the correct height: the derailleur's outer plate usually sits 1–3mm above the largest chainring.

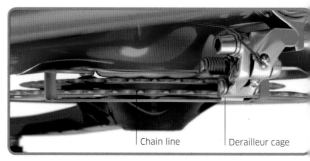

Chain line

Derailleur cage

3 **Look from above** at the chain line. Move the derailleur toward or away from the frame of your bike by hand. Ensure that the inner and outer plates are sitting parallel to the chainrings.

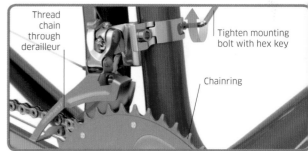

Thread chain through derailleur

Tighten mounting bolt with hex key

Chainring

4 **When the derailleur is positioned** correctly, tighten the mounting bolt all the way to secure it in place. Refer to the manufacturer's instructions for the correct torque setting. Reattach the chain (see pp.158–59).

Workshop tip: Gear cables that are rusty, dirty, or frayed will make it harder for you to change gear correctly. It is therefore a good idea for you to replace old cables (see pp.132-35) at the same time as installing a new front derailleur.

Follow existing cable route

Leave cable end free

5 **Using the shifter**, set the chain on the smallest chainring, and the rear derailleur to the lowest gear (the largest cog) on the cassette. This is the farthest that the chain will need to travel.

6 **If you are installing** a new gear cable, set the front shifter to the lowest gear, and run the cable from the shifter following the original routing (see pp.132-35). Do not fasten the cable in place.

1-2mm

Low limit screw

Derailleur cage

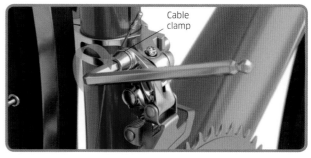

Cable clamp

7 **Using a Phillips screwdriver**, turn the "low limit" screw (marked "L" on some models) on the front derailleur, so that the inner plate of the derailleur cage sits about 1-2mm from the inside of the chain.

8 **Close any barrel adjusters** with your fingers. Feed the end of the gear cable through the cable clamp on the derailleur and fasten it in place with a hex key. Trim the cable and fit an end cap.

1-2mm

High limit screw

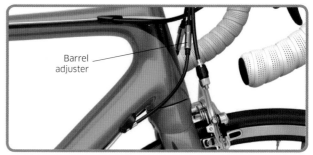

Barrel adjuster

9 **Using the shifters**, set the chain to the largest chainring and onto the smallest cog of the rear cassette. Turn the "high limit" screw until the outer plate of the derailleur is 1-2mm from the chain.

10 **Use the shifter** to move the chain from one chainring to another. If the chain does not pass smoothly between chainrings, turn the barrel adjusters in small increments to adjust the cable.

Rear derailleurs

The rear derailleur on your bike shifts the chain between the cogs on the rear cassette. It has an arm with a parallelogram mechanism that moves using pivots, and is controlled by the tension in the gear cable. When you press the gear-shift lever, the derailleur releases slack in the cable. The return spring in the derailleur then forces the parallelogram to move, taking up the slack, and pulls the bottom of the chain sideways. When you are not changing gear, the cable tension keeps the derailleur in position. Rear derailleurs vary in length—longer models are required for cassettes with a larger range of gears.

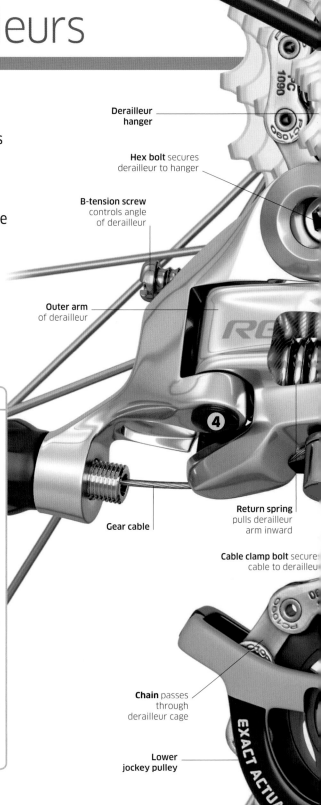

Derailleur hanger

Hex bolt secures derailleur to hanger

B-tension screw controls angle of derailleur

Outer arm of derailleur

Gear cable

Return spring pulls derailleur arm inward

Cable clamp bolt secures cable to derailleur

Chain passes through derailleur cage

Lower jockey pulley

 PARTS FOCUS

The rear derailleur comprises an arm with pivots, to move the chain, and jockey pulleys, to maintain tension on the chain.

(1) The **jockey pulleys** are held within a cage fixed to the derailleur arm. They keep the chain taut as it shifts between cogs on the cassette.

(2) The **hanger** supports the derailleur on the frame. It is a separate component on some bikes, while on others it can be part of the frame.

(3) The **limit screws** on the derailleur adjust the range of movement at either end of its range, and so prevent the chain from overshifting. The limit screws should be set correctly (see pp.148–49).

(4) The **pivots** allow the derailleur to move inward and outward beneath the cassette.

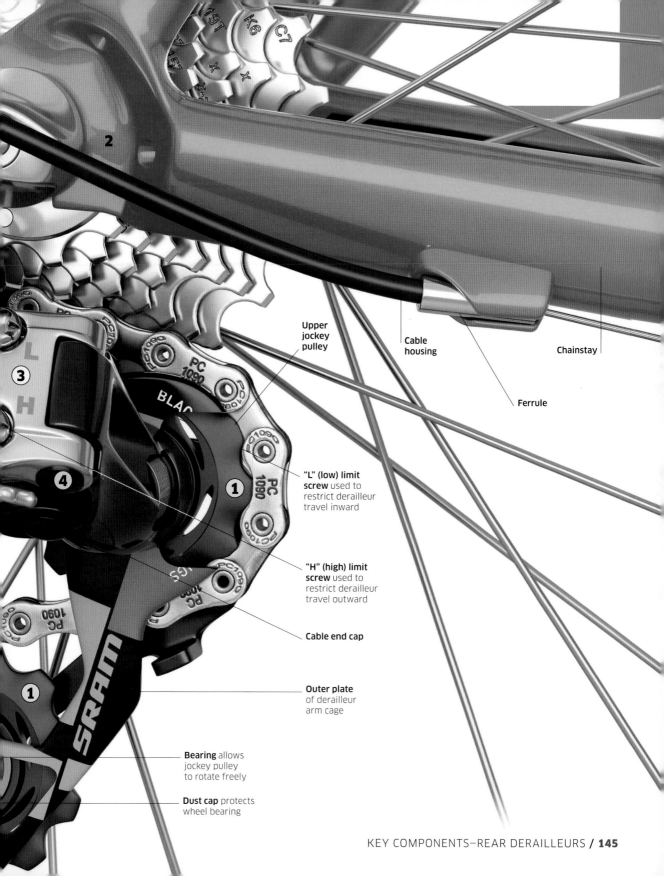

Upper
jockey
pulley

Cable
housing

Chainstay

Ferrule

**"L" (low) limit
screw** used to
restrict derailleur
travel inward

**"H" (high) limit
screw** used to
restrict derailleur
travel outward

Cable end cap

Outer plate
of derailleur
arm cage

Bearing allows
jockey pulley
to rotate freely

Dust cap protects
wheel bearing

Rear derailleurs

The rear derailleur (mech) shifts the chain between cogs on the cassette as you change gear. If the spring mechanism becomes worn down, it may seize, causing the bike to slip between gears, and you will need to replace the derailleur.

BEFORE YOU START

- Secure your bike in a frame stand
- Remove the chain (see pp.158–59)
- Remove the existing derailleur by disconnecting the gear cable, and reversing step 2

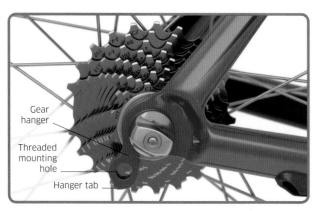

Gear hanger

Threaded mounting hole

Hanger tab

1 **Grease inside the threaded mounting hole** on the gear hanger to ensure that the derailleur will move freely. If your bike has a bolt-on hanger, check that it is sitting straight and fits securely.

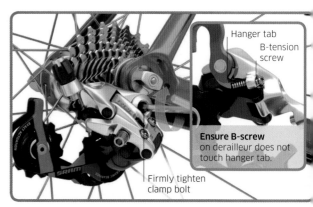

Hanger tab

B-tension screw

Ensure B-screw on derailleur does not touch hanger tab.

Firmly tighten clamp bolt

2 **Angle the rear derailleur** at 90 degrees to its normal position, and insert its clamp bolt into the mounting hole. Tighten it with a hex key. To check that it is secure, push it to see if it springs back into position.

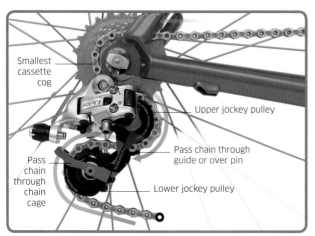

Smallest cassette cog

Upper jockey pulley

Pass chain through guide or over pin

Pass chain through chain cage

Lower jockey pulley

3 **Rest one end** of the chain on the smallest front chainring. Pass the other end over the back of the smallest cassette cog, the front of the upper jockey pulley, and the back of the lower jockey pulley.

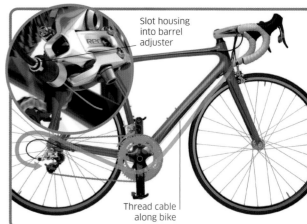

Slot housing into barrel adjuster

Thread cable along bike

4 **Attach the gear cable** (see pp.132–35) and route it along the frame, adding cable housing where required. Feed the cable through the barrel adjuster, and secure the last section of housing.

TOOLS AND EQUIPMENT

- Frame stand
- Grease
- Set of hex keys
- Chain tool or quick-release link
- Phillips screwdriver
- Oil

Cable clamp

Barrel adjuster

End of chain

5 **Thread the cable** into the cable clamp on the derailleur. Pull the cable taut and tighten the clamp bolt using a hex key.

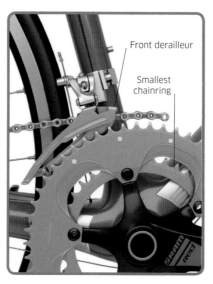

Front derailleur

Smallest chainring

6 **Feed the other end** of the chain through the front derailleur, and pass it over the front of the smallest chainring.

Chainstay

Bring ends of chain together

7 **Bring the two ends** of the chain together below the chainstay. Gravity will help to keep it in position on the bike.

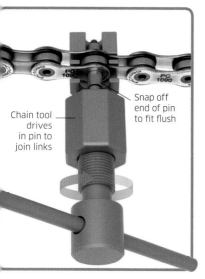

Chain tool drives in pin to join links

Snap off end of pin to fit flush

8 **Join the ends** of the chain together, according to the type of chain you have. Most use pins (as above) or quick-release links.

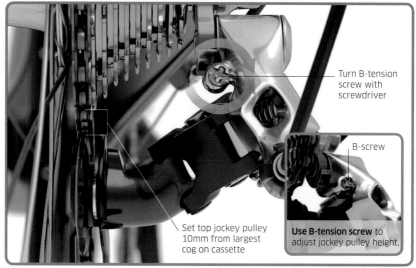

Turn B-tension screw with screwdriver

B-screw

Set top jockey pulley 10mm from largest cog on cassette

Use B-tension screw to adjust jockey pulley height.

9 **Shift the chain** onto the largest cog on the rear cassette. Adjust the B-tension screw on the rear derailleur so that the top jockey pulley is about 10mm away from the largest cog. This will ensure that the derailleur acts effectively, without interfering with the cogs.

Rear derailleurs

Mechanical bicycle gears are controlled by the tension of the gear cables. When the cables are correctly adjusted, the gears will shift smoothly and easily. If the chain rattles or slips into another gear while you are pedaling, or if the gear does not change at all, this indicates that the tension in the gear cables has changed, and the rear derailleur (mech) needs to be indexed.

 BEFORE YOU START

- Replace gear cables if worn down or damaged (see pp.132–35)
- Clean the rear derailleur and apply oil to the spring
- Secure your bike in a frame stand, rear wheel off the floor
- Shift the chain on to the smallest chainring

Cable clamp bolt

Barrel adjuster

2 **Loosen the cable clamp bolt** with a hex key to release the cable and pull it free. Wind the barrel adjuster clockwise until it no longer turns, then rotate it counterclockwise by a one full turn.

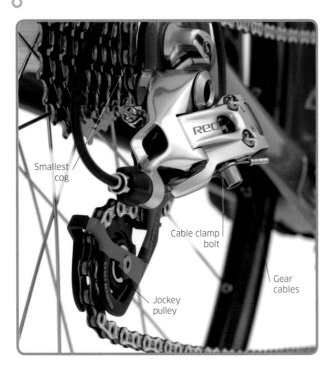

Smallest cog

Cable clamp bolt

Gear cables

Jockey pulley

1 **Use the gear-shift levers** to set the chain on the smallest cog on the cassette (the highest gear), and the smallest ring on the chainring. This will reduce tension in the gear cables, and offer you some slack.

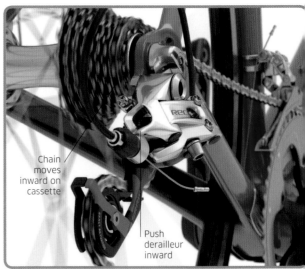

Chain moves inward on cassette

Push derailleur inward

3 **Turn the pedals** slowly with one hand. Use your other hand to push the body of the rear derailleur inward, so that the chain moves to the second smallest cog on the cassette.

TOOLS AND EQUIPMENT

- Cloth
- Oil
- Frame stand
- Set of hex keys
- Phillips screwdriver

Workshop tip: The B-screw controls the angle of the derailleur and its distance between the top jockey pulley and the cogs. It should be close to, but not touching, the cassette. To adjust it, shift it to the largest cog. Wind the screw in to move the wheel closer.

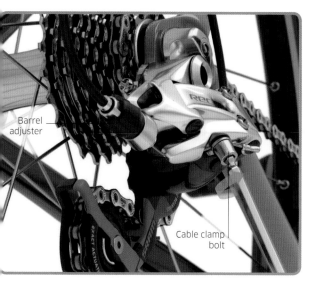

Barrel adjuster

Cable clamp bolt

4 **Insert the gear cables** into the cable clamp, pull it taut, and tighten the cable clamp bolt. Check the top jockey pulley is aligned with the second smallest cog. If not, turn the barrel adjuster counterclockwise.

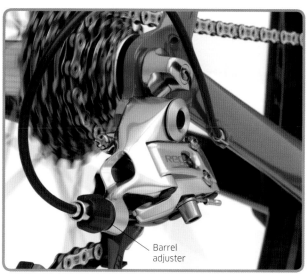

Barrel adjuster

5 **Turn the pedals** and shift through the gears from lowest to highest. If the chain skips two gears, turn the barrel adjuster clockwise. If the chain is slow to move to higher cogs, turn it counterclockwise.

Turn "H" screw with Phillips screwdriver

6 **Set the "H" (high) limit** on the derailleur to stop the chain jumping off the end of the smallest cog. Shift to the highest gear, and turn the "H" screw until the top jockey pulley sits directly under the smallest cog.

Turn "L" screw with Phillips screwdriver

7 **Set the "L" (low) limit** to prevent the chain from overshooting the cassette in the lowest gear. Shift to the lowest gear, and turn the "L" screw until the top jockey pulley sits directly under the largest cog.

Hub gears

A hub gear comprises a set of gears housed within a sealed unit attached to the rear wheel. The number of gears ranges from two or three in a traditional Sturmey-Archer hub, or six to eight in a Shimano hub, to 14 in a Rohloff hub. Gear sets comprise "planet" gears that rotate around a fixed "sun" gear, all held within a ring gear. Hub gears work on most types of bicycle, although they are rather heavy for racing bikes. They are known for reliability and longevity, as the components stay clean and dry inside the hub shell. Hub gears are simple to install, but need professional maintenance owing to their complexity.

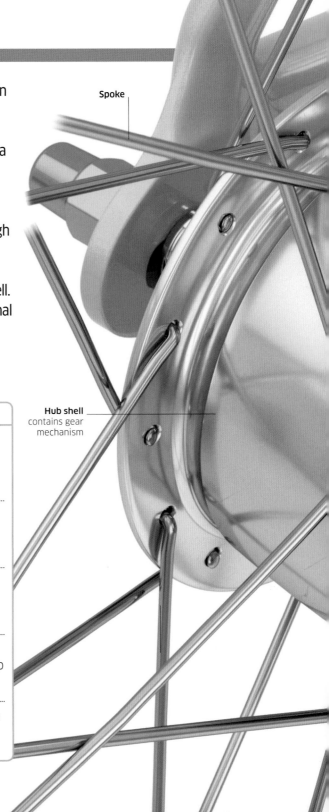

Spoke

Hub shell
contains gear
mechanism

 PARTS FOCUS

Hub gears such as a Shimano Alfine 8 (right) have few serviceable parts. Only the cable needs occasional adjustment (see pp.152–55).

① The **yellow bars** visible in the observation window slip out of alignment when the gear cable tension needs to be adjusted.

② The **cable pulley** changes the gear inside the hub gear as the gear cable is pulled or relaxed by the gear-shift lever on the handlebar.

③ The **utility hole** on the cable pulley allows you to relax the gear cable and remove the cable clamp bolt in order to take off the wheel (see pp.82–83).

④ The **cable holder** on the cassette joint supports the cable housing, allowing the cable to be set at the correct tension.

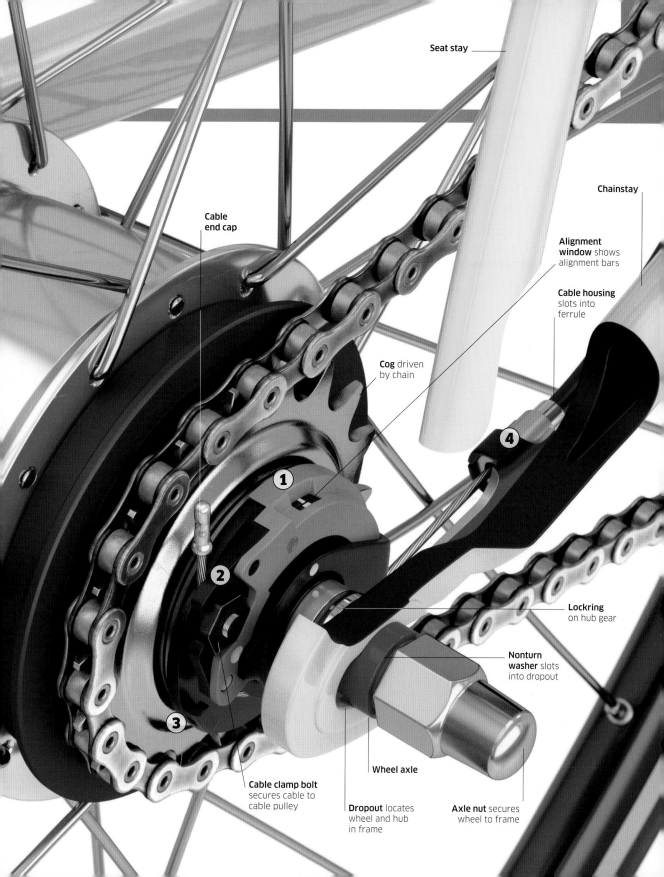

Seat stay

Chainstay

Cable
end cap

Alignment
window shows
alignment bars

Cable housing
slots into
ferrule

Cog driven
by chain

4

1

2

Lockring
on hub gear

Nonturn
washer slots
into dropout

3

Cable clamp bolt
secures cable to
cable pulley

Wheel axle

Dropout locates
wheel and hub
in frame

Axle nut secures
wheel to frame

Shimano Alfine 8

Hub gears are renowned for their reliability, and require little maintenance once set up. Gear cables can stretch over time, however, causing problems when you shift between gears. This issue is simple to fix, and requires no tools.

BEFORE YOU START

- Clean your hub gear with an alcohol-based cleaner
- Turn your bike upside down if it is an older model; support it upright if it is a newer model
- Prepare a clear space with plenty of room to work

1 **Locate the observation window** on the hub gear—it should be on the underside or the top of the hub itself. Two yellow bars should be visible. Clean the window, if required.

Shift through gears from first to fourth

2 **Put the hub** into its "adjustment mode" by changing into first gear and then back to fourth using the shifter. Fourth gear is shown as the number 4 on the gear-shift lever on some models.

Aligned bars signify that hub gear needs no further adjustment.

3 **Check the two yellow bars** in the window. If they are misaligned (as shown), the hub is out of alignment and you will need to adjust the cable. If they are aligned (inset), no adjustment is needed.

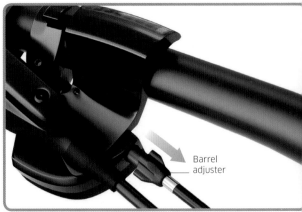

Barrel adjuster

4 **To fix the hub alignment**, locate the cable barrel adjuster, which is usually found on the gear-shift lever. Unlock the barrel mechanism by pulling the collar outward. The barrel will now turn.

TOOLS AND EQUIPMENT

- Alcohol-based cleaner
- Cleaning cloth

Caution! If your hub gear continues to have problems even though the yellow bars align, take it to a bike repair shop. Hub gears are complex, and are not designed to be taken apart. You may damage the hub permanently if you attempt any repairs yourself.

Turn barrel clockwise or counterclockwise to align bars

Change to first gear to take shifter out of adjustment mode

5 **Turning the barrel lock** causes the bar on the right of the window to move. Turn the barrel clockwise or counterclockwise until the bars in the hub observation window align.

6 **Once you are happy** with the adjustment, take the shifter out of adjustment mode by changing into first gear. Then shift into the highest gear, before finally shifting back into fourth.

Bars aligned

Misaligned bars signify that hub gear is still not correctly aligned.

7 **Check the alignment of the bars** in the observation window again. If they are still misaligned, repeat steps 2–6, turning the barrel and shifting the gears until the bars line up correctly. Once aligned, take the bike for a ride, then check the yellow bars once more.

VARIATIONS

Shimano Alfine hub gears are available with 4, 7, 8, or 11 gears, and all models are adjusted in the same basic way. There are a number of small differences to be aware of, however. You should also refer to the owner's manual for your hub.

- Shimano Alfine hubs with 4, 7, or 8 gears are adjusted with the shifter set in fourth gear. The 11-speed model is adjusted in sixth gear.

- The alignment bars on the Alfine 8 hub are yellow. On other models, they are red or green.

Sturmey-Archer three-speed

Sturmey-Archer hub gears have been used for decades on a wide range of bicycles, from utility road bikes to modern folding ones. The hub is very reliable, but it cannot be maintained at home. The gear cables can stretch, hindering gear selection, but this is an easy problem to fix.

BEFORE YOU START

- Secure your bike in a frame stand
- Make sure that the rear wheel is centered in the forks
- Wipe away any dirt and grease from the area around the hub gear
- Check the gear cable for any damage

Adjustment gear indicated by circle on gear-shift lever

1 **Set the hub gear** into "adjustment mode" by selecting the second gear on the gear-shift lever. (This gear is commonly used as the adjustment gear on modern shifters.)

Protective cover

2 **The hub linkage** and fulcrum on modern bikes may be concealed by a protective cover. If so, unclip the cover from the bike to access the linkage, taking care not to snap the retaining clips.

5 in (12.5 cm)

Fulcrum clip

3 **If the bike has** a separate fulcrum clip, check that this is secure and positioned at least 5 in (12.5 cm) from the hub. To adjust it, loosen the screw on its rear, reposition the clip, and retighten the screw.

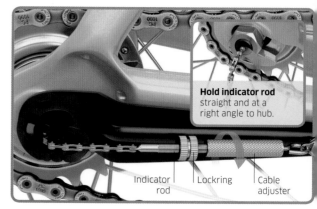

Hold indicator rod straight and at a right angle to hub.

Indicator rod | Lockring | Cable adjuster

4 **Unscrew the cable adjuster** from the indicator rod to disconnect it. Hold the indicator rod so that it points straight out of the hub, turn it clockwise to tighten it all the way, and loosen it by half a turn.

Caution! You may damage the hub if you use it with misaligned gears. If you have problems selecting a gear, or the hub slips, check that the tension in the gear cable is correct. If the problems persist, take the bike to a bike shop for specialized attention.

Lockring

Indicator rod

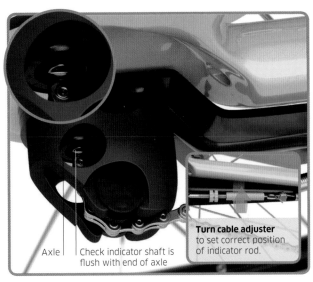

Axle | Check indicator shaft is flush with end of axle

Turn cable adjuster to set correct position of indicator rod.

5 Check the indicator rod for any damage. Clean and grease its threads, then screw the rod back into the cable adjuster by hand. Loosen the lockring on the indicator rod by a few turns.

6 With second gear still selected on the shifter, turn the cable adjuster until the end of the indicator shaft is exactly level with the end of the axle when seen through the observation window.

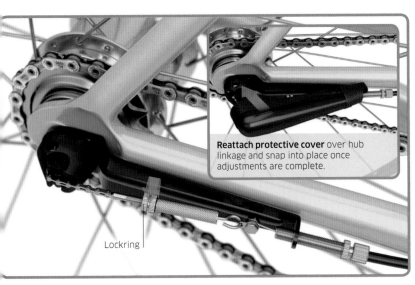

Reattach protective cover over hub linkage and snap into place once adjustments are complete.

Lockring

7 Tighten the lockring on the cable adjuster to secure the new setting. Shift between the gears to check that they work with no slipping. Reattach the cover over the hub linkage. Take the bike for a test ride in a safe area, and make any further adjustments if required.

FIVE-SPEED HUBS

A Sturmey-Archer five-speed hub gear is adjusted in a similar way to the three-speed model.

- Select the second gear on the shifter and turn the cable adjuster so no more than 1 in (2.5 mm) of the indicator shaft protrudes over the axle end.

- Tighten the lockring against the cable adjuster.

- Select fifth gear, turn pedals, then reselect second gear.

- Check the position of the indicator rod, and readjust if required.

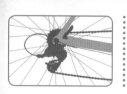

▶ KEY COMPONENTS
Chains and cassettes

The chain and cassette–the cluster of cogs on the rear hub–transfer drive from the crankset to the rear wheel, converting your pedaling energy into forward motion. A chain consists of more than a hundred links, each of which is made up of two plates that are joined by pins and rollers, which allow the links to rotate and flex. Chains vary in width depending on the number of cogs–ranging from 8 to 12–on the cassette. Each link fits snugly on either side of a tooth on the cog, which is stamped with "ramps"–grooves that allow the chain to shift more smoothly from one cog to the next.

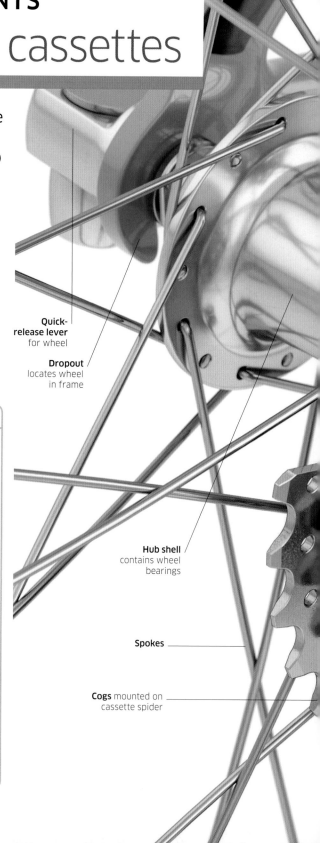

Quick-release lever
for wheel

Dropout
locates wheel
in frame

Hub shell
contains wheel
bearings

Spokes

Cogs mounted on
cassette spider

PARTS FOCUS

The **cassette** consists of up to 12 cogs with a varying number of teeth–from 10 to 50– offering a multitude of gear ratios.

① The **lockring** holds the cassette onto the free hub. You will need a special tool to remove it if you change your cassette (see pp.160–61).

② A series of **cogs** in different sizes make up the cassette, which each provide a different ratio. The smallest cog gives the highest gear.

③ Cassettes feature **spacers** that ensure the correct distance between cogs. The number of spacers depends on the type of cassette.

④ The **rear derailleur** is not part of the cassette, but performs the vital function of shifting the chain across the cassette, allowing you to change gear.

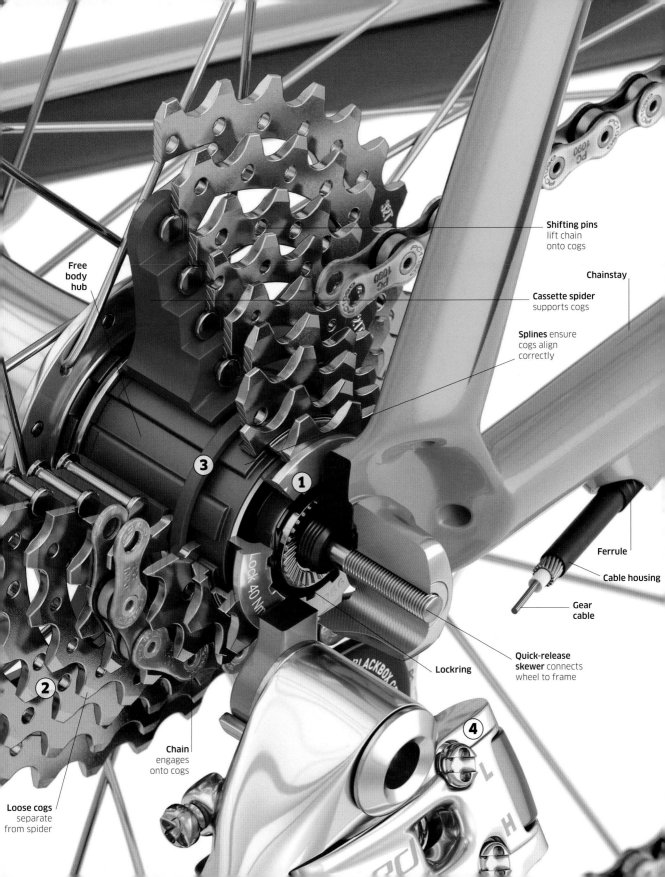

Shifting pins lift chain onto cogs

Chainstay

Cassette spider supports cogs

Free body hub

Splines ensure cogs align correctly

Ferrule

Cable housing

Gear cable

Lockring

Quick-release skewer connects wheel to frame

Chain engages onto cogs

Loose cogs separate from spider

Bicycle chains

Your bike chain takes a lot of wear and tear, as it is constantly twisted and put under strain. It requires oil to work smoothly, which in itself attracts grit and grime. Slipping gears may be a sign that your chain needs to be replaced.

⚙ BEFORE YOU START

- Ensure that the chain is on the smallest cog at the back and the smallest chainring at the front to provide enough slack
- Place a chain wear indicator onto the chain. The indicator pins should slot into the links; if not, the chain has stretched

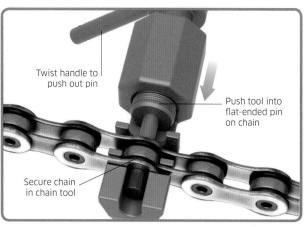

Twist handle to push out pin

Push tool into flat-ended pin on chain

Secure chain in chain tool

1 Lift the chain off the chainring and onto the bottom bracket. Select a link on the lower length of chain, and locate the chain in the chain tool. Wind the handle to push the pin out, and remove the chain.

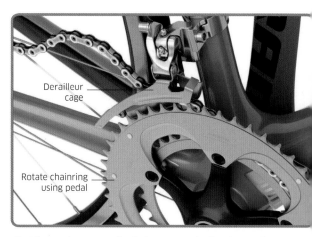

Derailleur cage

Rotate chainring using pedal

2 Thread one end of the new chain through the front derailleur (mech) cage until it catches on the teeth of the chainring. Turn the pedals and draw the chain downward.

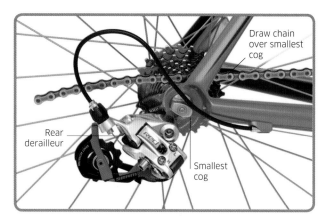

Draw chain over smallest cog

Rear derailleur

Smallest cog

3 Pull the other end of the chain toward the rear derailleur so that it rests on the smallest cog of the cassette. It is now ready to be threaded through the rear derailleur.

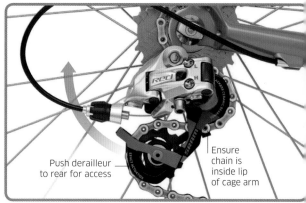

Push derailleur to rear for access

Ensure chain is inside lip of cage arm

4 Thread the new chain through the rear derailleur. Feed the chain downward carefully—clockwise over the top jockey pulley, and counterclockwise over the bottom jockey pulley.

- Chain wear indicator
- Chain tool (ensure it is the correct size)
- Grease and oil
- Needle-nose pliers
- Chain links and pins

Workshop tip: A new chain may need to be shortened, as if it is too long, it may jump off the chainring. Chains vary in length. To find the optimum length, wrap the chain around the biggest cog at the back and the biggest front chainring at the front, and add two links.

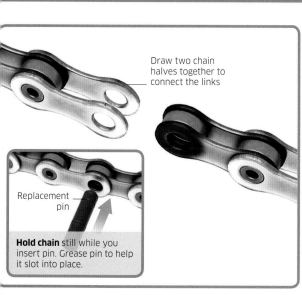

Draw two chain halves together to connect the links

Replacement pin

Hold chain still while you insert pin. Grease pin to help it slot into place.

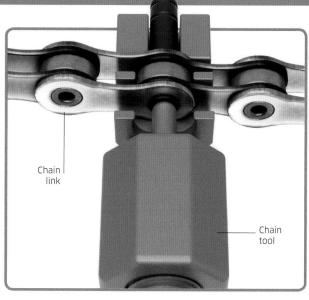

Chain link

Chain tool

5 **Bring the two ends** of the chain together underneath the chainstay. Push the thin end of the replacement pin between the two links to hold the chain together.

6 **Slot the chain** into the guide on the chain tool. Twist the handle of the tool to push the replacement pin into the links, and securely join the lengths of chain together.

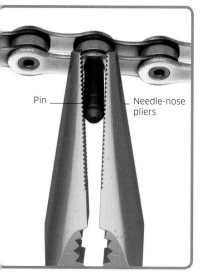

Pin

Needle-nose pliers

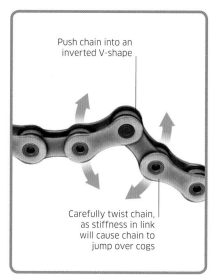

Push chain into an inverted V-shape

Carefully twist chain, as stiffness in link will cause chain to jump over cogs

7 **Snap off the end** of the pin using needle-nose pliers. Some chain tools can also be used to shorten the chain pin.

8 **The chain will feel** stiff at the join. Apply oil to the link and manipulate the chain with your hands until the link moves freely.

CHAIN LINKS

Many manufacturers now make special chain connectors that mean you can remove and replace your chain easily—sometimes without tools.

- The SRAM "PowerLink" has two halves with a built-in pin. Snap the link into place and apply tension to secure it. The link can be released manually.

- Shimano chains feature a hardened connecting pin with a flared end for extra strength.

- Campagnolo's Ultralink comes with a chain segment so several links can be replaced at once.

Rear cassettes

Cassettes are susceptible to wear, especially if you allow dirt, grease, and road salt to build up, causing your chain to slip and jump. Although cassettes can be cleaned in situ, they are best removed to do a more thorough job.

BEFORE YOU START

- Prepare a clear space where you can lay out the parts
- Remove the rear wheel from your bike (see pp.80–81)
- Select the correct lockring tool for your cassette

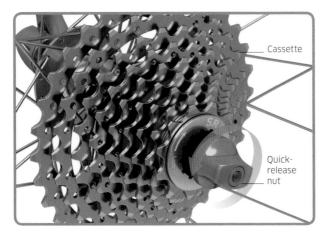

Cassette

Quick-release nut

1 **Remove the skewer** by unscrewing the quick-release nut all the way in order to access the lockring. Then slide the skewer out of the hub, being careful not to lose the conical springs on each side.

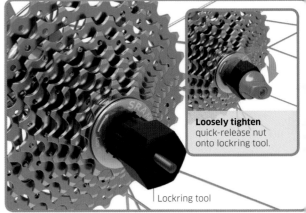

Loosely tighten quick-release nut onto lockring tool.

Lockring tool

2 **Using the correct lockring tool**, insert the serrated edge of the tool all the way into the lockring on the cassette. Replace the quick-release nut to hold the tool in place as it is turned.

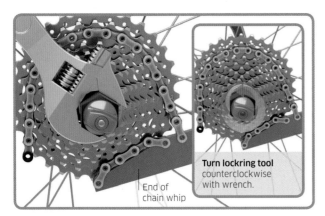

Turn lockring tool counterclockwise with wrench.

End of chain whip

3 **Install a chain whip** around the second-largest gear of the cassette. Holding the chain whip firmly to stop the cassette turning, grip the lockring tool with an adjustable wrench, and unscrew the lockring.

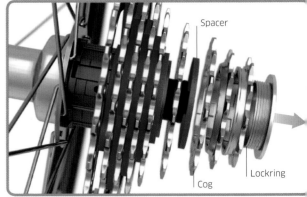

Spacer

Lockring

Cog

4 **Undo the quick-release nut**, remove the tool, and unscrew the lockring. Slide the cassette from the freehub. Some cogs may be loose when removed; make a note of their order and any spacers used.

Workshop tip: A thin layer of grease applied to the grooves of the freehub body will prevent rust. If any corrosion is already present, use a stiff brush or scouring pad to clean it off gently.

Clean in gaps

Brush cogs firmly

Clean the cassette and cog teeth with a hard-bristled brush and degreaser. Wash off the dirty fluid with soapy water.

PARTS FOCUS

Many cassettes are only compatible with specific hubs, so check this when buying new components.

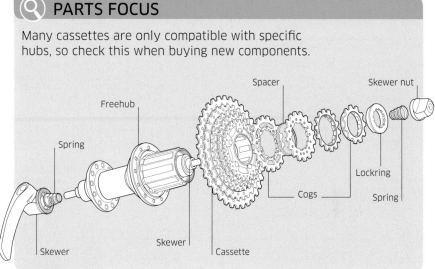

Spacer
Skewer nut
Freehub
Spring
Lockring
Spring
Cogs
Skewer
Skewer
Cassette

Grooves on freehub body ensure cassette aligns correctly.

Line up the cassette body, known as the spider, with the grooves on the freehub. They will only fit in one arrangement.

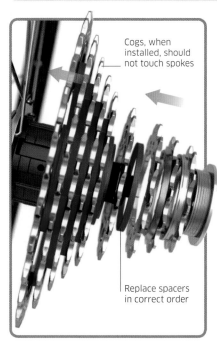

Cogs, when installed, should not touch spokes

Replace spacers in correct order

Push the cassette and cogs onto the freehub body. Ensure that you return the spacers in the correct order.

Reattach the cassette to the hub using the lockring tool and a wrench to tighten it. You can now replace the wheel and chain.

Cranksets

The crankset comprises the crankarms, chainrings, and bottom bracket (BB). When choosing a crankset, consider the size of the chainrings and the number of teeth, which affects the gearing, and select a crankarm length to suit your leg length, which will make pedaling easier. You should also choose a crankset to suit the style of riding you are intending to do.

TYPE	SUITABILITY	KEY COMPONENTS
FAST ROAD Fast road cranksets should be light but very stiff. These cranksets are often equipped with bigger chainrings, offering a higher range of gears for race riders.	■ **Racing** and other competitive road events.	■ **The crankarm and spider** are made as a single piece. ■ **The two chainrings** must work with 10- to 11-speed chains. ■ **The axle** is press-fitted on splines on the right side and secured with a pinch bolt on the left side.
TRAINING/CYCLO-CROSS/ENDURANCE These mid-level cranksets provide similar performance to more expensive versions, so are suitable for more general riding, although they are stiffer and tend to weigh more than premium models.	■ **General road riding**, training, or endurance. ■ **Cyclo-cross racing**. ■ **Gravel riding**.	■ **The crankarm and spider** are usually made as a single piece. ■ **The two chainrings** must work with 10- to 11-speed chains. ■ **The axle** is press-fitted on splines on the right side and secured with a pinch bolt on the left side.
TRACK/FIXED/SINGLE-SPEED These cranksets have wider teeth and only one chainring. They are very stiff in order to cope with high pedal forces.	■ **Track** cycling and racing. ■ **Single-speed** city riding.	■ **The crankarm and spider** are usually made as a single piece. ■ **The wider chainring** is usually only compatible with wider 0.125 in (3.18 mm) chain. ■ **The axle** is typically installed into the frame with the BB.
MOUNTAIN BIKE Mountain bike cranksets vary from triple-ring cranksets, which provide a wide range of gears, to double-ring sets, which offer a saving in weight, and single-ring sets, often favored for simplicity.	■ **Hill climbing**, if the bike has a triple-ring crankset that includes low gears. ■ **Downhill riding** on a single-ring crankset.	■ **The crankarm and spider** are usually made as a single piece. ■ **The two chainrings** must work with 10- to 11-speed chains. ■ **The axle** is press-fitted on splines on the right side and secured with a pinch bolt on the left side.

Many components are made of lightweight aluminum, but the highest-end road bike cranksets have components of carbon to save weight. You may need a much tougher crankset if you are intending to do any heavy off-road riding, to reduce the risk of debris from the trail damaging or even breaking the chain mid-ride.

MATERIALS

- **Crankarms and spiders** are usually aluminum. Crankarms are hollow.
- **High-end cranksets** have carbon-fiber crankarms and hardened alloy chainrings.
- **Axles** are hollow and generally lightweight steel.

VARIATIONS

- **Crankarms are** 165–175 mm to suit different leg lengths. They are typically 172.5 mm.
- **Popular chainrings** have 53–39 teeth or mid-compact 52–36 teeth.

MAINTENANCE

- **Breakages** are rare, but after a knock, the crankarms should be checked for cracks.
- **Hooked chainrings** indicate excessive wear and should be changed.

- **Crankarms and spiders** are usually aluminum.
- **Crankarms** are often hollow but may be solid on budget cranksets.
- **Axles** are hollow and generally lightweight steel.
- **Entry-level bikes** may be installed with a square taper BB.

- **Crankarms are** 165–175 mm to suit different leg lengths. They are typically 172.5 mm.
- **Popular compact chainrings** have 50–34 teeth.
- **Cyclo-cross rings** may use 46–34 teeth.

- **Breakages** are rare, but after a knock, the crankarms should be checked for cracks.
- **Hooked chainrings** indicate excessive wear and should be changed.

- **Crankarms and spiders** are usually aluminum.
- **Axles** are hollow and generally lightweight steel.
- **Chainrings** may be made of aluminum or steel.

- **Crankarms are** 165–175 mm long.
- **Longer cranksets** may hit the ground when you are pedaling through corners or banking on a track.
- **Popular chainrings** have 48–49 teeth.

- **Off-road riding** accelerates wear on the chainrings, so check chainrings and chain regularly.
- **Check crankarms** for damage or cracks.

- **Crankarms and spiders** are usually aluminum.
- **Crankarms are often** hollow but may be solid on budget cranksets.
- **Axles** are square taper and use a square taper BB.

- **Crankarms are** 165–175 mm to suit different leg lengths. They are typically 172.5 mm.
- **Popular chainrings** have 40–28 teeth or mid-compact 38–26 teeth.
- **Triple cranksets** have 40–32–22 teeth.

- **Breakages are rare**, but after a knock, the crankarms should be checked for cracks.
- **Play at the BB** and a slack chain should be checked and changed.

Cranksets

The crankset rotates around the bottom bracket (BB) when you turn the pedals; it consists of the crankarms and chainrings. Square taper units (see pp.168–69) are bolted to the BB axle, while modern cranksets (see pp.166–71) are bonded to a one- or two-piece axle. Touring bikes and some mountain bikes have three chainrings for a wider range of gears. Road bikes have two chainrings to reduce weight, while some cyclo-cross, gravel, and mountain bikes use a "1x" (single) chainring. Cranksets are made of carbon or a solid piece of aluminum, so that they are strong enough to transmit your pedaling forces without flexing.

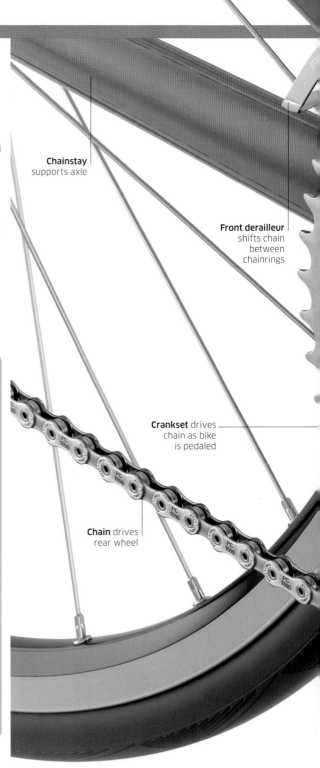

Chainstay supports axle

Front derailleur shifts chain between chainrings

Crankset drives chain as bike is pedaled

Chain drives rear wheel

⚙ PARTS FOCUS

The **crankset** consists of the crankarms and 1–3 chainrings, which have between 22 and 53 teeth for the chain links to slot onto.

① The two **crankarms** transmit the pedaling action of the rider to the chainring and chain, which in turn rotate the cassette and rear wheel.

② The **spider** is part of the drive (right) side crankarm, and consists of a number of arms onto which the chainrings are bolted.

③ The **axle** joins the crankarms and is bolted to, or integrated with, the BB. A larger-diameter axle will improve the stiffness of the crankset.

④ The **BB cups** screw or press into the frame and support the axle, allowing the crankset to rotate smoothly and without loss of torque.

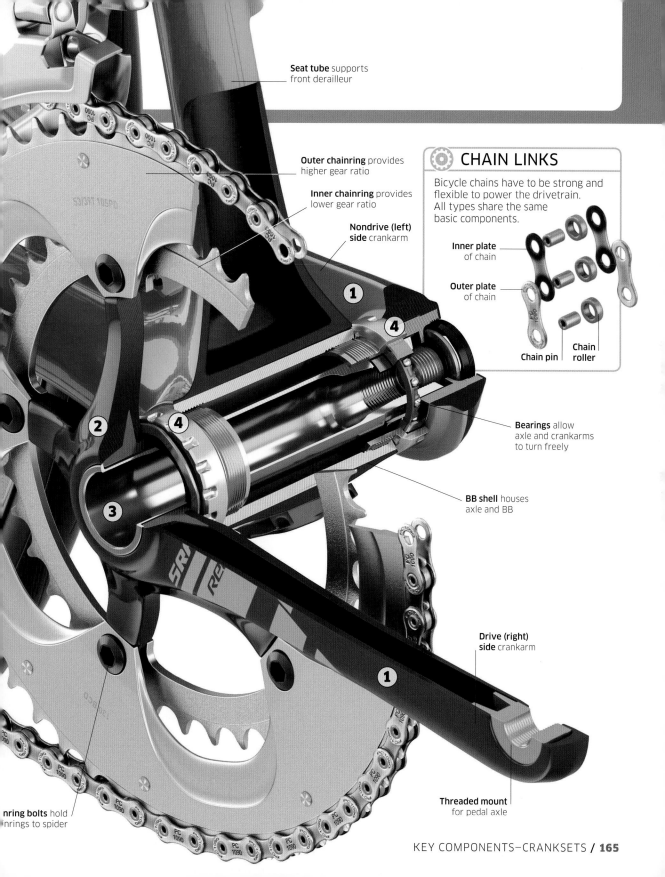

Seat tube supports
front derailleur

Outer chainring provides
higher gear ratio

Inner chainring provides
lower gear ratio

Nondrive (left)
side crankarm

1

4

S3/39T 10SPD

2

4

3

SRAM
RED

1

nring bolts hold
nrings to spider

CHAIN LINKS

Bicycle chains have to be strong and
flexible to power the drivetrain.
All types share the same
basic components.

Inner plate
of chain

Outer plate
of chain

Chain pin

Chain
roller

Bearings allow
axle and crankarms
to turn freely

BB shell houses
axle and BB

Drive (right)
side crankarm

Threaded mount
for pedal axle

Shimano HollowTech II

Shimano HollowTech cranksets feature a hollow axle that is connected permanently to the right-hand crank, and to which the left-hand crank is also attached. You will need to remove the crankset if you want to replace or perform maintenance on your bottom bracket (BB).

BEFORE YOU START

- Secure your bike in a frame stand
- Prepare a clear space where you can lay out the parts
- Place a drop cloth down to catch any grease
- Refer to the manufacturer's instructions for the correct pinch bolt torque setting

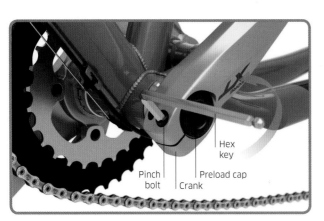

Hex key

Pinch bolt | Crank | Preload cap

1 **Using a 5 mm hex key,** loosen but do not remove the two pinch bolts on the nondrive (left) side crank. The bolts should be positioned on the left-hand side of the bike frame.

Push safety tab upward with a flat-head screwdriver.

Preload cap tool

2 **Remove the preload cap** using the specific preload cap tool by unwinding it counterclockwise. Then, using a small flat-head screwdriver, disengage the safety tab by pushing it upward.

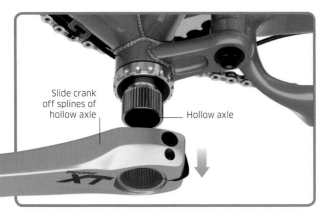

Slide crank off splines of hollow axle

Hollow axle

3 **With the safety tab disengaged,** slide the nondrive (left) side crank from the splined axle. If it does not move freely, you may need to wiggle it from side to side in order to dislodge it.

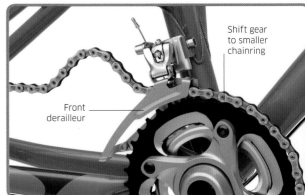

Shift gear to smaller chainring

Front derailleur

4 **Shift the front derailleur** (mech) to the smaller chainring. Lift the chain away from the chainring and allow it to hang freely so that it does not get twisted when you remove the crankset from the frame

TOOLS AND EQUIPMENT

- Frame stand
- Drop cloth
- 5 mm hex key
- Preload cap tool
- Flat-head screwdriver
- Rubber hammer
- Cloth and grease
- Torque wrench

Workshop tip: To make things easier when you are removing the nondrive (left) side crank, completely remove the pinch bolts and the safety tab. This will ensure there is no tension in the clamp.

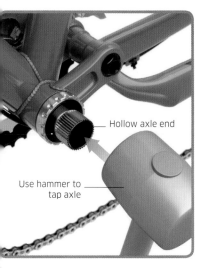

Hollow axle end

Use hammer to tap axle

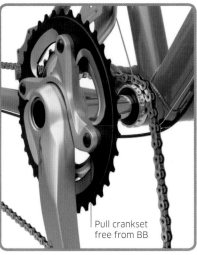

Pull crankset free from BB

SHIMANO TOOLS

Removing and reinstalling a Shimano HollowTech II crankset requires specific tools and information you may not have.

- The preload cap tool is supplied with the crankset, and is vital for installing and removing it. If yours is lost or damaged, you must buy a replacement.

- If you install the crankset using a torque wrench, the torque settings required are printed next to the pinch bolts. If they are missing, find them online at Shimano's Tech Resource.

5 **Using a rubber hammer**, firmly but carefully give the hollow axle a few taps until it passes through the BB.

6 **Gently pull the crankset** from the drive (right) side of the BB. Rest the chain on the BB to avoid it touching the ground.

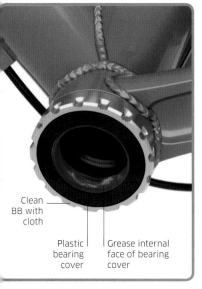

Clean BB with cloth

Plastic bearing cover

Grease internal face of bearing cover

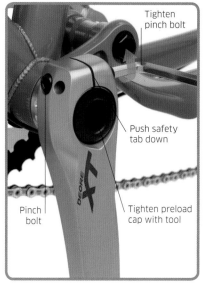

Tighten pinch bolt

Push safety tab down

Pinch bolt

Tighten preload cap with tool

7 **Clean the inner surfaces** of the plastic bearing covers on the BB where the axle sits, and apply fresh grease using your fingers.

8 **Push the crankset** through the BB, doing as much as possible by hand and finishing with the rubber hammer, if necessary.

9 **Reinstall the nondrive (left) side** crank and replace the preload cap. Push the safety tab into place and tighten the pinch bolts.

Square taper types

Square taper cranksets are common on older bikes, and those equipped with square taper bottom brackets (see pp.178-79). The crankset and crankarm attach onto the square bottom bracket (BB) spindle; you will need a crank puller tool to remove them. Detach the crankset whenever you are maintaining, or replacing, the BB.

BEFORE YOU START

- Secure your bike in a frame stand
- Prepare a clear space where you can lay out the parts
- Clean around the BB
- Spray oil on to the crank bolts to help to loosen them

Clean crank bolt threads

2 **Clean and lubricate the threads** inside the crank. Use a cloth to clean the thread on the removed bolt. Check that the bolt and any washers are in good condition, and apply fresh grease to the bolt.

Chainring

Turn crank bolt counterclockwise

1 **If the crank has** plastic bolt covers, remove these on both sides. Take out the bolt and any washers on the drive (right) side using a hex key. Hold the arm of the crank still as you work.

Crank puller

3 **Making sure that the end** of the crank puller tool is unscrewed all the way, carefully screw the threaded end into the crank by hand. Screw it in tightly—turning clockwise—with your fingers.

Caution! To avoid damaging the threads of the crank, ensure they are clean before inserting the crank puller tool. Also make sure that the crank puller is postioned straight onto the threads to prevent cross-threading.

Insert hex key into crank puller

Rest chain on BB

Remove chain

4 **With the crank puller tool** attached to the crank, use a wrench or a hex key to turn the end clockwise. The crank puller tool will push the crank off the frame and away from the BB spindle.

5 **Once the crank puller tool has pushed** the chainring off the BB spindle, lift the chainring away from the bike, taking care not to drop it. Lift the chain off the chainring, and rest it on the BB.

You will feel resistance as crank puller tool pushes against spindle.

Crank puller tool pushes crankarm off spindle

Set crankarms at 180 degrees to each other

Insert hex key all the way before turning

6 **Unscrew the crank puller tool** from the crankset using a wrench or hex key. Clean the threads of the crank puller tool.

7 **On the nondrive (left) side,** remove the crank bolt, screw in the crank puller, and tighten as before to remove the crankarm.

8 **Reinstall the crankset,** starting with the nondrive (left) side crankarm, reversing steps 1–7, as shown here.

Campagnolo Ultra-Torque

Campagnolo's drivetrain systems are widely used. Their Ultra-Torque and Power Torque cranksets utilize similar technology, and are installed in the same way. If there is any creaking or play in the crankset, you should remove it to diagnose the issue. You will also need to take off the crankset when replacing a bottom bracket (BB).

BEFORE YOU START

- If the crank bolt is corroded, spray it with penetrating oil
- Put the chain on the inner chainring

Remove bolt all the way, then clean and grease it, before reusing later.

Hex key

2 **Insert a long-arm 10 mm hex key** into the center of the spindle on the drive (right) side. Ensuring it is engaged all the way, turn it counterclockwise to loosen the crank bolt from the center.

Safety clip

1 **Temporarily lay your bike** on its side for easier access to the safety clip. Remove the safety clip using needle-nose pliers, and keep it safe. Secure the bike in a frame stand for the remainder of the task.

Remove chain from chainring

Turn chainring as chain is removed

3 **Remove the chain** from the chainring by lifting the rear derailleur (mech) to release tension from the chain. Rotate the chainring and lift the chain from it. Rest the detached chain on the BB.

Workshop tip: Before reinstalling, apply grease to the thread of the crank bolt. This will prevent the bolt from rusting or degrading over time, and make future removal easier. Hold the drive (right) side crankarm steady when loosening or retightening the crank bolt.

Chain will hang loose

4 **Ease the drive-side crank** out of the BB. Take care not to damage the crank or drop any of the components.

PARTS FOCUS

Because several crankset systems exist, parts from different manufacturers are often incompatible with one another.

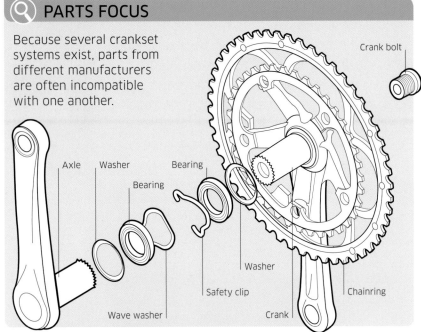

Crank bolt

Axle

Washer

Bearing

Bearing

Wave washer

Safety clip

Washer

Crank

Chainring

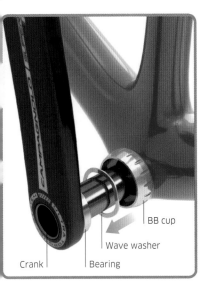

BB cup

Wave washer

Crank

Bearing

5 **Remove the other crankarm** and the wave washer (the "brown" washer on Campagnolo Power Torque cranksets).

Ensure chain is installed properly

Reinstall and clip in safety clip fully before riding.

6 **To reinstall the crankset**, first clean the axle and the bottom bracket, then regrease them. Check that the wave (or brown) washer has not flattened over time, and replace it if necessary. Reinstall the crankset by reversing steps 1–5.

Made from lightweight carbon fiber, SRAM Red cranksets feature a hollow axle, which is connected permanently to the drive (right) side crankarm, and which the left-hand crankarm attaches onto. You will need to remove the crankset if the bottom bracket (BB) needs cleaning or replacement. If replacing, make sure the new BB is the correct size for the SRAM crankset.

BEFORE YOU START

- Secure your bike in a frame stand
- Prepare a clear space where you can lay out the parts

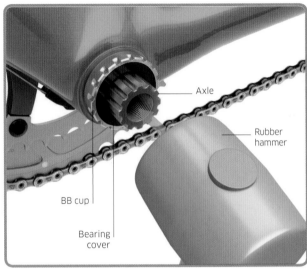

Axle

Rubber hammer

BB cup

Bearing cover

2 **Gently tap the axle** with a rubber hammer to push the crankset from the BB. The bearing covers may come away from the BB cups as the axle is removed. If this happens, push them back in using your fingers.

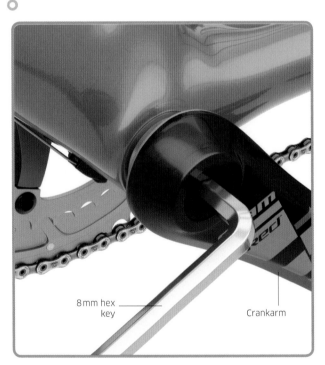

8 mm hex key

Crankarm

Pedal

Unhook chain to stop it getting tangled

Chainrings

1 **Insert an 8 mm hex key** into the crankarm bolt on the nondrive (left) side and turn it counterclockwise to release the crankarm from the axle. Remove the crankarm and set aside.

3 **Unhook the chain** from the chainrings and allow it to fall freely away. This is important, as you need to avoid the chain twisting when the crankset is pulled through the BB. Rest the chain on the BB.

Workshop tip: If the crankarms spin less freely after reinstalling, it may be due to the fresh grease in the BB seals. This will resolve itself as the BB beds in, so be patient.

Axle

Bearings protected by bearing cover

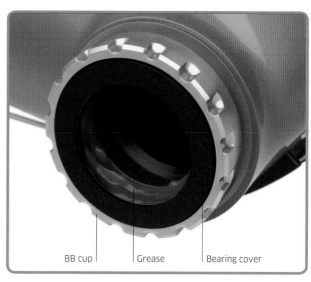

BB cup | Grease | Bearing cover

4 **Pull on the chainring** to slide the axle from the BB. If there is any sign of play or looseness in the crankarms, or noise from the bearings, you may need to replace the BB (see pp.176-77, 180-81).

5 **Clean the BB** thoroughly with degreaser and a cloth. Apply liberal amounts of fresh grease to the inner surfaces of the BB, including the bearing covers where the axle sits.

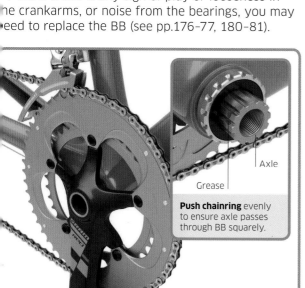

Axle

Grease

Push chainring evenly to ensure axle passes through BB squarely.

Grease

Tighten crankarm bolt all the way by turning hex key clockwise.

Crankarm

6 **Grease the axle** to help the crankset slide back into place easily and prevent corrosion. Push the crankset back through the BB from the drive (right) side, passing it through the chain first.

7 **Grease the spindle** of the nondrive (left) side crankarm and slide it onto the axle, ensuring that the splines line up. Tighten the crankarm bolt with a hex key. Hook the chain back onto the chainrings.

REMOVING AND REINSTALLING A CRANKSET–SRAM RED / **173**

Bottom brackets

An essential component on every kind of bike, the bottom bracket (BB) secures the crankarms to the frame via an axle, which is supported by bearings that allow it to rotate freely. Square taper (see pp.178–79) and Shimano Octalink BBs use an axle built into a "cartridge" unit, to which the crankarms are attached. Large-diameter axle systems—such as Campagnolo Power and Ultra-Torque (see pp.176–77), Shimano HollowTech (see pp.180–81), and SRAM GXP—have an axle built onto the crankarms that slides inside the bearing cups, which are located on either side of the frame's BB shell. These systems use sealed bearings for durability and ease of maintenance.

Drive (right) side crankarm includes spider for chainring fitting

Outer chainring has more teeth, giving higher gear ratio

Inner chainring has fewer teeth, giving lower gear ratio

Chain transmits propulsion from chainrings to rear wheel

 PARTS FOCUS

BBs are screwed or pressed into the BB shell of a frame, and allow the crankarms to rotate freely.

① The **crankarm bolt** sits inside the axle, securing the nondrive (left) and drive (right) side crankarms together.

② The **axle** sits inside the BB shell and cups, and rotates when the crankarms are turned. It may be built into a cartridge BB (see pp.178–79) or the drive (right) side crankarm (see pp.180–81). Alternatively, it may be split into two halves that are bonded to each crankarm (see pp.176–77).

③ The **BB cups** contain the bearings, and screw or press into either side of the BB shell.

④ The **bearings** sit inside the BB cups and are contained inside sealed units for added protection.

Safety clip
unique to
Campagnolo
BBs

Wave washer
is unique to
Campagnolo BBs

BB shell houses
axle and BB

**Large-
diameter axle**
for improved
power transfer

**Nondrive
(left) side** crank-
arm connects
pedal to BB axle

▶ REPLACING A BOTTOM BRACKET
Campagnolo Ultra-Torque

Campagnolo Ultra-Torque cranksets have bearing cups that sit on the frame's bottom bracket shell, with replaceable bearings secured onto the axle. Vibrations or noise are signs that the bearings are worn down and will need to be replaced.

Cloth

Axle

1 **Using a cloth** and degreaser, thoroughly clean the drive (right) side crankarm. Wipe away any grit and dirt from the axle, and clean inside it. Wipe the inside of the BB shell to remove any grease and dirt.

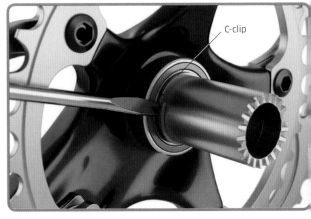

C-clip

2 **The drive (right) side crankarm has** a "C-clip" to stop the axle from moving laterally in the BB. Pry it from the bearing with a flat-head screwdriver, then pull it off the axle by hand. Take care not to lose it.

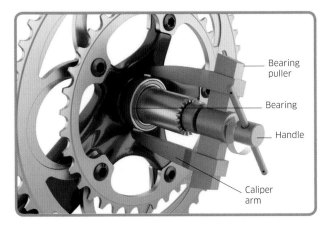

Bearing puller

Bearing

Handle

Caliper arm

3 **Secure the bearing puller** over the axle so that the tips of the caliper arms pinch underneath the bearing. Turn the handle clockwise. As the tool presses on the axle, the caliper arms will pull the bearing free.

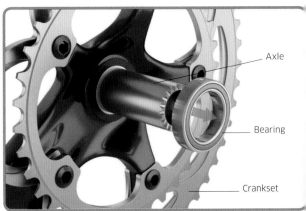

Axle

Bearing

Crankset

4 **Once the bearing is** loose, remove the bearing puller and pull the bearing off the axle with your fingers. If there is any damage to the axle surface, you may need to replace the crankset.

<table>
<tr><td>

TOOLS AND EQUIPMENT

- Frame stand
- Cloth and degreaser
- Flat-head screwdriver

- Bearing puller
- Grease
- Bearing installer

- Rubber hammer

</td></tr>
</table>

Workshop tip: Put a cloth underneath the crankarm before using the bearing puller and bearing installer tools. This will protect the arm from scratches during the removal and reinstallation process.

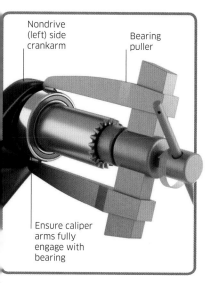

Nondrive (left) side crankarm

Bearing puller

Ensure caliper arms fully engage with bearing

Axle

Bearing cup

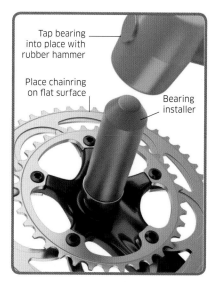

Tap bearing into place with rubber hammer

Place chainring on flat surface

Bearing installer

5 **Attach the bearing puller** onto the nondrive (left) side axle, with the arms engaged with the bearing. Free the bearing as in steps 3–4.

6 **Using a cloth**, thoroughly clean both sides of the axle and the bearing cups with degreaser. Check the parts for signs of wear.

7 **Slide the new bearing** onto the drive (right) side axle. Sit the bearing installer over the axle and lightly tap the bearing into place.

C-clip

Grease on bearing cup

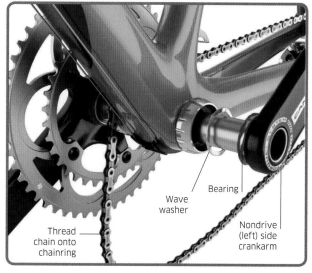

Thread chain onto chainring

Wave washer

Bearing

Nondrive (left) side crankarm

8 **When the bearing is** completely seated on the axle, apply grease to the bearing cup and the area around it. Put on the C-clip. Slide it onto the axle, up against the bearing, so that it fits snugly.

9 **Attach the second bearing** to the nondrive (left) side crankarm using the bearing installer, as in step 7. Hang the chain on the BB, and reinstall the crankset and nondrive (left) side crankarm (see pp.170–71).

REPLACING A BOTTOM BRACKET–CAMPAGNOLO ULTRA-TORQUE / **177**

▶ REPLACING A BOTTOM BRACKET
Cartridge types

A cartridge bottom bracket (BB) unit has a sealed chamber for the bearings. These bearings can become dry and worn down through use, causing the BB to creak when you pedal. A worn cartridge unit cannot be serviced and should be replaced.

BEFORE YOU START

- Secure your bike in a frame stand
- Remove the crankset (see pp.168–69)
- Secure the chain to the chainstay
- Prepare a clear space where you can lay out the parts

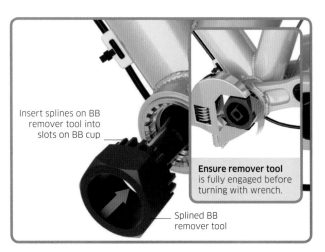

Insert splines on BB remover tool into slots on BB cup

Ensure remover tool is fully engaged before turning with wrench.

Splined BB remover tool

1 **Insert the splined BB remover tool** into the cup on the nondrive (left) side of the BB. Fasten the adjustable wrench over the tool and turn it counterclockwise to loosen the BB cup.

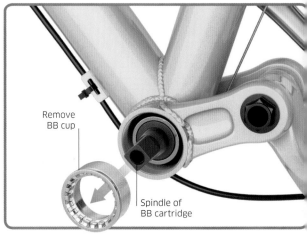

Remove BB cup

Spindle of BB cartridge

2 **Continue to loosen the BB cup** using the wrench, until you can unscrew it the rest of the way by hand. Remove the old cup from the nondrive (left) side of the frame.

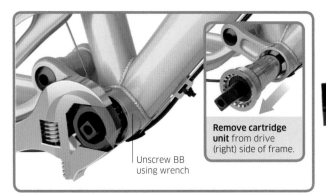

Remove cartridge unit from drive (right) side of frame.

Unscrew BB using wrench

3 **Insert the BB remover tool** into the drive (right) side. BB cups are marked with an arrow to indicate the direction in which to tighten them. To loosen them, turn the wrench the opposite way.

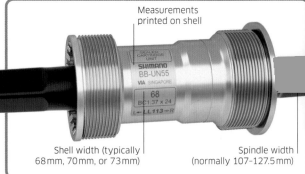

Measurements printed on shell

SHIMANO
BB-UN55
VIA SINGAPORE
68
BC1.37 x 24
L—LL113—R

Shell width (typically 68mm, 70mm, or 73mm)

Spindle width (normally 107–127.5mm)

4 **Check the shell** and spindle width on the old BB unit. If these figures are not on the shell, measure the widths with a measuring caliper. (You must replace the BB unit with one of the same dimensions.

Caution! BBs may be Italian or English threaded, which means they are tightened in opposite directions. Arrows on the BB cups show direction to tighten them.

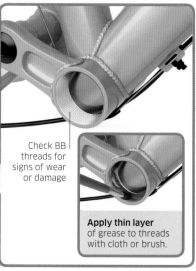

Check BB threads for signs of wear or damage

Apply thin layer of grease to threads with cloth or brush.

Screw new BB unit in by hand at first

Line up BB unit squarely

Turn tool backward until you hear a click as threads engage

5 **Check the BB threads** for damage and remove any dirt or debris using some degreaser and a cloth or small paintbrush.

6 **On the new BB unit**, remove the left-hand cup (marked "L"). Insert the unit into the drive (right) side of the bike frame.

7 **Use the remover tool** to screw in the unit. To avoid cross-threading, first turn it the "wrong" way until the threads engage.

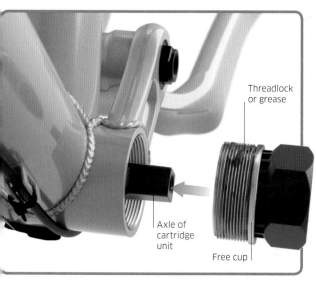

Threadlock or grease

Axle of cartridge unit

Free cup

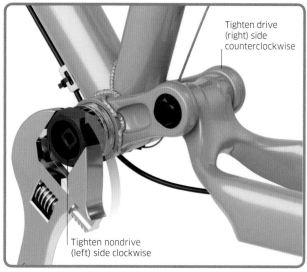

Tighten drive (right) side counterclockwise

Tighten nondrive (left) side clockwise

8 **Grease the thread** of the free cup. Check that the cartridge unit is centered inside the bike frame—there should be equal space all around the unit. Screw the cup in by hand until it is finger tight.

9 **Once both cups are** finger tight, use the BB remover tool together with the adjustable wrench to tighten each side as firmly as you can. Finish by reinstalling the crankset (see pp.166–73).

Shimano HollowTech II

The Shimano HollowTech II bottom bracket (BB) is widely installed on many modern bikes and works in conjunction with the HollowTech II crankset (see pp.166–67). Noise, roughness, and side movement indicate your BB is worn down.

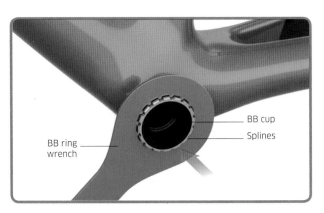

BB cup
Splines
BB ring wrench

1 Starting on the nondrive (left) side of the bike, attach the BB ring wrench over the splines of the BB cup. Loosen the cup by turning it in the opposite direction to the "tighten" arrow printed on it.

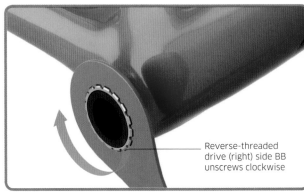

Reverse-threaded drive (right) side BB unscrews clockwise

2 Repeat on the drive (right) side of the bike, this time turning the BB ring wrench clockwise. The drive side is reverse thread, which prevents the cup from unscrewing as it is being ridden.

PARTS FOCUS

A Shimano HollowTech II BB consists of these components.

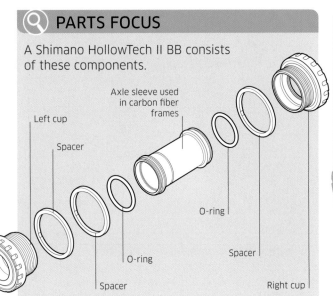

Axle sleeve used in carbon fiber frames
Left cup
Spacer
O-ring
O-ring
Spacer
Spacer
Right cup

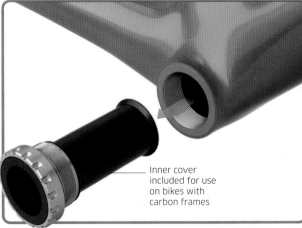

Inner cover included for use on bikes with carbon frames

3 Unscrew both external cups until the whole BB unit comes out—once they are loose enough, unscrew them by hand. The drive (right) side cup may be attached to an axle sleeve, if included.

TOOLS AND EQUIPMENT

- Frame stand
- Cloth
- Grease
- Bottom bracket ring wrench
- Degreaser

Caution! If you find there is any damage to the threads of the BB shell, or you accidentally cross-thread the BB, you may need to have the frame rethreaded by a professional mechanic.

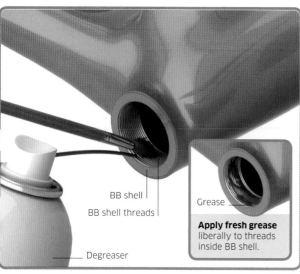

BB shell
BB shell threads

Degreaser

Grease

Apply fresh grease liberally to threads inside BB shell.

4 **Thoroughly clean out the threads** of the BB shell with degreaser and a cloth, and wipe dry. Check for corrosion and remove it, then generously grease the BB shell threads.

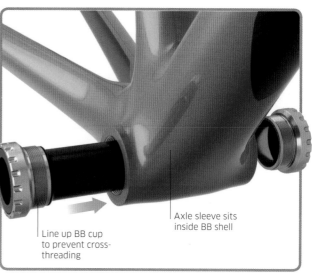

Line up BB cup to prevent cross-threading

Axle sleeve sits inside BB shell

5 **Screw the drive (right) side** of the new BB into the shell, turning it counterclockwise. Do this by hand as far as possible, as too much torque may damage the threads if they are not correctly aligned.

BB cup   Splines

6 **Screw in the nondrive (left) side cup** in the direction of the "tighten" arrow printed on it. Ensure that the cup is aligned with the thread on the shell. Tighten the cup until it is finger-tight.

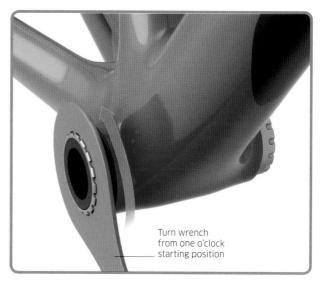

Turn wrench from one o'clock starting position

7 **Using the BB ring wrench**, tighten the BB cups all the way on both sides. Make sure that the wrench is squarely on the splines, as if it slips off under pressure, it may damage the splines.

Pedals

Many new bikes come with basic flat pedals, and some may have toe clips and straps. However, many modern pedals are designed to lock into the bottom of a cycling shoe, allowing you to generate force through the complete revolution of the pedal stroke, vastly improving pedal efficiency. Once your shoe has clicked into place, it can also be adjusted for varying

TYPE	SUITABILITY	OPERATION
FLAT PEDALS These basic pedals have no means of holding the foot in place. They are very easy to use and are especially popular on downhill mountain bikes, as they allow riders greater control of the bike through the pedals.	■ **Everyday utility cycling** or for commuting short distances. ■ **Mountain biking**, especially rides involving technical downhilling. ■ **Cargo bikes**, as they give riders greater control, allowing them to counterbalance their cargo.	■ **Made from a simple pedal plate** with no option to strap in. ■ **Despite the simplicity** of its design, it is possible to push down just as hard on a flat pedal as any other pedal.
CLIPLESS ROAD The most popular type of clipless pedal, these can only be used with a rigid-soled road shoe and a mounted shoe plate specific to the brand of pedal used.	■ **All types of road racing**, competitive endurance riding, and training.	■ **The clipless system** is installed on one side of the pedal, usually with a retaining lip at the front and a spring-loaded locking mechanism at the back. ■ **The system** makes it possible to customize the amount of float.
DOUBLE-SIDED CLIPLESS Entry on both sides makes this type of pedal easy to click into. Favored for off-road riding, they are also popular for general road riding, as the shoe used for this pedal has a grip sole that can be walked in.	■ **General road**, commuting, or off-road riding, as the pedal is designed to shed mud and uses smaller clears that are recessed into the tread of some shoes, making them more suitable for walking in.	■ **The raised clipless mechanism** works with a small, metal cleat that attaches to your cycling shoe with two bolts and pushes back a retaining lip on the pedal. ■ **The clipless style** has varying degrees of float and some quick-release tension options.
TOE CLIPS AND STRAPS New riders often prefer to start with pedals equipped with toe clips and straps because they can be used with noncycling shoes and do not lock the shoe to the pedal. The straps can be adjusted for a very loose fit.	■ **New cyclists** who want added power but are unsure about clipless pedals. ■ **For distance riders**, as the toe clips and straps make it possible to ride long distances on the road in stiff-soled shoes.	■ **Toe clips** stop the foot sliding forward, and the straps can be tightened to hold the shoe on the pedal. ■ **A shoe plate** can be slotted over the back of the pedal for serious road use.

degrees of "float"—the distance by which your foot can move on a pedal before it detaches and which you can adjust to suit your riding requirements. There are road and off-road versions of clipless pedals to suit every level of rider, and simple strap and cage pedals are available for those who prefer more traditional options, too.

KEY COMPONENTS

- **The body** is made from steel alloy or plastic with plates bolted to the front and rear.
- **Pedals** on mountain bikes typically have a bigger platform with small spikes that are screwed in to aid grip.

- **The body is** made from carbon fiber, with an integral quick-release in steel, plastic, or composite.
- **The clip mechanism** is spring- or tension-operated.

- **The body** is made from alloy with steel or titanium with a spring-operated mechanism.
- **The minimalist design** prevents mud clogging the pedal.

- **The body** is made from steel alloy or plastic with shoe plates bolted to the front and rear.
- **The toe clip and straps** hold the shoe in place.

SHOE TYPE

- **Any flat-soled shoes** are suitable for flat pedals, but leather or very hard soles may not grip well and could cause the foot to slip off, unbalancing the rider.

- **Lightweight road shoes** with smooth, rigid soles made of carbon or composite, and drilled for universal shoe plate, three-bolt, threaded inserts.
- **Shoes are vented to** keep feet cool.

- **Road or off-road style** shoes with rigid lug or grip soles designed for walking or running in cyclo-cross races.
- **Sliding two-bolt** shoe-plate mount is recessed in the shoe's sole, allowing a rider to clip-in if they wish to.

- **Any kind of shoe** can be used on flat pedals, and on pedals with toe clips and straps, but no shoe plates.
- **Traditional,** leather-soled cycling shoes must be used if pedals have shoe plates.

ADJUSTMENTS

- **There are no adjustment options** on a flat pedal.

- **The level of float** is changed in various ways, depending on the model of pedal, but it is usually adjustable via a grub screw on the spring mechanism or a tensioned plate.

- **Can be customized** to increase or decrease the level of float in various ways, depending on the type of pedal.

- **The strap wraps around** the shoe and can be tightened and released using quick-release on the strap.

Greasing axle bearings

Pedals rotate thousands of times per ride, and when close to the ground, they are exposed to water and dirt, causing wear. Worn-down pedals do not spin freely and make cycling less efficient. Maintaining pedals is a quick task, and you should check your pedals for wear every 12–18 months.

BEFORE YOU START

- Inspect each pedal to that ensure the body is not cracked
- Check that the pedal axle is not bent; if it is, replace it
- Put the chain onto the largest chainring
- If the pedal is stiff, spray it with penetrating oil
- Prepare a clear space where you can lay out the parts

Crankarm

Hex key

Pedal axle

1 Remove the pedals from the crankarms using a hex key or wrench, according to the pedals you have. The drive (right) side pedal unscrews counterclockwise, the nondrive (left) side clockwise.

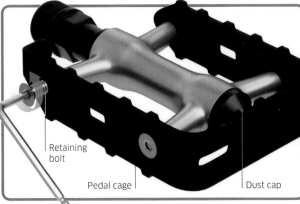

Retaining bolt

Pedal cage

Dust cap

2 Remove the pedal cages using a hex key, unscrewing the retaining bolts counterclockwise. If the bolts are stiff, spray them with penetrating oil. Clean the bolts and threads, and set them aside.

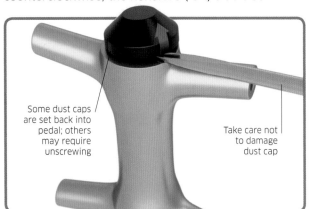

Some dust caps are set back into pedal; others may require unscrewing

Take care not to damage dust cap

3 Hold the pedal vertically with the dust cap up and the axle down. Pry off the dust cap with a flat-head screwdriver to get access to the bearings. Put the dust cap safely to one side.

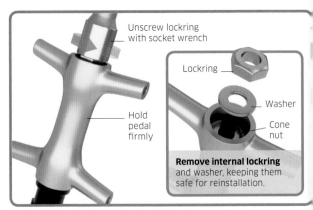

Unscrew lockring with socket wrench

Lockring

Washer

Hold pedal firmly

Cone nut

Remove internal lockring and washer, keeping them safe for reinstallation.

4 Insert a socket wrench onto the internal lockring Hold the pedal firmly and turn the lockring counterclockwise. Remove the lockring and the metal washer beneath it to reveal the cone nut.

TOOLS AND EQUIPMENT

- Penetrating oil
- Set of hex keys or wrenches
- Cloth and degreaser
- Flat-head screwdriver
- Socket wrench
- Magnetic tool or tweezers
- Grease and grease gun

Workshop tip: If you do not have a grease gun, you can use an old spoke to help push grease into tight gaps, such as pedal axles.

Locate socket wrench fully

Turn socket wrench counterclockwise to undo cone nut

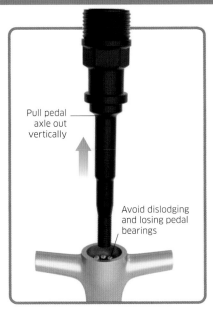

Pull pedal axle out vertically

Avoid dislodging and losing pedal bearings

Use magnetic tool if bearings are loose, or tweezers if held in clip

Check for worn bearings and replace, if necessary

Bearing race

5 **Use a socket wrench** to unscrew the cone nut counterclockwise from the end of the axle. Hold the axle steady.

6 **Turn the pedal** over and pull the axle out of the pedal body. Take care not to dislodge the bearings inside the pedal.

7 **Remove the bearings** using a magnetic tool or tweezers. Clean the bearings, axle, and the bearing races inside the pedal.

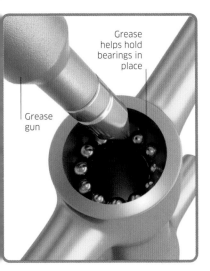

Grease helps hold bearings in place

Grease gun

Lockring

Washer

Cone nut

Ensure cone nut, washer, and lockring are re-installed in correct order.

Take care not to dislodge bearings when inserting axle

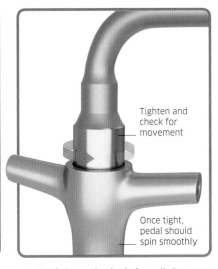

Tighten and check for movement

Once tight, pedal should spin smoothly

8 **Grease the inside** of the pedal. Insert the bearings back into the races on both sides of the pedal, and apply more grease.

9 **Slide the pedal axle** back into the pedal body. Install the cone nut, tightening it loosely. Reinstall the washer and the lockring.

10 **Tighten the lockring** all the way and reinstall the pedal cage. Grease the thread on the pedal axle before attaching it to the crankarm.

▶ FITTING CLEATS
Cycling shoes and cleats

If you use clipless pedals, you will need to fit cleats to your cycling shoes. Cleats are usually supplied together with clipless pedals. Make sure new cleats are compatible with your shoes and your pedals. To ride effectively and avoid knee injury, you will need to set the position and angle of the cleats to work with your feet.

🔧 BEFORE YOU START

- Remove any old cleats and clean the cleat bolt holes with a small brush
- Sit down, wearing your normal cycling socks
- Feel along the inside edge of each foot to locate the bony knuckle at the base of your big toe
- Put on your cycling shoes and find that same bony knuckle

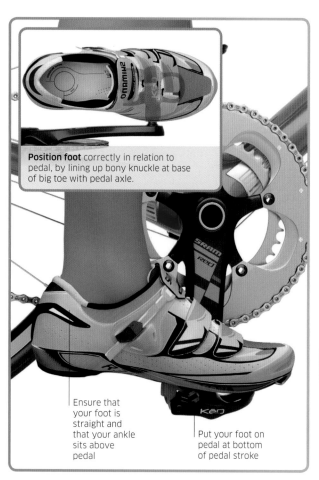

Position foot correctly in relation to pedal, by lining up bony knuckle at base of big toe with pedal axle.

Ensure that your foot is straight and that your ankle sits above pedal

Put your foot on pedal at bottom of pedal stroke

1 **Wearing your cycling shoes**, sit on your bike; you may need to lean against a wall or a support. Place your feet on the pedals with the balls of your feet directly over the pedal axle.

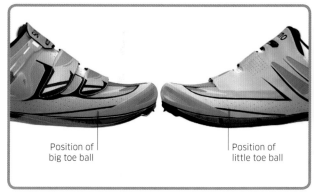

Position of big toe ball

Position of little toe ball

2 **To determine the position** of the cleats, with your shoes on, use a nonpermanent marker to mark out the position of the balls of your little toe and big toe on each shoe. Take your shoes off.

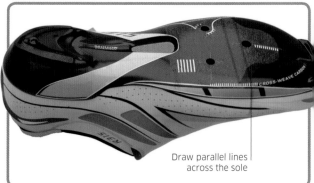

Draw parallel lines across the sole

3 **Turn each shoe** over in turn, and using a ruler, draw a line across the sole from the big toe mark and a parallel line from the little toe mark. The center of the cleat should sit between these lines.

Caution! Ensure that your cleats are compatible with your shoes. There are two main forms: twin-bolt cleats are typically used on mountain bikes, and three-bolt forms on road bikes. Some shoes for twin-bolt forms offer two pairs of bolt holes for precise fitting.

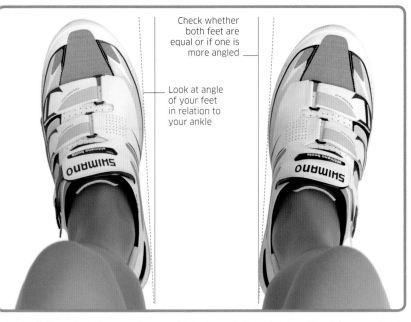

Check whether both feet are equal or if one is more angled

Look at angle of your feet in relation to your ankle

 **FINE-TUNING**

You can make fine adjustments to match your riding style.

- Moving the cleat sideways will affect how close your foot sits to your bike's centerline. If you ride with your knees wide at the top of the pedal stroke, move your cleats inward so your feet move outward. If you ride with narrow knees, move the cleat outward.

- Cleats are color-coded to show the amount of "float" (movement possible when the cleat is engaged with the pedal). Zero-float or fixed cleats keep the shoe locked in; those with 6- or 9-degree range allow feet to twist while pedaling.

4 To determine the angle at which to set the cleats, sit with your feet hanging freely off the ground. Check whether your feet naturally point outward (duck-footed), inward (pigeon-footed), or straight ahead (neutral). Note the approximate angle of each foot.

5 Grease the cleat bolt threads and loosely screw the cleats in, aligning the center of each cleat with the marks on the sole.

6 Twist each cleat so that the base sits within the marks you drew in step 3. Angle the front to match the angle of your feet.

7 Tighten the cleat screws equally, one by one. Try out the cleats while sitting on the bike as in step 1. Adjust them if required.

SUSPENSION

Suspension

Suspension is designed to absorb shocks and improve traction over bumps and dips on rough terrain. Therefore, it is mainly used on mountain bikes and some hybrid ones. Parts may include telescopic front forks, rear shocks, suspension seatposts or stems, and flexible frames. As always, before purchasing any of these parts, consider the type of riding you will be doing.

TYPE	SUITABILITY	OPERATION
SUSPENSION FORKS Almost all mountain bikes, and many hybrid bikes, have telescopic forks. Bikes with only front fork suspension are called "hardtail" mountain bikes. Forks are measured by their travel (the amount they move).	■ **Off-road riding** on rough or rocky terrain. ■ **Downhill and freeride bikes** that use longer-travel suspension (up to 9 in/230 mm of travel). ■ **Cross-country bikes** that use short-travel forks (3–4 in/80–100 mm).	■ **Suspension** is provided by compressed air or metal springs; it is often adjustable and includes a lockout function. ■ **The fork** can usually be set for the rider's weight using a preload adjuster.
REAR SHOCKS Many mountain bikes have both front suspension forks and a rear "shock"; this is called "full suspension." They vary in the amount of travel, the springs used, and the pivot system (the most common types being single-pivot and four-bar).	■ **Off-road riding** on very rough or rocky terrain, especially on technical downhills.	■ **The rear triangle**, or swingarm, holds the rear wheel and is joined to at least one pivot point on the main triangle of the frame. ■ **A shock absorber (shock)** controls movement in the swingarm. ■ **Many shocks** can be locked-out for road riding or climbing.
FLOATING DRIVETRAIN This rear suspension system has multiple pivots and linkages, and a bottom bracket that is secured to a link between the front and rear triangles so that it can move with the suspension.	■ **A wide range of terrain types;** a floating drivetrain provides sensitive traction and allows highly efficient pedaling.	■ **The rear triangle**, or swingarm, is joined to pivot points on the main triangle of the frame. ■ **A shock absorber (shock)** controls movement in the swingarm. ■ **The BB and crankset** sit on a separate link between the front and rear triangles.
SUSPENSION SADDLE/SEATPOST Suspension seatposts and saddles can be an easy, inexpensive way to improve ride quality for general riding. Even springs under the saddle offer basic shock absorption for utility bikes.	■ **Rough road riding** on uneven metallic surfaces or cobblestones. ■ **Long rides**. ■ **Hardtail mountain bikes**, if a full rear suspension system is not desired.	■ **The most basic form** of shock absorption is given by metal springs under the saddle. ■ **Suspension seatposts** have a spring set on a piston to provide shock absorption.

Even if you are intending only occasional riding on rougher roads, adding suspension to your seatpost can make cycling easier and more comfortable. For more serious trail riding, or even downhill and cross-country sessions, you should consider upgrading to suspension forks or even to a full-suspension set-up.

KEY COMPONENTS

- **The fork body** comprises a steerer tube, crown, fork stanchions, sliders, and an axle.
- **The springs utilize** inner chambers of pressurized air or metal coils.

- **The rear shock unit has** pressurized air springs or a metal spring.
- **The pivot system** enables the rear triangle to articulate independently of the rest of the frame.

- **The rear shock unit** utilizes pressurized air springs or metal coils.
- **A pivot system** enables the rear triangle to articulate with the rest of the frame.

- **The body of the seatpost** may include an internal spacer, internal spring, piston, and outer casing.
- **On some seatposts**, arms and pivots allow the saddle to move down and back.

VARIATIONS

- **Single-crown forks**, used on most mountain bikes, have one crown at the base of the steerer tube.
- **Dual-crown forks** have a second crown at the top of the steerer tube. They give extra stiffness for downhill bikes.

- **Single pivots** have a swingarm that connects to the front triangle at one pivot point, usually just above the bottom bracket (BB).
- **A four-bar system** has twin pivots with a linkage. A shock is located between the linkage and a fixed bracket on the frame.

- **Various types exist**, including the i-Drive, Freedrive, and Monolink systems.

- **Suspension seatposts** have an integral, damped tube. Posts may be made of aluminum, with stainless steel for pivots.
- **Elastomer dampers** may be attached to suspension seatposts or used alone.
- **Simple sprung saddles**.

MAINTENANCE

- **The fork stanchions** should be inspected for scratches, nicks, or leaks, all of which can indicate damaged seals.
- **After a front-end impact,** the fork should be checked for bends or damage.

- **The shock** must be checked to stop oil leaking past the seals.
- **There should** be no wear in the pivot points, linkages, or frame bearings.
- **The swingarm tubes** or spars may take damage and need repairing after a collision.

- **The shock** must be checked to stop oil leaking past the seals.
- **There should** be no wear in the pivot points, linkages, or frame bearings.
- **The swingarm** or linkages may take damage and need repair after a collision.

- **For suspension seatposts,** the spring should be regularly lubricated to prevent stiffness and squeaking.
- **Elastomer inserts** must be changed if they are worn down or start to harden with age, or if a firmer or softer ride is required.

Suspension forks

Suspension forks act by compressing and rebounding to absorb vibration and bumps. They help to keep the front wheel in contact with the ground over rough terrain and ease rider fatigue. The forks contain a steel coil spring or an air spring. The speed of the spring's action is controlled by damping from a piston within an oil reservoir. Both the damping and the spring action can be adjusted according to rider weight, preference, and terrain. You should keep suspension forks clean and maintain them after every 20 hours of riding (see pp.198-99). Some types also need specialized maintenance once a year.

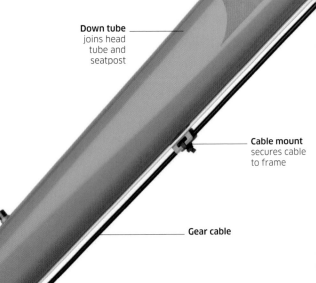

Down tube joins head tube and seatpost

Cable mount secures cable to frame

Gear cable

PARTS FOCUS

Suspension forks comprise an air spring (shown here) or metal coil, fixed fork stanchions, and mobile sliders. Many also have a lockout.

① The **fork stanchions** are fixed to the crown and contain the suspension mechanism, including the damper piston and air chamber or coil spring.

② The **sliders** are connected to the front wheel, and move vertically up and down the fork stanchions as the suspension compresses and decompresses.

③ The **air chamber** provides pressure within the fork stanchion. This pressure can be increased or reduced to adjust the suspension (see pp.194-95).

④ The **lockout** mechanism locks the suspension so that the forks do not compress. It is used to save pedaling energy when riding on smooth surfaces.

FRONT SAG

Suspension compresses a small amount under a rider's weight. This is shown on the O-ring (see pp.194-95) and can be adjusted if desired.

Head tube

Fork crown

Fork stanchion

Brace

O-ring

Slider

Headset

Air valve allows air to be added or released from air chamber

Top cap sits at top of air chamber

Air chamber used to pressurize suspension

Fork crown joins fork stanchions to steerer tube

Lockout dial locks forks

④

Compression damper controls fork rebound speed

①

③

O-ring used to set suspension sag

Tire

Spring seal keeps out dirt

Fork seal protects suspension from dirt

②

Piston head sits at top of slider

Oil chamber contains suspension oil

Damper piston compresses oil in chamber

Head seal on air chamber

Flow valve regulates damping

Damper shaft pushes damper piston

Damper head seal at base of piston

Disc brake caliper

Disc rotor

Dropout holds wheel axle

Rebound control allows fork rebound to be adjusted

Setting the front sag

Sag is the amount by which the suspension compresses under a rider's weight, which you can alter to suit different riding styles or terrain. The steps shown here are for air-filled forks, which are the most common. Coil-sprung forks can be adjusted by changing the preload setting.

BEFORE YOU START

- Add air to the shock absorbers to the pressure that the manufacturer recommends for your weight
- Recreate your normal riding weight: put on your usual riding clothes, shoes, helmet, and backpack, and attach any water bottles, hydration packs, or panniers

O-ring or rubber band

Base of fork stanchion

1 **Slide the O-ring** down to the base of the fork stanchion. If the fork stanchion does not have an O-ring, tie a rubber band to the base. Never use a cable tie, because it could scratch the fork stanchion.

Apply bodyweight to handlebar

Fork completely compressed

2 **Hold the front brake** firmly, ensuring that the bike cannot move forward. Push down on the handlebar with your full weight to compress the suspension fork as far as it will go.

50% 100% 75% 25%

O-ring indicates amount of movement

Using tape measure, note how far O-ring has been moved by fork stanchion.

3 **Release your weight** from the fork, allowing the suspension to return to its original extended position, then measure the distance from the base of the fork stanchion to the position of the O-ring.

O-ring at base of fork stanchion

4 **Push the O-ring** back down to the base of the fork stanchion. Mount your bike and, standing on the pedals with your weight over the handlebar, travel a short distance. Do not use the brake or pump the fork

Caution! If the fork has a travel-adjustment dial, ensure that you position it at the "full-travel" setting before performing these steps. If the fork has a "lock out" switch, set it "open" to allow the fork to compress and decompress all the way.

New position of O-ring

25%

25% of full extent of fork travel

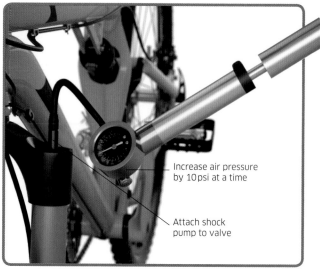

Increase air pressure by 10 psi at a time

Attach shock pump to valve

5 **Dismount carefully** and note the new position of the O-ring. For cross-country or trail riding, it should be at 20-25% of the total sag measured in step 2, and at 30% for downhill riding.

6 **If the sag is** greater than your required setting, attach a shock pump to the valve at the top of the stanchion and pump in air at increments of 10 psi. Repeat steps 3-5 to check the new setting.

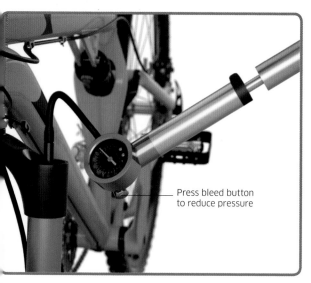

Press bleed button to reduce pressure

Desired amount of sag

Valve at top of fork stanchion

Position of O-ring

7 **If the sag is** lower than your desired setting, release some air from the fork—10 psi at a time—by pressing the bleed button on the shock pump. Repeat steps 3-5 to check the new setting.

8 **Take the bike** for a ride, then retest the amount of sag by running through steps 3-5 again. If necessary, adjust the amount of air pressure once more, as in steps 6-7.

Tuning suspension forks

Suspension forks can be adjusted to provide comfortable, controlled steering for your weight and the terrain on which you are cycling. One form of adjustment is "damping" to control the rate of the fork's compression (downward travel) and rebound (return to normal). Correct damping ensures that the forks will respond quickly and smoothly on uneven ground.

⊙ BEFORE YOU START

- Refer to the manufacturer's instructions for the recommended suspension settings
- Prepare a clear space where valve caps can be laid out
- Keep a notebook and pen to hand so you can jot down different settings as you try them out

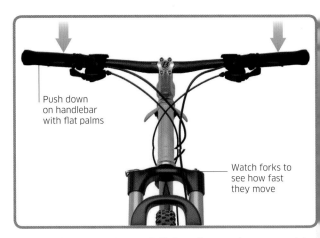

Push down on handlebar with flat palms

Watch forks to see how fast they move

2 **Unwind the rebound dial** and reset it at one-third of its full extent. Then test the rate at which the forks rebound by pushing down on the handlebar, keeping the palms of your hands flat.

Fork blade

Rebound dial

1 **Open the rebound dial** at the base of the fork blade by turning it counterclockwise as far as it will go. Then screw it clockwise, counting the clicks it makes until it is closed again. Divide this number by three.

Turn rebound dial clockwise to increase damping and slow rebound speed.

Tire will bounce if there is excessive rebound

3 **Check your front tire** to see if it stays in contact with the ground. If it skips off the ground, the rebound is too high. Turn the rebound dial clockwise to increase the damping and stop the bouncing.

Workshop tip: Some suspension forks can have the distance they travel vertically increased or decreased by inserting or removing plastic spacers inside the fork blades. Refer to the manufacturer's instructions if this applies to your forks.

Turn rebound dial counter-clockwise to reduce damping and increase rebound speed.

Tire stays in contact with ground

Feel how smoothly or roughly the fork reacts when braking

Note how fast forks travel— they should not "dive" or "bob" over bumps

Forks should absorb small impacts smoothly

Tire should have good contact with the ground

4 **If the fork rebounds** too slowly, turn the rebound dial counterclockwise to reduce the damping and increase the speed at which the fork reacts. The reaction should be smooth and not stiff.

5 **Put on your normal riding gear** and go for a ride over bumpy terrain to check how the suspension feels. Make further adjustments as needed, moving the dial by small amounts until you are happy.

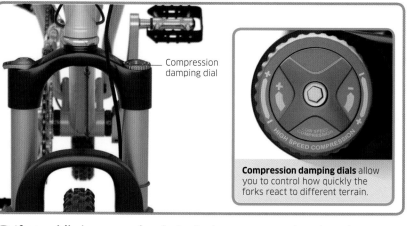

Compression damping dial

Compression damping dials allow you to control how quickly the forks react to different terrain.

6 **If your bike's suspension forks** feature compression damping, you may need to tune it to prevent them from compressing all the way or "bottoming out" while riding. Compression damping is adjusted by turning the dial on the top of each fork. Test and correct as necessary.

AIR-SPRUNG FORKS

Some air-sprung forks have an adjustable negative spring to control the fork's sensitivity to small bumps. Initially, the spring should be at the same air pressure as the main spring.

- Inflate air-sprung forks to the correct pressure for your weight.

- There are two types of shock pump: high pressure and low pressure. Use the correct pump for your suspension.

The lower legs

Suspension forks bear the brunt of rough terrain, so they need regular maintenance to ensure that they perform properly, and to prolong their lives. You should inspect the lower legs after every 25 hours of riding time, and you should ideally replace the seals and oil after 200 hours.

BEFORE YOU START

- Remove the stem and forks (see pp.54–57)
- Remove the front wheel (see pp.78–79)
- Remove the rim brake calipers, if included (see pp.114–15)
- Ensure that the forks are clean, and free of dirt and grit
- Refer to the fork manufacturer's instructions (see step 8)
- Lay out a drop cloth to catch any excess oil

Release air using a hex key

Slider

Fork stanchion

Release air from forks using hex key or shock pump so they can be compressed.

1 Fasten a shock pump to the air valve on the fork, and note the pressure. Release the air using the bleed button on the pump, or by pressing the valve on the fork with a hex key.

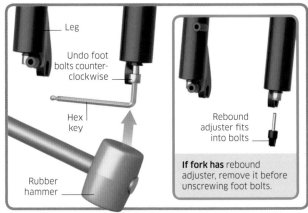

Leg

Undo foot bolts counter-clockwise

Hex key

Rubber hammer

Rebound adjuster fits into bolts

If fork has rebound adjuster, remove it before unscrewing foot bolts.

2 Insert a hex key into the foot bolts at the base of each leg and unscrew by three turns. With the hex key still in the bolt, tap it using a rubber hammer to loosen the damper shaft within the lower legs.

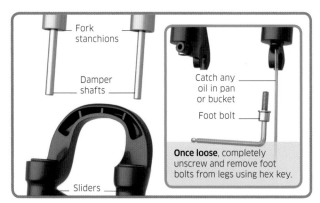

Fork stanchions

Damper shafts

Catch any oil in pan or bucket

Foot bolt

Sliders

Once loose, completely unscrew and remove foot bolts from legs using hex key.

3 Completely unscrew the foot bolts, then pull the lower legs to ease the sliders from the fork stanchions. If stiff, tap them free with a rubber hammer. Clean the fork stanchions and inspect the surface for scratches.

Spring ring

Foam rings sit inside seals

Wiper seal

Work a cloth around inside wiper seal to remove grease and dirt.

4 Remove the spring ring from the top of each wiper seal on the slider, and use a screwdriver to ease out the foam ring inside. Clean the rings and the inside of the seals with an alcohol-based cleaner.

Ensure lint-free towel does not get stuck in slider

5 Wrap a lint-free towel over a long screwdriver. Insert it into he sliders and wipe the inside of them thoroughly.

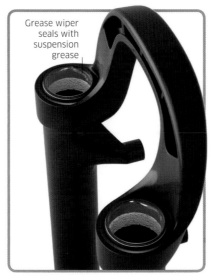

Grease wiper seals with suspension grease

6 Reattach the foam rings and spring rings to the wiper seals, then apply suspension grease around the inside of the seals.

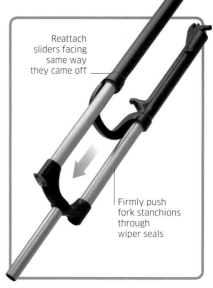

Reattach sliders facing same way they came off

Firmly push fork stanchions through wiper seals

7 Rotate the forks so that the fork stanchions are positioned diagonally. Push the sliders halfway onto the fork stanchions.

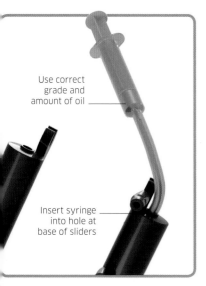

Use correct grade and amount of oil

Insert syringe into hole at base of sliders

8 Inject suspension oil into the sliders using a syringe. Refer to the fork manufacturer's instructions on which oil to use.

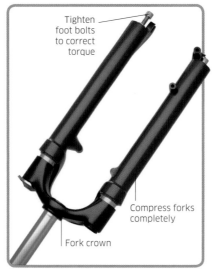

Tighten foot bolts to correct torque

Compress forks completely

Fork crown

9 Compress the forks and hold them in place. Replace both foot bolts and the rebound adjuster, if included. Clean any spilled oil.

Attach shock pump to air valve

Add air to fork to correct pressure

10 Repressurize the fork to its original pressure using a shock pump. Reattach the forks to the bike (see pp.54–57).

Rear suspension

Rear suspension systems keep the rear wheel in contact with the ground over rough terrain to maximize traction and give a smoother ride. Rear shock units, the central part of the system, contain a steel coil spring or an air spring, which allows the suspension to compress or rebound to absorb bumps and dips. The speed of the spring's action is controlled by damping pistons inside oil- or nitrogen-filled chambers. The spring action and the damping can be adjusted according to your weight, personal preference, and the terrain you are riding on. You need to keep the shock unit clean and maintain it after every 20 hours of riding. Some types also need specialized maintenance annually.

⚙ REAR LINKAGE

There are several designs of rear linkage, and the location of the rear shock will vary accordingly. The shock still performs in the same way, however.

Seatpost

Linkage

Rear shock

⚙ PARTS FOCUS

Rear suspension systems have a shock unit that acts on pivots and linkages on the frame to allow the rear wheel to move up and down.

① On some systems (such as the one shown here), one or more **linkages** join the rear shock to the rear triangle of the bike frame.

② **Pivots** between the linkages and/or on the frame allow the rear triangle to rotate around them so the rear wheel can move up and down.

③ The **shaft** forms the lower half of the shock unit. It contains the nitrogen and oil chambers, and the pistons that provide damping.

④ The **air chamber** occupies the top half of the shock. Air can be added or released to adjust air pressure when setting the sag (see pp.202–03).

Hex bolts secure linkage to pivots

Linkage allows suspension to move

②

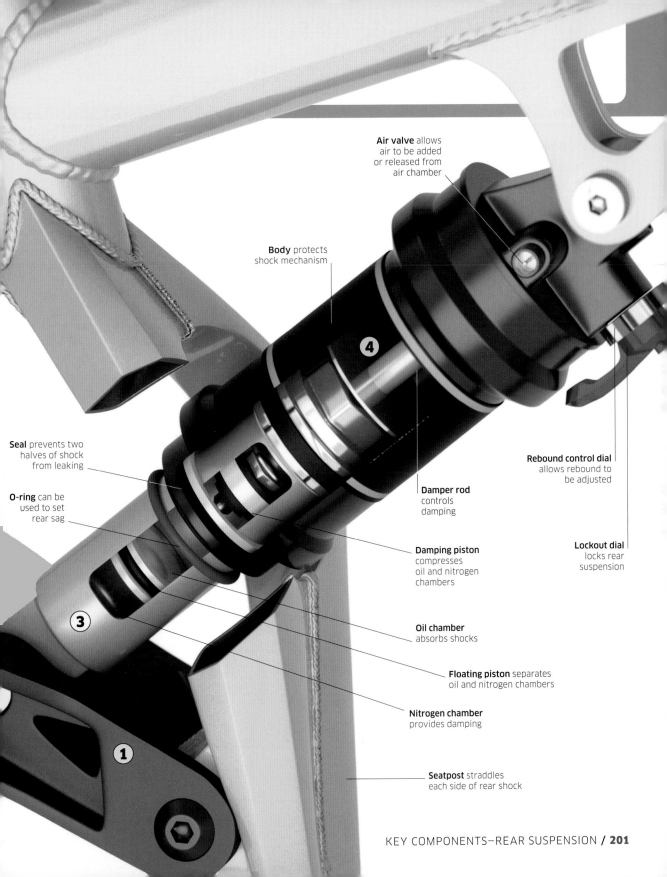

Air valve allows air to be added or released from air chamber

Body protects shock mechanism

④

Seal prevents two halves of shock from leaking

O-ring can be used to set rear sag

③

①

Damper rod controls damping

Rebound control dial allows rebound to be adjusted

Damping piston compresses oil and nitrogen chambers

Lockout dial locks rear suspension

Oil chamber absorbs shocks

Floating piston separates oil and nitrogen chambers

Nitrogen chamber provides damping

Seatpost straddles each side of rear shock

Setting the rear sag

Rear suspension is designed not only to give a comfortable ride but also to keep the back wheel on the ground for maximum grip and pedaling efficiency. To do so, shock absorbers (shocks) need to be able to compress and expand to cope with bumps and any dips you encounter.

BEFORE YOU START

- Position your bike against a wall
- Add air to the shock absorber to the manufacturer's recommended setting for your weight with a shock pump
- Put on your normal riding gear (see pp.196–197)

Shock body moves along shaft to allow compression and rebound

Main body of rear shock

Shock seal

O-ring

If O-ring is missing, tie cut rubber band around shaft, ensuring it is tight.

1 **Slide the O-ring** up the shaft until it sits against the rubber shock seal of the shock body. If the bicycle has no O-ring, tie a cut rubber band around the shaft, and push it against the shock seal instead.

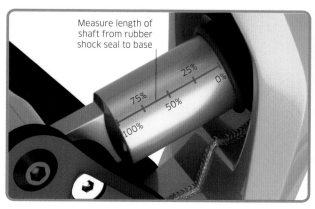

Measure length of shaft from rubber shock seal to base

25%

0%

75%

50%

100%

2 **Measure the shaft**, and divide its length by 4. Most shocks require 25% sag, but as a precaution check your shock manufacturer's instructions to determine the recommended amount of sag.

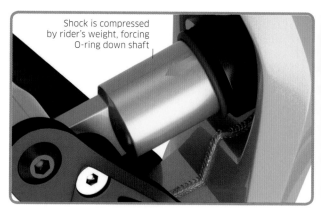

Shock is compressed by rider's weight, forcing O-ring down shaft

3 **Wearing your riding gear**, mount the bike carefully so that the rear suspension is compressed by your full weight as it would be on a normal ride. Avoid bouncing the shock as you get on.

Workshop tip: Before you start to adjust the rear sag, ensure that any lockout or propedal switch on the shock is turned off so that the shock can move through its full distance of travel.

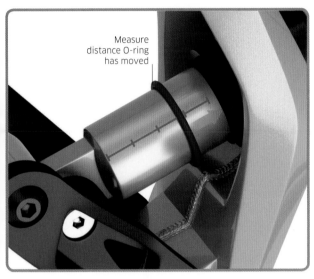

Measure distance O-ring has moved

If O-ring has moved beyond 25% along the shaft, sag is too high

25%

4 **Dismount carefully**, so that the shock decompresses, and check the position of the O-ring on the shaft. It should have traveled between 20% and 30% along the exposed length of the shaft.

5 **The optimum extent of shock travel** is around 25% along the shaft. If the O-ring or band has moved beyond 25%, then the sag is too much; if it has moved less than 25%, then the sag is too low.

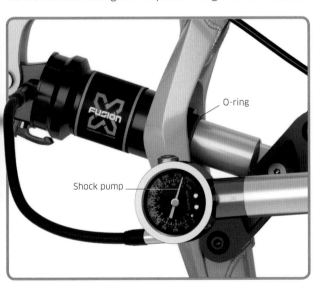

O-ring

Shock pump

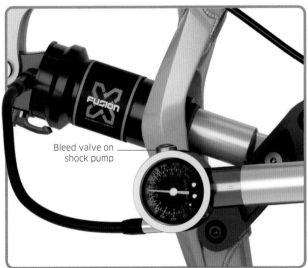

Bleed valve on shock pump

6 **Attach a shock pump** to adjust the air pressure inside the shock. If the sag is too low, increase the air pressure at increments of 10 psi at a time. Retest the sag and add more air as required.

7 **If the sag is** too high, use the bleed button on the shock pump to release air from the shock and reduce the air pressure. Retest the sag (see steps 1–4), and repeat as necessary.

OWNER'S GUIDE

REGULAR MAINTENANCE
Planner

A maintenance timetable can be a useful way to keep on top of any work you need to do on your bike. By scheduling regular sessions for basic fixes, you will reduce the likelihood of wearing out parts prematurely or having an accident on the road.

⚙ EVERY WEEK

DRIVETRAIN
As one of the most complex parts of a bike, the drivetrain needs constant maintenance.

- **Check chain** for wear (pp.40–41).
- **Ensure gears** are shifting properly (pp.40–41, 130–38).
- **Inspect cables** for fraying or wear (pp.40–41).
- **Tighten crankarms** and chainring bolts (pp.40–41, 166–73).
- **Oil chain** and jockey pulleys if bike was ridden in the rain (pp.44–45).

STEERING AND WHEELS
Wheels and steering may require frequent attention if you are riding more on trails than on roads.

- **Check headset** is correctly adjusted and allows for easy steering (pp.40–41).
- **Check quick-release** levers are functioning (pp.40–41).
- **Ensure wheels** are in true and have no broken spokes (pp.40–41, 88–89).
- **Inspect handlebar** and stem for cracks and ensure stem bolts are tightened (pp.40–41).

BRAKES
Brakes can prevent all manner of accidents, so regular maintenance checks and repairs are crucial.

- **Inspect inner cables** for fraying and outer cables for wear, then oil with lube (pp.44–45).
- **Ensure pads** are aligned and not worn down (pp.40–41).
- **Tighten disc** and caliper bolts (pp.100–01, 118–19).
- **Check for cracks** in brake parts (pp.40–41).
- **Inspect hydraulic hoses** for wear or leaks (pp.40–41).

SUSPENSION
Regularly checking suspension systems can prevent small problems from developing into larger ones.

- **Check over fork** and shock exterior surfaces for cracks (pp.40–41).
- **Inspect fork stanchions** under shock boots for cracks (pp.192–93).
- **Tighten top caps**, crown bolts, and shaft bolts (pp.196–99).
- **Lubricate fork stanchions** with wet lube (pp.44–45).

ELECTRONICS
Motor performance will be more efficient if your bike runs smoothly.

- **Ensure battery** is fully charged.
- **Clean bike** so there is less resistance when cycling and battery drains more slowly (pp.142–43).

The sample schedule below gives an idea of how often you should check over your bike if you ride often. A heavily used model will need much more attention, while a bike for infrequent, short road journeys will require far less maintenance.

EVERY MONTH

- **Check bottom bracket** runs smoothly (pp.174–81).
- **Oil chain** and jockey pulleys (pp.44–45)
- **Tighten pedals,** if needed (pp.184–85).
- **Check cog teeth** on chain/cassette ring are not worn down or missing (pp.156–57).
- **Ensure rear derailleur** hangers are fixed (pp.144–49).
- **Spray derailleur hangers**, cables, and clipless pedal-release mechanism with lubricant (pp.44–45).

- **Check hubs** for any roughness, tight spots, or play on axles (pp.44–45).
- **Ensure there are no splits** on rubber hub seals (pp.90–91).
- **Inspect headset covers**, if installed (pp.52–53).
- **Oil hub seals** (pp.90–91).

- **Ensure discs** are aligned and not worn (pp.40–41).
- **Grease inner cables** and oil inside outer cables (pp.44–45).
- **Replace brake pads** of frequently ridden mountain bikes (pp.120–21).

- **Eliminate any play** in forks and shocks (pp.196–99).
- **Check fork stanchions** to see if oil line is visible (pp.192–93).
- **Inspect fork and shock seals** for cracks or slackness (pp.198–99).
- **Ensure there is no fork** or shock sag (pp.194–97).
- **Turn bike upside-down** and store overnight so oil can spread through fork.

- **Check electronics cables** outer for wear or splits.

EVERY SIX MONTHS

- **Check for play** in freewheel (pp.78–83), freehub body (pp.90–91), and rear derailleur frame bolt (pp.144–45).
- **Ensure jockey pulleys** are not worn down (pp.144–45).
- **Oil hub gear** and check pedals do not feel rough or notchy and are not worn down (pp.44–45).
- **Replace chain** if used less regularly (pp.158–59).
- **Replace cogs** (pp.160–61) and inner and outer cables (pp.132–35).

- **Inspect bearings** in open-bearing hubs for wear (pp.94–95).
- **Check for wear** in bearings and bearing surfaces in headsets (pp.54–55).
- **Grease open bearing** hubs (pp.94–95) and headsets (pp.54–55).
- **Replace handlebar tapes** and grips (pp.62–63).

- **Grease** brake bosses (pp.44–45).
- **Replace** inner or outer cables (pp.132–35).

- **Remove headset** to check fork steerer assembly for cracks (pp.54–57).
- **Replace fork oil** (pp.44–45).
- **Have suspension** maintenance done by trained technician.

- **Check working** of electronic gear-shift levers (pp.136–37).

Steering, saddle, wheels

The stationary components on your bicycle deserve the same careful maintenance as its moving parts. The handlebar, stem, saddle, and seatpost bear your weight and provide comfort, while the wheels and headset must turn smoothly and without play.

⚠ PROBLEM

🔍 POSSIBLE CAUSES

Steering does not respond as expected when you move the handlebar. Other symptoms might include:

- **Steering feels delayed** or imprecise.
- **Cracked or bubbling paintwork**, cracks in the frame around tube junctions, or soft or springy carbon.

- **Handlebar** may be bent or not aligned correctly.
- **Headset** is too tight, too loose, or worn down.
- **The forks** or frame may be bent.

Seatpost wobbles loose or slips down gradually during riding. You might also notice:

- **Saddle** is not straight.
- **Pedaling is harder** when sitting down due to the lower-than-normal saddle height.

- **Seatpost diameter** may be too small for frame.
- **Saddle clamp** might be loose.
- **Seatpost clamp** may be loose, or have slipped up the seatpost.

Bicycle handles uncertainly when riding around corners. Other symptoms include:

- **Wheel rattles** on the hub or wobbles in the frame.
- **Brakes rub** against the wheel.

- **Tires** could be underinflated.
- **Bearings** of the cup-and-cone hubs may be loose.
- **Wheel** may be out of true.
- **Worn down** or incorrectly adjusted headset.

Wheel rim or tire rubs against the brake, frame, or fork whenever you are riding. Symptoms might include:

- **Loose or broken spokes** rattle in the wheel.
- **Wheel is buckled**, most often following a crash.

- **Wheel** might be out of true after an impact due to spokes loosening.
- **Wheel** may have been incorrectly inserted in the dropouts.
- **Tire bead** could be incorrectly seated inside the rim.
- **Brake** is misaligned.

Resistance when riding, whether coasting or pedaling. You might also notice:

- **Grinding or squeaking** from either wheel.
- **Tire rubs** against the frame or brakes.

- **Hub bearings** could be dirty, worn down, or too tight.
- **The wheel** might be out of true, or the tire bead incorrectly seated inside the rim.
- **Brakes** may be misaligned.

Problems with these parts can cause significant discomfort or difficulty when riding. If you are unable to steer properly or feel your wheels are not running smoothly, it is essential to identify the cause of the problem and possible remedies as quickly as possible.

POSSIBLE SOLUTIONS

Check alignment of the handlebar. The stem should be in line with the wheel, so the bar is at 90 degrees to the wheel. Replace bent handlebar (pp.60–61).

See if the headset moves freely and without play. Adjust it if necessary, and/or grease or replace the bearings and races (pp.54–57).

Inspect the frame and forks for rippled paint, cracks, or bent tubes. Replace them unless made of steel, which can be fixed by a frame builder.

Swap the seatpost for one with the correct diameter. To find the right size, measure the internal diameter of the seat tube (pp.68–69).

Tighten the saddle clamp, ensuring that the jaws of the clamp are in the correct position around the saddle rails (pp.68–69).

Remove the seatpost clamp and clean it, as well as the top of the seat tube. Reassemble clamp, grease and reinsert the seatpost, and tighten appropriately (pp.68–69).

Check that the tire is not flat–patch or replace the inner tube, if so. Then inflate to the manufacturer's advised pressure (pp.48–49).

Adjust the cup-and-cone hub's bearings so that they are tight, with no lateral play.

True the wheel so that the rim runs straight, adjusting the tension of the spokes in the out-of-true area with a spoke wrench (pp.88–89).

Spin the wheel to gauge the severity of the buckled wheel. Replace the broken spokes and true the wheel, or replace the wheel entirely (pp.88–89).

Remove the wheel and reinsert, correctly centered in dropouts. Tighten the axle nuts evenly on each side, or tighten the quick-release all the way (pp.78–81).

Deflate the inner tube, pinch your fingers around the tire to squeeze the bead inside the rim, then run your hands around the tire. Reinflate the tube (pp.84–87).

Overhaul the cup-and-cone hubs and check races, ball bearings, and cones for wear. If unworn, regrease and tighten. Replace worn down or pitted parts.

True the wheel so that it runs straight. Check that the tire bead is correctly seated in the rim–if not, deflate the inner tube and reseat the tire bead (pp.84–89).

Adjust the brake alignment with the rim, ensuring that the pads are parallel to the wheel rim. Check the centering and adjust if necessary (pp.112–117).

Although mechanically simple, fully functioning brakes are essential for safe cycling–failure can have dramatic and dangerous consequences.

Good, well-maintained brakes should deliver ample braking power to slow your speed quickly and effectively or bring you to a halt.

⚠ PROBLEM

Brakes make a noise when you pull the brake levers to slow your bike. Symptoms include:

- **Squealing or scraping** when the brakes are applied.
- **Shaking** when the brake pads hit the wheel rim.
- **Brake pads rubbing** against the rim.

Bicycle slows down when you pull the brake lever, but you cannot lock the wheel to stop the bike. You might also notice:

- **The brake lever hitting** the handlebar when you pull it.
- **Poor braking** in wet weather.

Brakes gradually or rapidly lose power, with no reduction in speed despite pulling hard on the levers. Other symptoms might include:

- **A sharp crack** from a snapping brake cable.

Brakes do not spring back all the way when you release the brake lever, and the pad sticks against or close to the rim. You might also experience:

- **A spongy feeling** when the brake levers are pulled.
- **More resistance** than you are used to when pedaling.

Brakes are stiff or difficult to apply when you pull the brake lever. Other symptoms include:

- **A grating sound** coming from the brake lever.
- **Resistance or sticking** from the brake cables when the brake lever is pulled.

🔍 POSSIBLE CAUSES

- **Squealing may be** due to the brake pads being angled flat or tail-in to the rim, or dirt and pad residue on the rim.
- **Scraping or grinding** may be caused by the pads being old and hard, or contaminated with dirt and grit.

- **Brake pads may be too far** from the rim due to pad wear, cable stretch, or the brake quick-release being open.
- **Poorly aligned brake pads** may be slipping under the rim.
- **Link wire on cantilever brakes** may be badly adjusted.
- **Pads or rims** may be worn down, dirty, or contaminated. Steel rims have poor friction when wet, and may be the issue.

- **Cable-clamp bolt** may be loose, or brake cable may have snapped.
- **Brake pads** might not be not secured tightly on brake arms.
- **Cable housing** end-caps might be missing.

- **Pivot bolts are too tight**, preventing brake arms from moving freely.
- **Dry, corroded, or worn down** brake cable and/or housing.
- **Brake pads** are out of alignment with rim, and have worn down unevenly with a lip of pad trapped under rim.
- **Spring tension** insufficient to push arms away from rim.

- **Brake pivots or bosses are worn down**, corroded, or dirty.
- **Cable is corroded** or routed incorrectly.
- **Brake lever** may be clogged with dirt or damaged.

Any problems with brakes pose considerable danger both to yourself and other road users, but if you spot the symptoms early and take quick action to identify and then resolve the problem, you drastically reduce the potential risk of a life-threatening crash or accident.

💡 POSSIBLE SOLUTIONS

Toe-in the brake pads so that front of pad is angled toward the rim, touching the rim first during braking. Check that the brakes are centered (pp.110–117).

Clean the rim using degreaser and a brush to dislodge any hardened pad residue, then rinse off with water (pp.42–43).

Replace the brake pads if worn down past the depth-marker grooves. If not, use a scalpel to level the pad, then sand it gently (pp.110–111).

Reset the brake pads by moving them toward the rim, or adjusting the cable at the clamp or barrel adjuster. Close the brake quick-release (pp.104–105, 112–117).

Check the pads and rims for wear and replace if there is evidence of scoring or wear to the rim. If not, clean the surface of both, and run sandpaper over the pads (pp.42–43, 110–111).

For cantilever brakes, loosen the cable clamp and adjust the link wire to the correct angle for optimum brake power (pp.114–115).

Tighten the cable-clamp bolt, replacing the brake cable in the case of a breakage (pp.104–105).

Replace the cable housing end-caps, and check the housing itself for rust or wear. Apply lubricant and replace the housing if necessary (pp.104–105).

Tighten the brake pads on the brake arm, ensuring they are centered and aligned with the rim (pp.110–117).

Loosen the pivot bolts until the brake arms can move unhindered. Lubricate the pivot points or apply grease to the brake bosses (pp.44–45, 116–117).

Lubricate or replace the brake cable and/or housing. If the pads are worn down, replace or cut off the lip with a scalpel, then reset to the rim (pp.44–45, pp.102–105, pp.110–111).

For V- or cantilever brakes, remove the brake arms and place the spring tension pin in the brake boss's uppermost hole (pp.112–115).

Clean and lubricate the brake pivots or bosses. Try wire wool or fine sandpaper to remove or smooth over rust corrosion (pp.42–43).

Clean or replace the brake cable and/or housing, ensuring the cables are correctly routed and seated into the cable stops, and the end-caps are fitted (pp.42–43, 102–105).

Clean the brake lever, lubricate its pivot point, and grease the cable housing where it meets the lever. Replace it if broken (pp.42–43, 102–105).

▶ TROUBLESHOOTING
Disc brakes

The most powerful and reliable form of bicycle brake, disc brakes are also popular because of the "modulation"–fine control over braking power– that they offer the rider. While discs are robust and effective even in poor conditions, take care of them to greatly improve their performance.

⚠ PROBLEM

Brakes squeal when you pull the brake lever to reduce your speed or halt the bike. You might also notice:

- **Reduced braking power** when you apply the brakes.
- **Vibrations or shaking** during braking.

Brake pads rub against the rotor when you are riding. Other symptoms might include:

- **Grinding or scraping** sounds when the wheel rotates.
- **Excessive wear** on pads and rotor.

Loss of braking power when you pull the brake lever, meaning you find it impossible to lock the wheel completely. You might also notice:

- **Increase in stopping distance** when braking.
- **Brake lever hits handlebar** without stopping the bike.

Brake pads do not spring back from the disc rotor after you have finished braking. You might also notice:

- **A scraping noise** once the brakes are released.
- **A grinding** from the cable as mechanical disc brakes are applied.

A spongy feeling at the brake lever when you apply the hydraulic disc brake. Other symptoms might include:

- **A different "bite point"**–the position in the brake lever's travel at which the brakes come on–each time you pull the lever.

🔍 CAUSES

- **Contamination from** lubricant, degreaser, brake fluid, or grease may have leaked onto the disc rotor or brake pads.
- **Rotor surface** may be worn down or roughened.
- **Caliper bolts** may be loose and vibrate when braking.

- **The rotor may be warped** due to an impact when riding, such as the bike falling on its side or getting damaged during storage or transit.
- **Brake calipers may be misaligned** with the disc rotor.
- **Brake pads may be too close** to the disc rotor.

- **Contamination from** lubricant, degreaser, brake fluid, or grease may have leaked onto the disc rotor or brake pads.
- **Pads may be** glazed over, worn out, or not "bedded in."
- **Brake lever "reach"**–distance between lever and handlebar–may be badly adjusted.
- **Air may have** entered brake system.

- **Brake cable and/or housing** may be dirty, frayed, or corroded, which inhibits brake-pad movement.
- **Hydraulic pistons may be dirty,** sticking within the brake caliper rather than moving freely.
- **Dirt has jammed** the lever arm of the mechanical disc-brake caliper.

- **Air may be in the system** if pumping the brake–repeatedly applying and releasing lever–improves braking power and results in a firmer feel.
- **Fluid may be leaking** from hydraulic hoses.
- **Brake fluid may have boiled** due to prolonged braking or natural entry of water over time.

As disc brakes are complex, it can be hard to identify which part of the system contains the fault. However, using this chart, it should be possible to narrow down the possible causes behind any difficulties with your disc brakes and identify the potential solution.

POSSIBLE SOLUTIONS

Clean the rotor with isopropyl alcohol, or replace it if badly worn down. Gently sand the pads and rotor with fine-grade sandpaper (pp.42–43).

Check the caliper-fixing bolts and rotor-fixing bolts, and tighten to recommended torque ratings (pp.120–121).

Consider using organic brake pads rather than metallic ones. Ensure that metallic pads are "bedded in" all the way (pp.120–121).

True the rotor by bending it back into line with an adjustable wrench. If the rotor is badly warped, replace it (pp.120–121).

Reset the caliper so the disc rotor is centered between the pads. Loosen the caliper-fixing bolts, center by eye, and retighten.

Adjust mechanical disc pads independently to prevent rubbing. Adjust the outer pad by tweaking cable tension, and the inner pad with the adjustment screw.

Burn contamination off the pad with prolonged braking down a safe slope. Or hold pad over a blowtorch or gas stove on low setting. Clean a contaminated rotor.

Bed in new pads by riding at speed, dragging the brake for 5 seconds, then locking the wheel. Repeat up to a dozen times. Sand off any pad glaze.

Adjust brake-lever travel by turning the reach adjuster or grub screw. For cable discs, tighten the barrel adjuster on the brake lever.

Clean and lubricate the cable and housing, or replace them. For best braking power, secure cable with the caliper arm set at fully open (pp.42–45).

Clean pistons. First, take out the pads and pump lever until pistons protrude from caliper. Clean then reset with a piston-press tool or screwdriver wrapped in a rag.

Strip and clean the lever arm and caliper body of a mechanical disc, removing the wheel and pads first.

Bleed the brake to expel air bubbles from the hydraulic system (pp.108–109).

Inspect hydraulic hoses, especially at joints. Tighten any leaking joints and bleed air from the brakes (pp.108–109).

Replace brake fluid with the same type of fluid–do not mix up mineral and DOT fluids. Then bleed air from the system (pp.108–109).

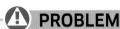

▶ TROUBLESHOOTING
Drivetrain

The drivetrain is the most complex system on your bicycle, with the greatest potential for faults to develop. From gear-shift levers to cables, crankarms to pedals, derailleurs to bottom brackets, cogs, chainrings, and chains, there is a lot to go wrong.

⚠ PROBLEM

The chain slips or skips, giving way under pressure when you pedal. You may notice:

- **Chain crunches** when pedaling out of the saddle.

Rear derailleur shifting is sluggish or inaccurate, with several pedal turns before changing gear. Other symptoms include:

- **Chain jumps** multiple cogs when shifting gears.
- **The chain falls** into the spokes or between the frame and smallest cog.

Front derailleur does not change gear correctly. Symptoms might include:

- **The chain falls off** into the BB or crankarm.
- **The chain will not shift** into smallest or biggest chainring.

Resistance when pedaling, which may cause fatigue and potential injury. You might notice:

- **The bicycle coasts freely** when you are not pedaling.
- **Creaking or crunching noise** from the BB, pedals, or chainrings.

The electronic shift system is not functioning correctly when you change gear. Symptoms include:

- **The gears change intermittently** or not at all.
- **A loss of power** at the derailleurs' electric motors.

⨀ POSSIBLE CAUSES

- **Chain links may be stiff,** indexing poorly adjusted, or– if skipping happens only in particular gears–cogs or chainrings may be worn down.
- **The derailleur hanger** or rear derailleur may be bent.
- **The chain may be dirty or worn down,** or chain links twisted due to jamming between frame and chainrings or cogs.

- **The cable or housing** may be dirty, worn down, or stretched.
- **You may be** using brake housing instead of gear housing.
- **A worn down or broken** shifter might cause poor shifting.
- **The rear derailleur pivots** or jockey pulleys may be worn down.
- **A dropped chain** may be due to badly adjusted indexing or limit screws, a loose cassette lockring, or an incorrect chain.

- **The front derailleur may be badly adjusted,** cable may have stretched or be incorrectly inserted in cable clamp.
- **The chain may be dirty,** preventing accurate gear-shifting.
- **The chainring(s) may be bent** or loose.
- **A worn down or broken** shifter may cause inaccurate shifts.
- **Cable or housing is dirty,** corroded, frayed, or split.

- **The BB may too tight,** dirty, or worn down, making it difficult to pedal.
- **The pedals may be too tight,** dirty, or worn down.
- **Chainrings might rub against the frame,** causing damage to paintwork and compromising strength of frame.

- **The electric cable connector may have come out** or been compressed at handlebar by bar tape or other clamps.
- **Battery may be flat** due to insufficient charging.
- **Incorrect limit-screw adjustment** will require greater force for derailleur to change gear, draining battery of power.

However, if you use this chart to spot the warning signs, you may be able to resolve problems before they become too large.

As with all of these charts, if, after consulting the releveant pages in the book, you still can't fix the problem, ask for help at a bike shop.

 POSSIBLE SOLUTIONS

Loosen stiff links by flexing the chain laterally. If the chain, chainrings, or cassette are badly worn, replace all three–worn parts cause new parts to wear down faster (pp.158-161).

Adjust indexing by turning the rear derailleur barrel adjuster until the chain stops skipping. Straighten or replace derailleur hanger; replace bent derailleur (pp.148-149).

Remove twisted chain links, ensuring the chain is long enough to reach the largest chainring/cog. Replace chain if worn; clean if dirty (pp.158-159).

Replace broken cables or housing; if in good condition, clean and lubricate. Ensure all ferrules are present, and gear housings are used (pp.148-149).

Check the gear-shift lever is clean and functioning correctly–replace if it is broken. If the pivots are worn, replace the derailleur. Replace jockey pulleys if they are worn.

Adjust the rear derailleur limit screws and indexing. Ensure the cassette lockring is tight. Replace with a chain of the correct width and brand. (pp.148-149, 158-159).

Loosen the cable and move the derailleur by hand to ensure it reaches all the chainrings. Adjust the limit screws if not. Clean the cable and fasten in clamp (pp.148-149).

Clean the chain, chainrings, cogs, and derailleurs. If a chainring is bent, use an adjustable wrench to straighten it. Tighten the chainring bolts (pp.42-43).

Check the gear-shift lever is clean and functioning correctly–replace if it is broken. Replace a broken cable or housing; clean and lubricate if not (pp.42-45, 132-135).

Overhaul or replace the BB, cleaning and greasing the bearings if possible. Tighten to ensure free movement but no play (pp.176-181).

Overhaul the pedals, cleaning the axle, bearings, and bearing surfaces. If the bearings or surfaces are worn down, replace them. Or replace the entire pedal (pp.184-185).

Adjust or replace the bottom bracket and/or the crankset to increase the clearance of the chainrings and frame (pp.158-159, 176-181).

Check that all cables and connectors are correctly inserted and unimpeded. If detached, reinsert them with the correct tool (pp.138-139).

Check the indicator light to verify the battery level. Remove and fully recharge the battery if necessary.

Adjust the limit screws to ensure that the movement of the derailleurs is not impeded (pp.138-139).

Glossary

Terms in *italic* within an entry are defined under their own headings within the glossary.

Allen key An alternative name for a *hex key*.

Axle The central shaft around which a bike wheel spins.

Barrel adjuster A small cup attached to the end of a cable that is used to lengthen cable housing and thus adjust cable tension.

Bead The edge of a tire that sits on a wheel.

Bearing A mechanism that usually consists of a number of ball bearings and circular channels, or races. It allows two metal surfaces to move freely while in contact.

Binder bolt A bolt integrated into the frame at the top of older style *seat tubes* which clamps the *seatpost* into the frame.

Bleeding The method of removing air from brakes.

Block Alternative name for *cassette*.

Boss Threaded metal fixture on a bike frame to which an item, such as a bottle *cage* or a *brake caliper* arm rack, is attached.

Bottom bracket (BB) Rotating unit that connects the *crankarms* on either side of the BB shell to each other.

Bottom out A term that describes the point when a *suspension* fork or shock absorber reaches the limit of its *travel*.

Brake lever The metal or plastic lever attached to the end of the brake cable and pulled to engage the brake.

Brake lever hood The body in which the *brake lever* sits, connecting it to the handlebar.

Brake travel The distance a *brake lever* moves before the brake pads engage the braking surface on the rim or *hub* of a wheel.

Cable end cap A small, metal cap, closed at one end, that fits over the cut ends of a cable to prevent fraying.

Cable mount A housing that keeps the cable housing stationary but leaves the inner cable free to move.

Cage A lightweight frame, usually of plastic, in which drinking bottles can be stored and easily accessed. Also a component of front and rear *derailleurs*, and pedals.

Caliper The arms on a *caliper brake* that clamp onto the wheel rim, thereby stopping the wheel's motion.

Caliper brakes Single brake mechanisms which bolt onto the frame and whose arms reach around the tire from above.

Cantilever brakes Brakes that attach separately to the fork on either side of the tire.

Cassette A series of *sprockets* attached to the *freehub* that range in size to give different *gear* ratios.

Chainring A toothed ring attached to the *crankarms*, which drives the chain and, in turn, the *sprockets* and the rear wheel of a bike.

Chainstay The frame tube joining the *bottom bracket* shell and rear *dropout*.

Cleat A plastic or metal plate that attaches to the sole of a cycling shoe and engages into a *clipless pedal* to hold the foot on the pedal.

Clinchers Tires that clinch to a wheel rim, fitting over the top of an inner tube.

Clipless pedal A pedal with a mechanism to engage the *cleat* on the sole of a cycling shoe and hold it securely in place. Called "clipless" because they replaced pedals that had toe clips and straps.

Derailleurs can be fitted to road and off-road bikes, and move the chain across the cassette and chainring when shifting gear.

Cog An alternative name for a *sprocket*

Compression The action of a *suspension* system when it absorbs an impact from the terrain. The term refers to the compression of the spring.

Cone Part of a cup-and-cone wheel hub that holds the *bearings* against the cup.

Crankarm The lever that joins the pedals to the *chainrings* and transfers energy from the rider's legs to the *drivetrain* of the bike.

Crankset The assembly of *chainrings* and *crankarms*.

Damping The process that absorbs the energy of an impact transmitted through a *suspension* system. It controls the speed at which any form of suspension responds to uneven terrain.

Derailleur A component that shifts the chain between *sprockets* on the cassette (rear derailleur) and between *chainrings* attached to *crankarmss* (front derailleur); it allows multiple gearing on bikes. See also *Mech*.

Derailleur hanger A metal extension that is attached to the rear *dropout* allowing the rear *derailleur* to be mounted on the bike.

Dishing The act of centring a wheel on its *axle*.

Double-butted tubes Bike tubes that are thick at the ends but thin elsewhere.

Down tube The frame tube that joins the *bottom bracket* shell to the *head tube*.

Drivetrain The assembly of pedals, *crankset*, chain, and *sprockets* that drives the bike forward by transmitting leg power into wheel rotation. See also *Transmission*.

Drop out A slotted plate at the end of the *fork* blades and stays, into which the *axle* of a wheel is attached.

Drops The lower straight part of a road handlebar that extends back toward the rider.

Dual-pivot brakes A version of a *caliper brake* in which each brake arm moves on a separate pivot.

Expander bolt A bolt that draws up a truncated cone or triangle of metal inside a metal tube in order to wedge the tube in place. Commonly found inside the stem of a threaded *headset*.

Dual-pivot brakes offer greater stopping power than traditional single-pull calipers. They are common on modern road bikes.

Ferrule A cap placed on the end of cable housing to secure it to cable mounts or components.

Forks The part of the bike that holds the front wheel, typically consisting of two blades joined at the crown.

Freehub A mechanism, part of the *hub*, that allows the rear wheel to rotate while the pedals remain stationary.

Freewheel A mechanism that does the same job as a *freehub* but can be screwed on or off the *hub*.

Gear An expression of the *chainring* and *sprocket* combination, linked by the chain, that propels the bike.

Gear satellite A disc on a hub *gear* that rotates when the gear cable is shifted, moving the *sprockets* within the *hub* to change gear.

Gear-shift lever The control mechanism, usually on the handlebar, used to initiate gear-shifts.

GPS Global Positioning System, a satellite-based navigational network used in cycling for navigation and to record speed and other ride data, via a handlebar-mounted device.

"Granny ring" The smallest *chainring*, used to engage low-ratio small *sprockets* for climbing steep hills.

Groupset A matched set of components from a single manufacturer which are engineered to work together. The groupset features both *derailleurs*, *crankset*, *gear-shift levers*, brake *calipers*, a chain, and a *cassette*.

Grub screw A headless, threaded bolt with a single diameter throughout its length.

Headset The *bearing* unit that attaches the *forks* to a frame and allows them to turn. There are two varieties: threaded and threadless.

Headset spacers Circular rings made of alloy or carbon that sit above the *headset* and can be used to raise or lower the *stem* to change a rider's position.

Head tube The frame tube through which the *steerer tube* runs.

Hex bolt A threaded bolt with a hexagonal depression in the center of its head.

Hex key Hexagonal-shaped tool that fits *hex bolts*.

Hexagonal bolt or nut A threaded bolt with a hexagonal-shaped head, or a hexagonal-shaped nut that fits onto a threaded bolt.

Hub The central part of the wheel, through which the *axle* runs and which allows the wheel to spin freely.

Hydraulic A mechanical system that uses compressed fluid to move an object.

Interference kit A fastening that relies on friction to keep parts together.

Jockey pulleys The part of the rear *derailleur* that shifts the chain between *gears*.

Link wire A small cable that connects the two arms of a *cantilever brake*.

Lockring/locknut A ring or nut used to tighten onto a threaded object and secure it in place.

Mech Short for mechanism. Device that pushes the chain onto a larger or smaller *chainring* or *sprocket*. See also *Derailleur gears*.

Negative spring A device that acts against the main spring in a *suspension* system. In *compression*, for example, a negative spring works to extend the *fork*, helping to overcome the effects of *stiction*.

Nipple The piece of metal attached to the end of a cable that secures the cable in the control lever.

Pawl The curved bar or lever that engages with the teeth of a ratchet to ensure it can turn only one way.

A seatpost supports the saddle and is inserted into the seat tube. Set the height of your seatpost to suit your riding style.

Play A term used to describe any looseness in mechanical parts.

Presta valve A high-pressure *valve* found on road bike inner tubes.

Presta valve nut A *locknut* found just above the *valve core* thread. The nut must be opened to pump up the inner tube.

Quick-release mechanism A lever connected to a skewer that locks or releases a component from the frame.

Quill A type of *stem* that fits inside the top of a *steerer tube* and is held in place internally.

Rear triangle The rear of a bicycle which includes the *seat stays*, the *chainstays*, and the *seat tube*.

Rebound A term to describe the action of a *suspension* system after it absorbs an impact from the terrain. It refers to the extension of the system's spring.

Rotor A flat metal disc that rotates alongside the bike wheel and provides the braking surface for disc brakes.

Seatpost A hollow tube that holds the saddle and is inserted into the *seat tube*.

Seatpost clamp A piece of plastic attached to the frame that holds the *seatpost* in position.

Seat stay The frame tube joining the *bottom bracket* shell and rear *dropout*.

Seat tube The frame tube that holds the *seatpost*.

Shifter lever The lever pressed to shift *gears*.

Sidewall Part of the tire between the *tread* and rim.

Spider A multi-armed part that connects the *chainring* to the axle of the *bottom bracket* or the *cogs* in a *cassette*.

Spindle A part that attaches the *bottom bracket* to the *crankarms*.

Spring-tension pin The end of a *cantilever* or *V-brake* return spring that fits into a locating hole on the bike's brake mounting *bosses*.

Sprocket A circular metal object with teeth, sometimes used as an alternative term for *cog*. It usually describes the parts within a hub gear that can be combined to give different *gear* ratios.

Stanchions The upper legs of a *suspension fork*.

Steerer tube The tube that connects the *fork* to the *stem* and handlebar.

Stem The component that connects the handlebar to the *steerer tube*.

Stiction A term that combines the words static and friction. It describes the tension between moving and static parts at rest, such as the seals and *stanchions* in a *suspension* fork.

Suspension An air/oil or a coil/oil system that absorbs the bumps from a trail or road. The system is either integrated into the *fork* or connected to the rear wheel via a linkage.

Threads The spiral grooves cut into metal that allow separate parts to be screwed or bolted together.

Top tube The frame tube that joins the *seat tube* to the *head tube*.

Torx key A type of screw head with a six-pointed, star-shaped head sometimes used on *stem* bolts and clamps instead of a *hex key*.

Transmission A bike's transmission is made up of those parts that transfer the rider's energy into forward motion–the pedals, chain, *crankset* and *cogs*. See also *Drivetrain*.

Travel A term that refers to the total distance a component moves in carrying out its purpose. For example, travel in a *suspension* fork is the total distance the *fork* has available to move in order to absorb a shock.

Tread The central part of a tire that makes contact with the ground.

Trigger shifters *Gear-shift levers* that respond to the flick of a triggerlike *shifter lever*.

Twist shifters *Gear-shift levers* that respond to the twist of a special grip on the handlebar.

V-brake A type of *cantilever brake* with long arms on which the cable attaches to one side, and the cable housing to the other.

Valve The part of a tire tube that connects to the pump.

Valve core The inner parts of a tube *valve*.

Viscosity A rating system for oils, which also refers to the weight. A light oil has low viscosity and moves quicker than a heavy oil through a given *damping* mechanism. This results in a faster-acting *suspension* system or reduced *damping*.

Wheel jig A stand that holds a wheel so that its rim runs between two jaws. Used in trueing a wheel after replacing a broken spoke.

Wheel-retention tabs Small protrusions on front dropouts that prevent wheels from falling off frame when *quick-release mechanism* is open.

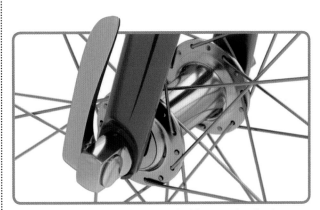

Quick-release levers can be opened without tools, allowing you to remove wheels and release brake cables quickly and easily.

Index

Page numbers in **bold** refer to main entries.

Acknowledgments

The publisher would like to thank the following for their kind permission to reproduce their photographs:

(Key: a-above; b-below/bottom; c-center; f-far; l-left; r-right; t-top)

14 Koga: (c). **15 Kalkhoff Bikes:** (bl). **17 Genesis Bikes UK genesisbikes.co.uk:** (tr). **Giant Europe B.V.:** (br). **Look Cycle:** (cl). **Ridley Bikes:** (bl). **Tandem Group Cycles:** (tl). **24 Condor Cycles Ltd:** (2/cl, 3/cl). **Extra (UK) Ltd:** (1/cr, 2/cr, 3/cr, 4/cr, 3/b). **Getty Images:** angelsimon (1/t, 2/t). **Tredz Bikes:** (1/cl, 1/b, 2/b, b). **25 Blaze.cc:** (1/bl, 2/bl). **Condor Cycles Ltd:** (2/t, 1/br, 3/br). **Hope Technology:** (bl). **Tredz Bikes:** (1/t, 3/t, 4/t, 2/cl, 3/bl, 2/br). **Wheelbase:** (5/t, 1/cl, 1, 3/cl). **26 Condor Cycles Ltd:** (2/tr, 2/cl, 3/cl, 5/cl, 3/b). **Getty Images:** mooltfilm (1/cl). **Lazer Sport:** (cr). **Tredz Bikes:** (1/tr, 4/cl, 1/cr, 2/cr, 3/cr, 1/b, 2/b). **27 Busch & Muller KG:** (2/cl). **Condor Cycles Ltd:** (1/tl, 1/bl). **Hammerhead:** (1/r). **ICEdot:** (2/bl). **LINKA:** (4/b). **Lumos Helmet lumoshelmet.co:** (4/r). **Scosche Industries Inc:** (2/r). **Tredz Bikes:** (2/tl, 3/tl, 1/cl, 3/b, 3/r). **28 Condor Cycles Ltd:** (1/tr, 3/tr, 1/b, 2/b). **ROSE Bikes GmbH:** (5/b). **Tredz Bikes:** (1/tl, 2/tl, 3/tl, 4/tr, 3/b, 4/b). **Triton Cycles:** (2/tr). **29 Extra (UK) Ltd:** (3/tl, 2/tr). **Radical Design:** (3/b). **Tailfin:** (4/tl, 5/tl). **Tredz Bikes:** (tl, 2/tl, 1/c, 2/c, 3/c, 4/c, 1/b, 2/b, 4/b). Wheelbase: (1/tr). **30 Condor Cycles Ltd:** (1/bc, 2/bc). **31 Condor Cycles Ltd:** (1/tl, 2/tl, 4/tl, 5/tl, 2/tr, 3/tr, 1/c, 2/c, 3/c, 4/c, 1/b, 2/b, 3/b, 4/b, b). **Extra (UK) Ltd:** *(5/c).* Tredz Bikes: (3/tl, 1/tr). *32 Tredz Bikes:* (1/b, 2/b). *33 Condor Cycles Ltd:* (3/b). *Tredz Bikes:* (1/t, 2/t, 3/t, t, 1/c, 2/c, 3/c, 4/c, 1/b, 2/b, 4/b, 5/b). **36 Extra (UK) Ltd:** (6/b). **Tredz Bikes:** (3/tr, 1/tr, 2/tr, 1, 2/b, 3/b, 4/b, 5/b, 7/b, 8/b, c). **37 Getty Images:** VolodymyrN (4/bl). **Tredz Bikes:** (1/tl, 2/tl, 3/tl, 1/tr, 2/tr, 3/tr, 4/tr, 5/tr, 1/bl, 2/bl, 3/bl, 5/bl, 6/bl, 7/bl, 8/bl, 1/br, 2/br)

All other images © Dorling Kindersley
For further information see: **www.dkimages.com**

In addition, Dorling Kindersley would like to extend thanks to the following contributors for their help with making the book: DK India for additional line artwork: Assistant animator Alok Kumar Singh, Production Co-ordinator Rohit Rojal, Audio Video Production Manager Nain Singh Rawat, Head of Digital Operations Manjari Hooda. Additional design assistance; Simon Murrell

Claire Beaumont, a former racing cyclist, is now the Marketing Manager and a lead creative at London-based, bespoke bicycle manufacturer, Condor Cycles. A consultant on DK's *The Bicycle Book*, Claire is also co-author of *Le Tour*: *Race Log* and *Cycling Climbs*, and has written about cycling for magazines, including *The Ride Journal*, *Cycling Weekly,* and *Cycling Active.*

Ben Spurrier, a passionate cyclist, is the head bike designer for Condor Cycles, London. Awarded by *Wallpaper* magazine in 2011 for a special edition range of bikes, Ben has been a member of the judging panel for the annual D&AD (Design and Art Direction) New Blood awards, and has spoken at The Design Museum, London, about bikes and design. He has also worked with many leading magazines, including *Australian Mountain Bike*, *Bike Etc*, and *Privateer.*

Brendan McCaffrey is an illustrator, designer, cycling enthusiast, and amateur bike mechanic based in Las Palmas in Gran Canaria, Spain. An industrial design graduate from NCAD, Dublin he has worked for the past 20 years producing illustrations for clients in the videogame, toy, and product industries. **www.bmcaff.com**

Model Credits:
3D Roadbike model by Brendan McCaffrey
3D Mountain Bike model supplied by Gino Marcomini
Additional models supplied by Brendan MCaffrey, Gino Marcomini, Ronnie Olsthoorn, and Moises Guerra Armas